San Francisco Memoirs
1835-1851

There is a romance attached to the early days of San Francisco's history, a real interest clinging to the men who lived here, and to the incidents of their lives during those strange, eventful days—something not so easily explained to those who were not here—a kind of freemasonry, binding fraternally all those who lived here in a time when the very sense of remoteness and isolation from all the rest of the world brought men closer together ... drawn to one field by eager, adventurous enterprise, such a long, weary way from home and loved ones, having something in common, so different from any previous experience known or read of ...

Men and Memories of San Francisco in the Spring of '50
by T. A. Barry and B. A. Patten
Published by A. L. Bancroft & Company
San Francisco, 1873

San Francisco Memoirs

～ 1835-1851 ～

Eyewitness accounts of the birth of a city

Compiled and introduced by

Malcolm E. Barker

LONDONBORN PUBLICATIONS

SAN FRANCISCO 1994

Londonborn Publications acknowledges the following publishers and individual holders of copyright for granting permission to reprint items as indicated:

Frances F. Beilharz and Carlos U. López: "Noise and confusion," "One way to win," "Pretty dames, fresh from New York," and "Sentence reversed." (All by Vicente Pérez Rosales, and reprinted from *We Were 49ers*. Translated and edited by Edwin A. Beilharz and Carlos U. López. © 1976.)

The Henry E. Huntington Library: "This land of gold and wonders." (From *Apron Full of Gold: The Letters of Mary Jane Megquier from San Francisco, 1849-1856*. Edited by Robert Glass Cleland. © 1949.)

Sacramento Book Collectors Club: "Christmas inferno." (From *The Adventures of a Young Swiss in California: The Gold Rush Account of Théophile de Rutté*. Translated and edited by Mary Grace Paquette. © 1992.)

Regents of the University of California and the University of California Press: "The Polka Saloon" and "A dandy transformed." (Both from *Three Years in California: William Perkins' Journal of Life at Sonora, 1849-1852* by William Perkins, et al. © 1964.)

Yale University Press: "A lady at the Montgomery House" and "Home again!" (From *A Frontier Lady: Recollections of the Gold Rush and Early California* by Sarah Royce. © 1932.)

Yale University Press: "The night they cried 'To arms!'" and "The governor's brawl." (Both from *The Cruise of the Portsmouth: A Sailor's View of the Naval Conquest of California* by Joseph T. Downey. © 1958.)

Londonborn Publications also acknowledges the following for permission to use items from their collections:

Robert Chandler: "Now is the time for making money." (From photocopy of letter by Ann Eliza Brannan.)

The Church of Jesus Christ of Latter-day Saints: "Through the eyes of a child." (From photocopy of a manuscript by James Horace Skinner, in their vault.)

The Church of Jesus Christ of Latter-day Saints: "Mormons at the Mission Dolores." (From photocopy of an original letter written by Mary Holland Sparks, in their vault.)

Library of Congress Cataloging-in-Publication Data
San Francisco memoirs, 1835-1851 : eyewitness accounts of the birth of a city / compiled and introduced by Malcolm E. Barker.
    p.   cm.
Includes bibliographical references and index.
ISBN 0-930235-04-5 (alk. paper)
1. San Francisco (Calif.)--History--Sources.
I. Barker, Malcolm E., 1933-   .
F869.S357S368 1994   94-26182
979.4'61--dc20   CIP

First printed September 1994

10 9 8 7 6 5 4 3 2

LONDONBORN PUBLICATIONS
P.O. Box 77246, San Francisco, 94107-0246

In loving memory of my mother
Phyllis Ann Barker
1903-1988

Acknowledgments

Librarians and their assistants top the list of individuals I want to thank for helping me bring together this book project. Not once did I sense any complaint as they went into their vaults to find the seemingly endless number of books, letters, documents, illustrations, and miscellaneous ephemera that I requested. On several occasions they unearthed items I did not even know I needed. Unfortunately, I do not have the names of all the people involved, and can only list them as follows:

Bancroft Library, University of California, Berkeley—especially Richard Ogar; California Room, California State Library, Sacramento—especially Gary Kurutz, Special Collections Director, and Mark Cashatt; Stanleigh Bry, formerly Library Director at the Society of California Pioneers; Stanley A. Carroll and his staff at the San Francisco Room, San Francisco Public Library; Jocelyn A. Moss at the Anne Kent California History Room, Marin County Free Library; Mechanics' Institute Library, San Francisco; J. Porter Shaw Library, San Francisco Maritime Museum; and the Historical Department at the Church of Jesus Christ of Latter-day Saints, Salt Lake City, Utah—especially Bill Slaughter and Ronald G. Watt.

I owe a great deal of gratitude to Jackie Pels, of Hardscratch Press, for her insightful job of editing my text, as well as for being a friend and supporter throughout the whole process of this book.

David Johnson deserves a special "thank you" for his work on the cover. The background is an original piece of watercolor artwork, not a computer-generated image!

Another good friend, John Boring, created the excellent map on page 24—and I thank him for that.

For help in locating illustrations, I thank especially Mrs. Lilian Kelly (for the *Brooklyn* photograph), Jocelyn A. Moss (for the portrait of Steve Richardson), and Mrs. M. P. Naud (for the George Burgess painting of 1850 San Francisco). Also, Kathleen Manning of Prints Old & Rare, and Peter Blodgett of Huntington Library, San Marino.

For their invaluable assistance in obtaining for me permissions to use copyrighted material, I thank Donna Anstey (Yale University Press), Mrs. Frances F. Beilharz and Dr. Carlos U. López (both for *We Were 49ers*), Robert Dickover (Sacramento Book Collectors Club), Karen Harms (Huntington Library Press), and Rose Robinson (University of California Press). Also, the Library of Congress for researching the copyright status of various items.

In addition to those people already mentioned, there are others I do not want to forget. To them, also, I extend my heartfelt thanks:

Walter Swarthout for his constant faith in this project; Edward L. Crossley for help and advice concerning the Spanish and Mexican eras; Peter Browning of Great West Books, and Nel Lancaster for their patience while guiding me through my problems with computers; Carlo G. Carlucci for help with Latin translations. Also, Will Bagley, fellow researcher into the life of Samuel Brannan; Rand Richards of Heritage House Publishers, and Michelle Vignes.

Last—but certainly not least—I reach back in time to salute the men and women who had the foresight to write in such detail about their experiences and feelings as they endured the rigors of a rapidly growing city. It was they who set the pace for the San Francisco we know and love today!

M.E.B.

Contents

Illustrations

*   These illustrations are from *San Francisco Annals*, a book that was published in 1855. In order to retain the fine detail, they have been scanned into a computer and printed as drop-out halftones.
**   These maps are from H. H. Bancroft's *History of California*, volume 6.
***The map on page 24 was created by John Boring / Envisagements, of Livermore, California, specifically for this volume.

Londonborn Publications acknowledges the following institutions and individuals for the loan of illustrations as indicated. Illustrations not listed here are in the author's private collection.
Bancroft Library, University of California: pages 63, 99, 101, 122, 125, 266.
Peter Browning: page 150.
California Academy of Sciences: page 27.
California State Library: pages 30, 50, 52, 54, 75, 178, 196, 226, 263.
Nancy A. Hacker: page 232.
Hirschl & Adler Gallery Inc., New York: pages 86, 240. (Private collections.)
Henry E. Huntington Library: pages 173, 220.
Dr. Carlos U. López: page 134.
Marin County Historical Society: page 64.
Mary Grace Paquette: page 270.
Rand Richards: page 281.
Sausalito Historical Society: page 36.

The curvature of the cove is apparent in this map from the 1850s. As wharves extended toward deeper water the areas between them were filled in.

Voices from a foreign time

UNDERSTANDING THE FOREIGNER WHO IS attempting to speak one's language is not always easy. Unfamiliar syntax and misplaced accents impede the pace of conversation, and every now and then the dialogue comes to a halt as, together, speaker and listener struggle to translate a word. Patience is imperative.

The same can be said of reading something written in a "foreign" time. Here one is confronted with words that are familiar, but encased in unfamiliar punctuation and with an added hazard: Some of the words have changed in meaning over the years, or have fallen from common usage.

Reprinting writings from an earlier era often raises the temptation to modernize the punctuation and to replace obsolete or rarely used words with today's counterparts in an effort to make them easier to read. Yet by doing so, are we not robbing the pieces of their uniqueness? Is it not like denying the foreign tourist the use of his or her distinctive accent?

In this book, therefore, apart from dividing unbroken blocks of type into more manageable paragraphs, the only editing I have done is in a very few instances where the text might be unclear, or where there were obvious typographical errors. I wanted these people to tell us their stories in their own individual styles, regardless of whether they now sound archaic or alien. Their accounts, strung together in generally chronological order as they are here, tell the story of the birth of San Francisco, revealing a myriad fascinating personal details that add a human dimension to the city's history.

My principal criterion in selecting these pieces was that each one should be an eyewitness account of a particular aspect of life in San Francisco during those early pioneer days. I wanted tales of human frailties to which we can relate, and that give us an emotional bridge to the past. In particular, I wanted "average" people rather than civic leaders and decision-makers.

Surely the story of the birth and growth of San Francisco is one of the most dynamic of any city on earth. To spring from a village of approximately 150 people to a multinational metropolis of 30,000 in the space of 3½ years, without the technology and tools we take for granted, is phenomenal. What was it like living in such tumultuous times, experiencing first-hand the city's growing pains?

It is apparent from their letters, diaries, and books that those pioneers were fully aware of the significance of their time and place. Often in recording their thoughts and actions they speculated about the future greatness of the town. Finding a market for their writings at that time was not difficult. People all over the United States—indeed, all over the world—hungered for stories about this new El Dorado. Publishers and editors eagerly set into print every account they could get, often without checking for accuracy. The French novelist Alexandre Dumas, of *The Three Musketeers* fame, was only one of several writers to set novels in California without ever visiting the state.

Few of the writers included in this book were historians. The majority were like most people who visit new and unfamiliar places and then set down their opinions without being fully aware of all the relevant facts. They were tourists, essentially.

Early in the project I realized that, if this collection were to be of lasting value, I would have to verify many details within the pieces—a task that had me going from one resource to another, peering at microfilm, reading through dozens of seemingly unrelated books, and talking with a number of scholars and historians. Instead of "correcting" the originals, however, I have added brief comments before and/or after each piece. And, rather than encumber the pages with footnotes, I have listed my resources by page number in "Resource notes" at the back of the book. In a few instances I have used brackets ([]) to interject immediate clarification in a text. All parenthetical notations in the pieces were made by the original writers.

New headings have been added throughout, except in the case of "Eldorado"—the only book title that seemed appropriate for the excerpt as reprinted here. Ellipsis points (...) within the text indicate that several words or sentences have been deleted from the original. Longer cuts—sometimes of several paragraphs—are indicated like this between paragraphs:

.   .   .

As already suggested, one of the hazards is that certain words have changed in meaning, or were specific to that particular period and today are unknown.

To us, it may seem strange that Sarah Royce would be so eager to move into a *tenement*, now that that word for an apartment building has negative connotations. Also strange is to read the same woman referring to the other tenants in her building as *fellow-inmates*. What are we to think when William Perkins writes, "having arranged our *traps*, I strolled up towards the hills"? Or of the sailors on Richard Henry Dana's ship clearing away the *kids* after dinner before settling down to make themselves new clothes? And speaking of clothes, what were the *frocks* worn by sailors on the *Portsmouth*?

We might well wonder what Perkins expected to snare in his traps, and why there were children on a ship that had no women—or perhaps Dana was referring to goats? Were the frocks anything like *frock coats*?

Of these words, probably *traps* (for personal belongings, or luggage) is the most easily recognized. Less well known are *kids* for the mess-tubs used by sailors, and *frocks* for the woolen sweaters those men wore.

These are only a few of the words that seemed to me to require "translating" as the 20th century reader goes through this book. Such words are defined with a footnote. Where appropriate, a more complete definition is given in the Glossary.

Another example of changing times/changing words is *locos*, as when Mary Jane Megquier says of an election, "the locos take the lead." In her time, *locos* was a popular nickname for Democrats, stemming from the brand name of matches used by a faction of Democrats to light candles when the gaslights were extinguished during a boisterous debate at New York's Tammany Hall in 1835. *Loco* was an abbreviation of *loco-foco*.

To a word lover, these are like gems found in a long buried treasure chest, and I have enjoyed dusting them off to share with my readers.

Bringing together writings from diverse sources and cultures presents another dilemma for the publisher: whether or not to standardize the spelling. Kearny Street, for instance, sometimes appears as *Kearney* Street. El Dorado often appears as *Eldorado*, even when not refering specifically to the gambling saloon of that name. And the word theater appears occasionally with the English spelling, *theatre*. Again, my choice has been to retain the original form.

Most of these pieces are excerpted from books that were first published more than 100 years ago. Some of the books have been reprinted, several appearing in the late 1940s as California approached its centennial. Fewer than half a dozen remain in print. However, some titles still can be found on the shelves of public libraries, while a search through used book shops—especially those listed in the Yellow Pages as antiquarian book sellers—often will reward the persistent seeker with an original copy.

My hope is that these excerpts will whet appetites. The books quoted are listed in the Bibliography at the back of this volume. For now, though, relax and enjoy a visit with these men and women as they recount their impressions of early San Francisco.

Malcolm E. Barker
San Rafael, California
July, 1994

What's in a name?

THE POPULAR NOTION THAT San Francisco was called Yerba Buena before the Americans renamed it in January 1847 is not as clear cut as it may seem. In truth, there was a San Francisco on the shores of the bay long before there was a Yerba Buena.

The name San Francisco appears in several Spanish documents dating back to the late 18th century. The British explorer Captain George Vancouver, who visited the area in 1792, called it "the Spanish town and settlement of St. Francisco." And during the early 1840s, various communiques were sent from Washington to the U.S. fleet in the Pacific urging the capture of "San Francisco" in the event of war with Mexico. No mention of Yerba Buena.

Another potential source of confusion is the name "Golden Gate." Some readers will be surprised to see so many references to the Golden Gate in journals written more than 100 years ago. "But surely the bridge wasn't built until 1937?" they may well ask.

The following is offered in an attempt to explain what was named when, where, why, and by whom. But first we must introduce a lesser-known issue: the other San Francisco, just 30 miles north of the Golden Gate.

In November 1595, Portuguese navigator Sebastián Cermeño sailed into a small bay just south of Point Reyes and named it *La Bahía de San Francisco*—the Bay of Saint Francis—for Saint Francis of Assisi, the founder of the Franciscan order. Despite a belief popular in England during the 17th and 18th centuries, the name had nothing to do with Sir Francis Drake who, reputedly, had visited the bay 16 years earlier to repair his ship, *Golden Hind*—although the English buccaneer

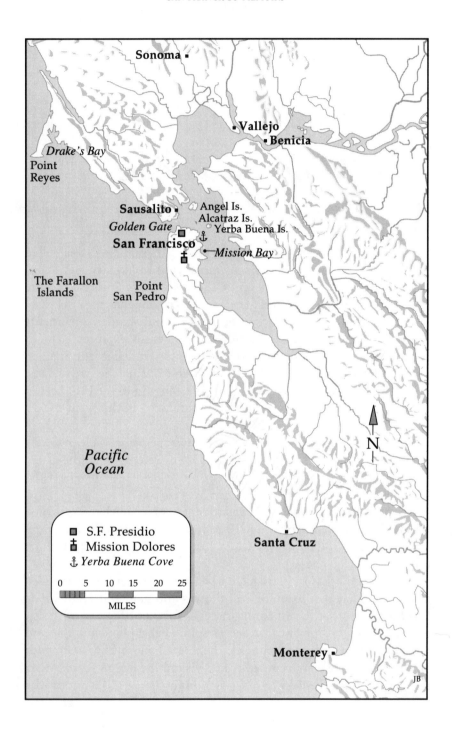

Sonoma

Vallejo
Benicia

Drake's Bay
Point
Reyes

Sausalito
Angel Is.
Alcatraz Is.
Golden Gate
Yerba Buena Is.
San Francisco
Mission Bay

The Farallon
Islands
Point
San Pedro

Pacific
Ocean

N

□ S.F. Presidio
✝ Mission Dolores
⚓ Yerba Buena Cove

0 5 10 15 20 25
MILES

Santa Cruz

Monterey

was honored nearly 200 years later, in 1792, when the bay was given the name by which we know it today, *Drake's Bay*.

San Francisco — the bay

In "A city is born" we'll see how a Spanish expedition coming by land from San Diego in 1769 discovered San Francisco Bay by accident. For now, we need only to know that two days before that discovery the explorers reached Point San Pedro and, according to the diary of the expedition's engineer, Miguel Costansó, looked up the coast and saw "a large bay formed by a point of land that extended a long distance into the sea" (Drake's Bay and Point Reyes), "seven rocky, white islands" (the Farallon Islands), and "the mouth of an estuary that appeared to extend inland" (the entrance to San Francisco Bay—the bay itself being hidden from their view at this point).

"It seemed to us beyond all question that what we were looking upon was the port of San Francisco," wrote Costansó.

The only San Francisco to appear on maps of the area at that time was the one named by Cermeño—the one we know as Drake's Bay. But from this and subsequent entries in Costansó's diary it appears that the Spaniards applied the name San Francisco to that "mouth of an estuary" and that they assumed that the immense bay they found a couple of days later was the Bay of San Francisco. In fact, neither that bay nor its entrance had been seen by Europeans before, and, consequently, neither was named on their maps. What the Spaniards were doing was transferring the name of a known bay to a previously unknown bay, and, in the process, instigating the confusion that was to linger for almost 200 years!

In 1775, the Spanish navigator Juan Manuel de Ayala sailed into the bay on the *San Carlos* and spent several weeks exploring and naming the various coves, inlets, and islands that he found there. By this time the Spanish authorities were convinced that the two San Francisco bays were one, and they instructed Ayala to seek the strait that linked them. Of course, he did not find it.

San Francisco — the town. Part I

In 1776, the Spanish built a fort near the entrance of the bay and a mission farther inland, near a small lake they called *Nuestra Señora de los Dolores*, "Our Lady of Sorrows," because they first saw it on the

Friday before Palm Sunday. They called the mission *San Francisco de Asís*, again in honor of St. Francis of Assisi.

Other missions were subsequently established along the Northern California coast, and, by 1823, it was apparent that San Francisco de Asís was lagging in its efforts to cultivate the land and convert the indigenous peoples to Christianity. Blame was placed on unhealthy weather and arid soil, and a search was made for a new site. On April 4, 1824, the mission church of *San Francisco Solano* (often referred to as "New San Francisco") was dedicated at Sonoma, 47 miles to the north, with the idea that the priests and neophytes at Old San Francisco would be transferred there. The Sonoma mission was not named after St. Francis of Assisi but after St. Francis Solano, who had served many years as a missionary in Peru.

By this time most of the friars and residents had dropped the *de Asís* from the old mission's name and were calling it simply *San Francisco*. But the presidio was also known as *San Francisco*. Now there was this *New San Francisco*.

To distinguish it from the newer one, people began referring to the old mission by its location, *Misión de los Dolores*—the mission at Dolores Lake. Eventually, it became Mission Dolores, the name it is popularly known by today.

Yerba Buena — the cove

In 1835, the Mexican governor, José Figueroa, decided to establish a civilian settlement in the area. William Richardson, an English sailor who had lived in California since leaving his ship in 1822, persuaded him that the ideal location would be the sandy cove which nestled halfway between the presidio and the mission, and which was known as *Yerba Buena*, after the sweet-smelling herb found growing there. The governor agreed, and he appointed an *ayuntamiento* (or, common council) to administer the *pueblo de San Francisco*, which extended down the peninsula to just above San Jose. At the same time, Figueroa made Richardson the port captain.

Richardson built a rough shack at the cove, and the following year he applied for—and was granted—"a lot of one hundred varas square [275 ft. x 275 ft.], in Yerba Buena, in front of the Plaza and anchorage of the ships." It is worth noting that he dated his request "San Francisco, June 1, 1836."

The cove and its surrounding chaparral-covered hills became known as Yerba Buena, even though it was all part of the pueblo of San Francisco. As more non-Spanish speaking people (mostly American and English) moved to the area in the late 1830s and early 1840s, they set up their shacks and tents at the cove and established a community of their own, separate from the mission and the presidio, both of which were now falling into ruin because of neglect. It was here at the cove that the American sloop of war *Portsmouth* anchored in 1846, during the U.S.-Mexico war, and where Captain John Montgomery first raised the American flag—thus giving us the names for Portsmouth Square and Montgomery Street.

The yerba buena plant, otherwise known as *Micromeria Douglasii*.

In late July 1846, the area's population was more than doubled with the arrival of an American ship bringing 238 men, women, and children, most of them Mormons. These people erected their tents and shacks on the hills around the cove, and some moved into the secularized mission buildings. Although the settlements at the cove, the mission, and the presidio were closing in on each other, most of these new arrivals clung to Yerba Buena as the name for their town.

San Francisco — the town. Part II

Ever since Ayala's first exploration in 1775, it had been apparent that several ports could be built within this one huge bay. Although most efforts were concentrated around Yerba Buena, a group of businessmen selected a location in the northern portion of the bay to build a rival port, which they planned to call *Francisca*, in honor of the wife of General Mariano Vallejo, on whose *rancho* it was located.

Town officials at Yerba Buena realized that the name would give the new port a decided advantage over theirs because of its similarity to the name of the bay. In a sudden and dramatic move, the following ordinance was printed in English and Spanish in the local newspaper, *The California Star*, on January 23, 1847, and repeated on January 30 [italics added]:

> Whereas the local name of Yerba Buena as *applied to the settlement or town of San Francisco* is unknown beyond the immediate district; and has been applied from the local name of the Cove on which the town is built,—Therefore, to prevent confusion and mistakes in public documents, and that the town may have the advantage of *the name given on the published maps*,
>
> It is hereby ordered that the name of San Francisco shall hereafter be used in all official communications, and public documents, or records appertaining to the town.

H. H. Bancroft, in his seven-volume *History of California* (published 1886-1890), pointed out that it wasn't truly a name change because *Yerba Buena* was "but a comparatively modern description for a part of San Francisco." Nevertheless, not everyone approved of the switch. The *Star's* publisher, Samuel Brannan, opposed it, and for several weeks his newspaper carried reports of events in "the town of Yerba Buena." It wasn't until March 20 that San Francisco finally replaced Yerba Buena in the *Star's* masthead.

As for the town of Francisca, that name was changed to *Benicia*— Señora Vallejo's second name.

The Golden Gate

Contrary to what many people think, there was a Golden Gate long before there was a Golden Gate Bridge. The name was applied originally to the entrance of the bay. Another misconception is that the name is somehow connected with the Gold Rush that attracted so many thousands of immigrants to sail between its heads. Again, there was a Golden Gate before there was a Gold Rush.

John C. Frémont was probably the most daring and romantic—though controversial—of all of California's early heroes, playing at various times the parts of explorer, Bear Flag Revolt leader, military governor, and U.S. senator. He is also responsible for naming the Golden Gate. In his *Geographical Memoir upon Upper California* (published 1848), he explained that he had been inspired by the Golden Horn, the harbor entrance of Byzantium (later Constantinople, now Istanbul). The shape, size, and location of the California bay and its entrance suggested to him the same great commercial possibilities that had inspired the builders of that ancient city to name their harbor entrance *Chryoceras* (Greek for *Golden Horn*). And so Frémont called his harbor entrance *Chrysopylæ*, or, *Golden Gate*.

The islands

Alcatraz Island was originally called Yerba Buena Island and Yerba Buena Island (which now anchors the center of the San Francisco-Oakland Bay Bridge) was called Alcatraz. Those were the names given them by Ayala during his 1775 exploration of the bay.

Apparently the herb yerba buena was growing wild on the island, as well as over most of the peninsula at the mouth of the bay, and there is some confusion as to where the name first settled—on the island or on the shore. What is known is that it was applied to the North Beach area as early as 1792, long before it was applied to Yerba Buena Cove, on the opposite side of Telegraph Hill.

Ayala named the other island *Isla de los Alcatraces* (Island of the Pelicans) because of the big-billed birds he saw there. But the two names were accidentally switched by a British ship's captain, Frederick Beechey, who surveyed the bay in 1826, and they have remained switched ever since. From 1895 until the early 1930s, Yerba Buena Island was generally known as Goat Island, because an enterprising farmer was rearing a colony of goats there.

While his crew was surveying the bay in a launch, Ayala remained on board the *San Carlos* anchored off a large island which he named *Isla de los Angeles* in honor of Our Lady of the Angels. For a while it was known as *Los Angeles Island*, but today we know it as Angel Island. It is now a state park.

What a difference a year—and the discovery of gold—makes!
San Francisco in November 1848 and in November 1849.

A city is born

THE STEADY BREEZE THAT FILLED the sails of the British sloop *Discovery* seemed powerless against the strong current that ran out from the bay, and for most of that afternoon in November 1792, the ship could not go faster than five knots. By the time Captain Vancouver had navigated the narrow entrance to the bay, the sun was setting. He and his crew peered across at the darkening shore, looking for lights of the Spanish town they expected to find there. But all they saw were clusters of men waving at them.

The traditional cannon salutes were exchanged, their volleys echoing around the hills as the ship inched along the shoreline in a vain search for signs of a town. At eight o'clock, when only the glow of a fire on the beach could be seen, the *Discovery* dropped anchor in a sheltered cove and awaited the morning.

Thus began the first visit to San Francisco by a foreign (that is, non-Spanish) vessel. At the time, San Francisco was a typical Spanish colonial settlement consisting of a fort—called by the Spaniards a *presidio*—near the harbor entrance and a mission a few miles farther inland.

In his journal, *A Voyage of Discovery to the North Pacific Ocean, and Round the World*, published in 1801, George Vancouver wrote that instead of a town he found only "a square area . . . inclosed by a mud wall, and resembling a pound for cattle" (the presidio), and a group of buildings forming "a small oblong square" (the mission).

Thatched-roof buildings adjoined one another along the inside of the presidio walls, each one the same size and appearance as the other, except the church, which was longer and whitewashed. No attempt had been made to cover or level the bare soil floors inside the houses, and there was no protection against rain or wind coming in from the openings that served as windows. After viewing the commandant's quarters, Vancouver commented that it was far from the "sumptuous manner" in which he had expected to find Spaniards living "on this side of the globe."

Of the mission, he said, "The houses formed a small oblong square, the side of the church composed one end, near which were the apartments allotted to the fathers. These were constructed nearly after the manner of those at the Presidio, but appeared to be more finished, better contrived, were larger, and much more cleanly."

The captain and his men, who were on a round-the-world exploration conducting geological, astronomical, and other scientific experiments, remained in the area almost two weeks. During this time their hosts did everything they could to make them welcome. The visitors were entertained at banquets at the presidio and the mission and were provided with wood and fresh supplies of water and food, including several head of cattle. They also were taken on a sightseeing excursion to the mission community of Santa Clara, south of San Francisco—another first in that no foreigners had penetrated so far into the interior before. And when they prepared to leave, the Spaniards refused to accept any money in payment.

This generosity is particularly noteworthy when we realize that, of all the mission-presidio settlements along the California coast, San Francisco was probably the poorest. It had been established 16 years earlier, in 1776, as the northernmost link in a chain intended to establish Spain's claim to the area at a time when California and Mexico were one country known as New Spain.

The theory behind these settlements was that the priests would cultivate the land and convert local Native American tribes to Christianity so that eventually they would form the nucleus of a town, while the soldiers would protect the country from foreign invasion. There were no civilian settlers, other than the military wives and children who lived at the presidio.

To Vancouver it seemed that the padres had devoted more attention and energy to the construction and decoration of their church than they had to their own homes.

"Even their garden, an object of such material importance, had not yet acquired any great degree of cultivation, though its soil was a rich black mould, and promised an ample return for any labor that might be bestowed upon it," he wrote. "The whole contained about four acres, was tolerably well fenced, and produced some fig, peach, apple, and other fruit trees, but afforded a very scant supply of useful vegetables; the principal part lying waste and overrun with weeds."

The mission church that he saw in 1792 had been completed only the previous year and is the same one that today stands on the corner of Dolores and 16th streets—the oldest intact building in San Francisco. Its adobe walls are four feet thick.

The story of San Francisco goes back to 1769, when a Spanish expedition led by Gaspar de Portolá, and including Franciscan friars Father Juan Crespí and Francisco Gómez, came by land up the coast looking for Monterey harbor, which Sebastián Vizcaíno had visited and praised highly in 1602. There they expected to meet the *San José*, which was sailing from San Diego with supplies for them to establish a presidio and a mission. Although their map indicated what Monterey looked like from the sea, they did not recognize it when they approached it from land, and they kept going until—on October 31, 1769—they saw a cluster of rocky islands just off the coast (the Farallones) and, farther north, the white cliffs of what is now called Drake's Bay. They also saw what appeared to be the entrance to a bay, although the hills restricted their view.

While the main party rested, some of the men climbed a nearby hill on a hunting expedition and suddenly found themselves overlooking a magnificent harbor and bay that stretched inland for several miles. Without realizing it, they were the first Europeans ever to see the bay of San Francisco. Ships had sailed up and down the coast outside the heads for several years, but none of the navigators knew the bay was there—probably because of the heavy fog that often enshrouds the narrow entrance, which today is spanned by the Golden Gate Bridge. Portolá and his men tried to reach the white-cliffed bay—some believing it to be Monterey—but were unable to cross or circumnavigate San Francisco Bay. Meanwhile, their food was running short, and several men were sick or injured. Disillusioned, the soldiers and priests returned to San Diego without fully appreciating the great significance of their discovery.

It would be another seven years before the Spanish returned to settle beside this new-found bay. And then, on June 29, 1776, beneath a makeshift shelter of branches beside a small lake which they named *Nuestra Señora de los Dolores*, they celebrated a Mass—an event that marks the official founding of the city of San Francisco.

Monterey was eventually located during Portolá's second land expedition, in 1770, and, seven years later, it became the capital of California.

As we learn from Captain Vancouver's account, life in San Francisco at the end of the 18th century was not very prosperous. It did not improve much in the years that followed—if anything, life got more difficult. With its troublesome South American colonies fighting for independence, Spain was reluctant to spend money and energy on the tiny settlement so far north on the California coast. Soldiers at the presidio received no pay at all and were totally dependent upon the mission for their meals. This didn't please the padres, who were still obliged to pay taxes on the small amount of money they made selling wool, soap, and tanned hides. Apart from these hardships, California in general, and San Francisco in particular, remained virtually untouched by the revolution that lasted for a decade before Mexico finally won its independence in 1823.

The fur trade that the Spaniards had begun in the 1780s, which was developed into a highly profitable business by Russian trappers at Fort Ross, north of San Francisco, was given a boost when the new Mexican government opened California ports for foreign trade. Ships from the United States, Russia, England, and France stopped off not only to refuel but also to trade in seal and other furs. (See "Three weeks before the mast.")

To encourage colonization, the Mexican authorities offered generous land grants that enabled several wealthy Mexican families to move to California and develop huge cattle and horse *ranchos*. For several years, these close-knit families formed the aristocracy of California, enjoying a luxurious lifestyle of sporting and social events and relying upon Native Americans to work on their ranchos.

The Spanish mission system, which had remained in place after the revolution, came under close scrutiny following reports that the Franciscans had been flogging and degrading the neophytes and treating them as slaves, rather than helping them to become responsible

Christian landowners. The mission at San Francisco was further criticized for failing in its obligation to supply adequate food for the presidio troops.

Finally, in 1833, secularization of the California missions began and, despite attempts by the padres to forestall it, the lands were subdivided and dispersed, with several plots being granted to the neophytes. Unfortunately, few of the Native Americans benefited. Years of subjugation and cultural deprivation had reduced them to such a state that many drifted aimlessly into a pathetic life of squalor. Some were able to find work on the Mexican ranchos, but even there many were treated no better than slaves.

The San Francisco mission remained secularized until 1859, when it was re-established as a Catholic church. In the interim it and its adjoining buildings served variously as housing, as a saloon, and as a site for bull-and-bear fights.

The presidio's troops were transferred to Sonoma in 1835, and its buildings were abandoned, eventually falling into decay.

Many of the early foreign settlers in California were sailors who remained after their ships had left. Some did so voluntarily, as deserters. Others were banished by their captains as troublemakers.

William Richardson was an officer on the British whaler *Orion* when it arrived in San Francisco in 1822, and he became the area's first foreign settler when the ship sailed on without him. According to Bancroft, he was left behind "under circumstances not explained."

According to his son's memoirs, however, he deserted the ship because he had met and fallen in love with Maria Antonia Martínez, the daughter of Ignacio Martínez, comandante of the presidio. The Mexican governor, Pablo Vicente de Solá, granted Richardson permission to stay on the condition he give lessons in carpentry and navigation to the young men of California.

In 1823, when he was 27, Richardson was baptized at the mission, and he adopted as his second name Antonio, the masculine form of Señorita Martínez's second name. The couple married in 1825 and for a while they lived with her father in the presidio, where their first child, Mariana, was born on April 9, 1826. They moved to southern California in 1829, the year before Richardson became a naturalized Mexican citizen. Two sons were born at San Gabriel Mission: Esteban in 1831, and Francisco in 1833.

Captain William Antonio Richardson.

Richardson returned with his family to San Francisco in 1835 and built the first private dwelling there—a temporary structure in a cove, the beach of which came up to where Montgomery Street is today. The cove became known as Yerba Buena, because of the fragrant plant of that name found growing in the area. It was there that most ships elected to drop anchor, rather than the wind-swept beachfront at North Beach, opposite the presidio, where the Mexican authorities preferred them to be.

In the town's first election, in December 1834, Francisco de Haro, who had arrived in California in 1819 as a young army officer, was chosen *alcalde*—a position that combined the duties of mayor and judge. One of his earliest acts was to mark out the first street, La Calle de la Fundación (literally, The Street of the Founding, or Foundation Street), which began at water's edge and ran in the direction of the presidio, passing directly in front of Richardson's house. This name was later changed to DuPont Street, but today it is known as Grant Avenue.

In 1836, an American trader, Jacob P. Leese, in partnership with Nathan Spear and William Hinckley, built a two-story wooden house and store on a lot near Richardson's, completing it just in time to celebrate the Fourth of July with one of the town's first social gatherings.

Richardson, who had been appointed port captain by Governor José Figueroa in 1835, played a significant role in the early development of San Francisco. He carried out extensive surveys of the bay and was very active in the rapidly growing shipping industry, often serving as pilot on vessels entering and leaving the harbor. At the same time, however, he ran a lucrative smuggling business from his 18,000-acre ranch across the bay, the Rancho Saucelito, to which he and his family moved in 1841. The ranch covered areas today occupied by Sausalito and Mill Valley. Richardson Bay, in Marin County, and Richardson Avenue, which links Lombard Street with Doyle Drive in San Francisco, were named for him.

Gradually, other newcomers arrived in San Francisco and built homes either at the cove or by the presidio. A few settled farther away, near the mission. Jean Jacques Vioget, a Swiss-born sailor and trader, built a house which he used briefly as a bar and billiard parlor, catering to the increasing number of ships' crews that visited the bay. He leased the operation to Bob Ridley, an English trader, who employed another Englishman, John Henry Brown, to run it for him. Originally called Vioget's House, the building later became famous as the Portsmouth House, one of California's earliest hotels. It is mentioned in several stories in this book.

Looking back from the comfort of 1918, when he set down his memoirs, Richardson's son Esteban (Steve) remembered the cove as a dismal wilderness of desolate, forbidding sand dunes with a "reputation for unhealthfulness." He also recalled how, as a small boy, he used to sit on the veranda of his father's *Casa Grande* and watch bears, wolves, and coyotes on what is now Montgomery Street. (See "Wolves, bears, and coyotes.")

Wild animals were not unusual at the cove in those days. According to William D. Phelps' *Fore and Aft* (1871), a panther carried off a boy in 1841, and a grizzly bear stole the dinner of a group of woodcutters. The German physician Georg Heinrick von Lansdorf, who visited the area in 1806, wrote in his *Voyages and Travels in Various Parts of the World* (1817) that lions, tigers, wolves, foxes, bears, and polecats were common.

Bancroft estimates that in 1845 there were 20 structures and 300 people in the area encompassing Yerba Buena and Mission Dolores. Of these people, he says, 150 were of Spanish blood, 50 were foreigners, and the rest were either Native Americans or Kanakas (Hawaiians).

Meanwhile, other nations were awakening to the exciting potential of this newly found harbor. Captains of American, English, and Russian ships were taking home glowing accounts of what they found there. To all of them, it was very apparent that the Mexicans had virtually nothing in the way of serious defenses along the coast.

For the Americans, this was an opportunity to fulfill what they considered their Manifest Destiny and occupy all lands extending to the Pacific Ocean. Least interested, perhaps, were the Russians, who had sold their Fort Ross property to Captain John Sutter in 1841 after almost exterminating the local sea otter population. However, English ships hovered in the Pacific, looking suspiciously like contenders for the prize should Mexico be forced to forfeit it.

As early as 1835, President Andrew Jackson's administration had tried to buy California along with Texas. In August of that year, the secretary of state wrote to the American chargé d'affaires in Mexico, declaring that the main object was "to secure within our limits the whole bay of St. Francisco" because it would be "a most desirable place of resort for our numerous vessels engaged in the whaling business in the Pacific, far preferable to any to which they now have access."

But Mexico would not sell. Ten years later the United States annexed Texas and tried again to purchase California, this time in combination with New Mexico. Again its proposition was refused. Conflicts broke out on the U.S.-Mexico border, and, on May 13, 1846, the United States declared war on Mexico.

In June 1845, Commodore John Sloat of the Pacific Squadron had been sent secret instructions from Washington to occupy San Francisco "if you ascertain with certainty that Mexico has declared war against the United States." This, and subsequent communiques, stressed the importance of taking possession with as little force as possible, and of establishing friendly relations with the people living there.

Two days after the American declaration of war, another communique was sent by the secretary of the Navy to Sloat, with the instruction: "You will consider the most important object to be to take and to hold possession of San Francisco, and this you will do without fail."

But Sloat hesitated before taking action. Even though he heard of battles being waged between Mexicans and Americans, he had not "ascertained with certainty" that war had been declared. Quite possibly he was afraid of making the same mistake another American commodore had made three years earlier. On that occasion, Thomas ap Catesby Jones, acting upon false reports that the United States and Mexico were at war and that England was about to invade California, had sailed into Monterey harbor, demanded surrender, and raised the stars and stripes for the first time on California soil. A couple of days later he realized his error, lowered the flag, and sailed for Los Angeles to apologize to the Mexican authorities there.

By the time Sloat arrived at Monterey on July 2, 1846, the *Portsmouth*, under the command of Captain John Montgomery, was already anchored in San Francisco Bay awaiting orders. Neither ship encountered any resistance. In fact, in neither port were there any Mexican troops or senior officials.

Finally, on July 6, Sloat's men marched into the empty customs house in Monterey, read the declaration of occupation, and raised the American flag. Word was sent to Montgomery, and he, on July 9, performed a similar ceremony near the beach at Yerba Buena cove. (See "Raising the flag.")

The United States had finally achieved its "most important public object"—the occupation of San Francisco. Although the war with Mexico continued until February 1848, when the Treaty of Guadalupe Hidalgo was signed, little evidence of it was felt in the Bay Area. The decisive battles were fought in southern California.

Ill health forced Sloat to sail for home on July 29, barely three weeks after he had been proclaimed the first American military governor of California. He appointed as his successor Commander Robert F. Stockton, of the *Congress*.

During the period of occupation before the peace treaty was signed, the Americans retained the Mexican laws, and the townspeople elected Washington A. Bartlett, a Spanish-speaking officer from the *Portsmouth*, as alcalde of San Francisco.

On July 31, 1846, just three weeks after the U.S. flag was raised, the town's population was more than doubled by the arrival of the 450-ton *Brooklyn*. On board were 238 men, women, and children who, when they sailed from New York six months earlier, had expected to establish a Mormon colony on the coast of Mexican California, far from the persecution they had endured at the hands of Americans in Missouri and Illinois. With a few exceptions, all of these passengers belonged to the Church of Jesus Christ of Latter-day Saints.

Although they probably were happy to get off the ship after their long voyage, many of the Mormons looked anxiously at the American flag that flew so confidently on the shore. Their charismatic elder, Samuel Brannan, reportedly muttered, "There's that damned flag again!" Gone now was any hope he might have entertained about his followers taking over the place themselves.

For the crew of the *Portsmouth*, the sight of several attractive young American women was certainly an unexpected delight, as seaman Joseph Downey tells us in his reminiscences. (See "The Mormons, and Sam Brannan.")

Finding accommodations for so many people in such a small town proved to be a challenge, but within a few days the new settlers were sharing existing buildings with the residents or constructing their own homes with canvas and lumber. Mary Holland Sparks lived in a tent to begin with but then moved into one of the secularized mission buildings, which reminded her of the castles she had read about as a child. (See "Mormons at the Mission Dolores.")

These Mormons had been sent as the advance party for a much larger group being led across the plains by Brigham Young, and they set to work building a town—to be called New Hope—on the Stanislaus River. When word reached them that Young had decided to settle in the Salt Lake area, the project was abandoned. Eventually some crossed the mountains to be with their leader, while others stayed in California.

Brannan soon recognized San Francisco's potential, and he began to take an active interest in its commercial and political affairs. On January 9, 1847, he published the town's first newspaper, *The California Star*, through which he campaigned vigorously for a schoolhouse. He eventually became San Francisco's first millionaire, and at one point he owned a large portion of the town's real estate. By then, however, he had been accused of misappropriating the Mormon funds and had been excommunicated by the church.

A report in the *Star* of March 13, 1847, predicted that San Francisco, which then had a population of 500, would become the Liverpool or New York of the Pacific. By August there were 41 places of business, including two hotels, one apothecary, three bakeries, three butchers, seven grocery stores, one gunsmith, and two printing offices. Four-fifths of the population was under 40 years of age. By the end of the year there were approximately 800 residents, including 473 men, 177 women, and 60 schoolchildren.

These figures were to rise dramatically when gold was discovered at Coloma, on the American River in the Sierra Nevada. The first nuggets were found in January 1848, but several months passed before the significance of the find became apparent. Most people were skeptical—first not believing it really was gold, then doubting that there was much more of it.

Brannan is credited with having set the rush in motion. He and a partner had a small store at Sacramento. When he realized that there was indeed an abundance of gold, he stocked the store with picks, pans, and other essential provisions, and then printed a story about the find in a special edition of his San Francisco newspaper, which he sent to the East Coast.

But the people of San Francisco remained skeptical, even apathetic. So one day, on Montgomery Street, he waved a bottle of gold dust and yelled, "Gold! Gold from the American River!" He then placed the bottle on display at his newspaper office for everyone to see. That did it. Within a few days the town was almost deserted, the vast majority of people having rushed to the foothills. Brannan waited for them at his store and then sold his goods at greatly inflated prices. One report says that his sales during the early Gold Rush years averaged $150,000 a month.

Samuel Brannan's house, corner of Washington and Stockton streets, in 1847.

As one of his enterprises thrived, another struggled, then died. With the exodus from San Francisco went the advertisers and readers of his newspaper, and in June his editor, Edward Kemble, published a small, single sheet announcing the *Star's* demise.

An editorial in one of the last issues, dated May 27, 1848, gave this sad description of the deserted town:

Never within the last three years has the town presented a less lifelike, more barren appearance than at the present time, never so inactive, so void of stir as at present.

Stores are closed and places of business vacated, a large number of houses tenantless, various kinds of mechanical labor suspended or given up entirely, and nowhere the pleasant hum of industry salutes the ear as of late, but as if a curse had arrested our onward course of enterprise, every thing wears a desolate and sombre look, every where, all is dull, monotonous, dead.

The streets, late the thoroughfares of a brisk and business people, no longer resound with the incessant tread of stirring feet, no more the scenes of pressing throngs, eager consultations and hasty passing and repassing, not now disturbed by lumbering dray and clattering hoof,—the rough wind sweeps down them silent and deserted, it whirls, in mad gusts, through unobstructed passages, and howls dismally around houses great and small, but alike empty and forlorn.

For a while it looked as if Benicia, San Francisco's rival on the Carquinez Strait, might benefit because it was more accessible to the mines. But when the winter rains began, the miners came back to San Francisco, many with pockets full of gold. The town was gripped simultaneously by boredom and anticipation as people anxiously awaited the spring so they could rush back to the diggings.

Meanwhile, Brannan's newspaper story had ignited a spark in Eastern cities, and in February the first steamship, the *California*, arrived laden with potential miners. Other American ships followed. Then, as sailors spread the word around the world, ships of every nationality soon were anchoring in the bay, and a fresh vitality seized the town.

Homes, hotels, restaurants, saloons, merchant stores, and entertainment centers opened to cater to the thousands of incoming gold-seekers. Prices escalated. Eggs sold for $1 each, potatoes for $1.50 a pound. Buildings that had sold cheaply during the initial mania now resold at astronomical prices.

The once-popular billiard saloons no longer appealed to the miners who had been exerting all their time and energies panning for gold. Rained out of the mines, these men had little or no enthusiasm for pocketing balls with a cue. What they now hungered for was another means of getting rich, and fast—like at the turn of a card, or the roll of dice.

They persuaded the saloon keepers to replace the billiard tables with faro, roulette, and other gambling tables, and for several years the gaudily decorated *hells*—as gambling dens were called—provided the major source of entertainment and revenue on the Pacific coast. They also contributed to a rapidly increasing crime rate, thus ending what the old-timers later looked back upon as the good old days when San Francisco was a sleepy village called Yerba Buena. (See "A different class of people.")

In the spring of '49, thousands left town for the mines, which were now scattered over a wide area in and around the Mother Lode region. But the gold-seekers were soon replaced by new arrivals as people began pouring in to San Francisco not only on ships but also in covered wagons, trekking across plains and mountain ranges. Shrewd business owners realized there were other fortunes to be made by staying in town.

At that time there were many more hills in San Francisco than there are today. Some reached close to the water's edge, restricting expansion. Another disadvantage of the town's location was the lack of landing facilities. Ships had to anchor in the bay while their crews and passengers were ferried to one of two rocky promontories, either Clark's Point at the foot of Broadway, or Rincon Point at the opposite end of Yerba Buena cove.

Such obstacles were soon challenged and defeated. Steam-driven shovels (dubbed "steam-paddies," apparently because they did the work of several Irishmen) were brought in to level some hills and to cut major thoroughfares through others. Huge wharves were constructed at Broadway, Clay, Washington, and other major streets, reaching out into deeper water where ships could dock and discharge their cargoes. Some of these wharves were lined with rows of wooden shacks. In time, the area between the wharves was filled, usually with sand excavated from the hills, creating entirely new areas to expand the commercial section of the town.

The principal streets of the town were graded and paved with wooden planks in 1850, and a year later they were lit by lamps, the earliest of which were paid for by neighboring business houses and gambling saloons.

In the fall of 1849, a convention of 48 delegates was held at Monterey to draw up a constitution and to elect representatives to go to Washington and seek statehood for California, bypassing the traditional territorial status. Despite its newfound wealth, however, California was not welcomed by all of the nation's lawmakers. At that time the 30 states were evenly divided for and against slavery, and California's strong anti-slavery constitution was a threat to that balance. The debate was long and emotional, and it set a precedent by continuing throughout the summer months.

Yet for all this activity there prevailed a sense of the temporary in San Francisco. According to many letters, diaries, journals, and other writings left by those argonauts, the stay in San Francisco was only a sojourn to pick up a fortune that would be carried home when the gold fields dried up. Few of the early structures built by these people were more than wooden frames covered with canvas. Some of the hotel rooms were merely 2½ ft. x 6 ft. cubicles with walls of calico, or of canvas decorated with colored papers. Some lodging houses consisted of large rooms fitted with wooden ledges which served as bunks, with guests supplying their own bedding. And many people still lived in tents, which they pitched wherever they could find a vacant piece of land.

A great many of the ships bringing gold-seeking passengers were stranded when their crews deserted, creating a forest of masts blanketing the bay. In November 1849, 600 vessels were counted, most of which never did sail again. Some of these were landlocked when the mud flats around the wharves were filled in. Holes were cut into their sides for doors and windows, and they were transformed into hotels, business premises, homes, warehouses. The *Euphemia* became a jail, and the *Apollo* a saloon.

The most famous of these ships was the *Niantic*, which was converted into a warehouse when it was beached at Clay and Sansome streets. (See "A heterogeneous population.") It burned to the ground in 1851 and was replaced by a 3-story wooden building, the ground floor of which was occupied by offices and shops and the upper floors by the Niantic Hotel. This was demolished in 1872 to make way for the Niantic Block, which was destroyed in the 1906 earthquake and fire. On each occasion workers found what they believed were the last remains of the old ship. Yet when the present office building was erected on the site in 1978 the skeletal beams of the hull were unearthed. Salvage efforts were abandoned because of a lack of funds, and the exposed beams were chomped up by bulldozers. But that was not the end of the *Niantic*. A small portion of the bow section protruded onto an adjoining lot and is still there today, buried beneath the Transamerica Corporation's tiny Redwood Park.

The *Euphemia* as a jail, and the *Apollo* as a saloon.

About six o'clock on the morning of December 24, 1849, a fire broke out in one of the gambling saloons on Portsmouth Plaza, in the heart of town. Although the weather was calm, flames spread rapidly through the adjoining tinder-box structures until 50 buildings had been devoured. This was the first of six major fires to sweep San Francisco during an 18-month period. As soon as the fires were out, people erected new buildings, only to see them destroyed by the next blaze.

Three entire blocks were destroyed on May 4, 1850, and a few weeks later, on June 14, 300 more buildings were lost. Another conflagration flared on September 17. But the most horrendous of all was the fire that roared out of control on May 3-4, 1851. It began near

Portsmouth Plaza and is believed to have been started by an arsonist. This is how Bancroft described it in his *History of California*:

> Aided by a strong north-west breeze, it leaped across Kearny st upon the oft-ravaged blocks, the flames chasing one another, first south-eastward, then, with the shifting wind, turning north and east. The spaces under the planking of the streets and side-walks acted as funnels, which, sucking in the flames, carried them to sections seemingly secure, there to startle the unsuspecting occupants with a sudden outbreak all along the surface. Rising aloft, the whirling volumes seized upon either side, shriveling the frame houses, and crumbling with their intense heat the stout walls of supposed fire-proof structures, crushing all within and without. The iron shutters, ere falling to melt in the furnace, expanded within the heat, cutting off escape, and roasting alive some of the inmates.
>
> .   .   .
>
> Of the great city nothing remained save sparsely settled outskirts. All the business district between Pine and Pacific sts, from Kearny to Battery, on the water, presented a mass of ruins wherein only a few isolated houses still reared their blistered walls, besides small sections at each of its four corners. West-ward and north-eastward additional inroads had been made, ex-tending the devastation altogether over 22 blocks, not counting sections formed by alleys, and of these the greater number were utterly ravaged, as shown in the annexed plan. [See next page.] The number of destroyed houses has been variously estimated at from over 1,000 to nearly 2,000, involving a loss of nearly twelve million dollars, a sum larger than that for all the preceding great fires combined.

Looting was rampant. A large cache of stolen goods was later recovered on Yerba Buena Island, although one ship is reported to have gotten away with loot valued at between $150,000 and $200,000.

A sixth fire erupted the next month. Bancroft adds that this one was "due partly to the flimsiness of the temporary buildings, and partly to the lack of time to establish preventive measures and weed out incendiary hordes." Strict new ordinances were passed, regulating materials to be used in rebuilding the ravaged parts of town, and, within a very short time, San Francisco was on its way again to be-coming a major metropolis.

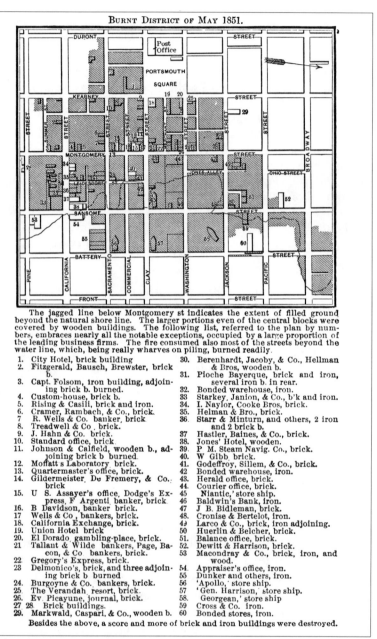

BURNT DISTRICT OF MAY 1851.

The jagged line below Montgomery st indicates the extent of filled ground beyond the natural shore line. The larger portions even of the central blocks were covered by wooden buildings. The following list, referred to the plan by numbers, embraces nearly all the notable exceptions, occupied by a large proportion of the leading business firms. The fire consumed also most of the streets beyond the water line, which, being really wharves on piling, burned readily.

1. City Hotel, brick building
2. Fitzgerald, Bausch, Brewster, brick b.
3. Capt. Folsom, iron building, adjoining brick b. burned.
4. Custom-house, brick b.
5. Rising & Casili, brick and iron.
6. Cramer, Rambach, & Co., brick.
7. R. Wells & Co. banker, brick
8. Treadwell & Co., brick.
9. J. Hahn & Co. brick.
10. Standard office, brick
11. Johnson & Calfield, wooden b., adjoining brick b burned.
12. Moffatt s Laboratory brick.
13. Quartermaster's office, brick.
14. Gildermeister, De Fremery, & Co., brick
15. U S. Assayer's office, Dodge's Express, F Argenti banker, brick
16. B Davidson, banker brick.
17. Wells & Co, bankers, brick.
18. California Exchange, brick.
19. Union Hotel brick
20. El Dorado, gambling-place, brick.
21. Tallant & Wilde bankers, Page, Bacon, & Co bankers, brick.
22. Gregory's Express, brick.
23. Delmonico's, brick, and three adjoining brick b burned
24. Burgoyne & Co. bankers, brick.
25. The Verandah resort, brick.
26. Ev. Picayune, journal, brick.
27 28. Brick buildings.
29. Markwald, Caspari, & Co., wooden b.

30. Berenhardt, Jacoby, & Co., Hellman & Bros, wooden b.
31. Pioche Bayerque, brick and iron, several iron b. in rear.
32. Bonded warehouse, iron.
33 Starkey, Janion, & Co., b'k and iron.
34. I. Naylor, Cooke Bros, brick.
35. Helman & Bro., brick.
36. Starr & Minturn, and others, 2 iron and 2 brick b.
37 Hastler, Baines, & Co., brick.
38. Jones' Hotel, wooden.
39. P M. Steam Navig. Co., brick.
40. W Gibb, brick.
41. Godeffroy, Sillem, & Co., brick.
42 Bonded warehouse, iron.
43. Herald office, brick.
44. Courier office, brick.
45 Niantic,' store ship.
46 Baldwin's Bank, iron.
47 J B. Bidleman, brick.
48. Cronise & Bertelot, iron.
49 Larco & Co., brick, iron adjoining.
50 Huerlin & Belcher, brick.
51. Balance office, brick.
52. Dewitt & Harrison, brick.
53 Macondray & Co., brick, iron, and wood.
54 Appraiser's office, iron.
55 Dunker and others, iron.
56 'Apollo,' store ship.
57 'Gen. Harrison,' store ship.
58. Georgean,' store ship
59 Cross & Co. iron.
60 Bonded stores, iron.

Besides the above, a score and more of brick and iron buildings were destroyed.

This plan accompanied H. H. Bancroft's description of the May 3-4, 1851 fire in his *History of California* (volume 6).

Appropriately, a phoenix rising from flames dominated the first seal adopted by the city, on November 4, 1852. Today's seal, with the phoenix in a less prominent but still significant position above a shield flanked by a miner and a sailor, was adopted in 1859 when San Francisco became a combined city and county.

On the morning of October 18, 1850, all of San Francisco turned out in an enthusiastic display of patriotism when the steamship *Oregon* sailed into the bay trailing a huge banner that proclaimed "California admitted!" The debate in Washington had ended on September 9 when President Millard Fillmore signed the California Bill, but only now was the news being received in San Francisco. Immediately, the booming of cannon echoed around the bay, and people gathered in happy clusters in the streets, laughing and congratulating one another. The stars and stripes waved from every vantage point. The emotions of that day are recaptured by Sarah Royce in "Home again!"

The excitement continued for several days and climaxed with a huge parade through the streets on October 29. The highlight was a tableau drawn by six white horses and featuring a young girl dressed in white with roses in her hair, representing California. Accompanying her were 30 boys, each carrying a shield inscribed with the name of one of the other states.

In his memoirs, written more than 60 years later, James Horace Skinner tells of taking part in a huge parade, which he recalled as being held to celebrate the ending of the U.S.-Mexico war. (See "Through the eyes of a child.") According to *The Annals of San Francisco* (published 1854), news of the peace agreed to in February 1848 did not reach Monterey until June 6 of that year, and it was commemorated in San Francisco on August 11 when "a cavalcade of citizens proceeded through the streets."

The brief account gives no hint of the grand procession described by Skinner. In fact, when we realize that in August most of the people were still at the mines, it is unlikely that such an extravagant spectacle could have been held in town then. His description matches contemporary newspaper accounts of the statehood parade. Furthermore, sketches of that historic event survive, depicting the towering float being drawn by six white horses. And so it seems that 8-year-old James Horace Skinner was one of the boys riding on that horse-drawn float on October 29, 1850.

Celebrating the admission of California as a state, October 29, 1850.

The gold mines attracted people through the 1850s and into the early 1860s. During this time San Francisco continued to grow and prosper. As sturdier buildings were built on the ashes of earlier structures, a greater sense of permanence enveloped the city. Recreational areas were developed. Prominent actors, musicians, and lecturers from New York, London, and Paris appeared at the theaters. Entire families moved in to stay, their presence stimulating men to drastically improve their manners and the way they dressed. The rough red shirts so commonly seen in earlier days were replaced by almost dandified clothing. And San Francisco's own brand of society, blending *nouveau riche* with established elite, began to emerge.

The city's first seal, adopted November 4, 1852.

San Francisco circa 1846-1847, when Montgomery Street was the waterfront. The large ship is the *Portsmouth.*

Yerba Buena
1835-1847

Richard Henry Dana, Jr., was 20 years old when he sailed into San Francisco Bay as a seaman aboard the brig *Alert* in December 1835. The ship, which was engaged in the hide and tallow trade that flourished on the California coast during the 1820s-1840s, remained in the bay for three weeks as the crew gathered hides from the missions and replenished the ship's supplies of wood and water.

After returning to Boston, Dana wrote of his experiences in *Two Years Before the Mast*—a book that has remained in print for the 150 years since. In this excerpt from the 1869 edition, Dana recalls spending two long, cold, rain-soaked nights in an open boat gathering wood on Angel Island, or as he and his crewmates called it, Wood Island.

His opening remarks that the presidio was "thirty miles from the mouth of the bay" and that Sir Francis Drake discovered the bay can be explained by the early belief that San Francisco Bay could be entered at Drake's Bay, farther up the coast. (See "What's in a name?")

This portrait was made about 1842, six years after Dana's voyage when, according to his daughter Elizabeth Ellery Dana, he was asked by the family to "put on his sailor dress for some special occasion."

RICHARD HENRY DANA (1815-1882)

Three weeks
before the mast

OUR PLACE OF DESTINATION HAD BEEN Monterey, but as we were to the northward of it when the wind hauled ahead, we made a fair wind for San Francisco. This large bay, which lies in latitude 37° 58', was discovered by Sir Francis Drake, and by him represented to be (as indeed it is) a magnificent bay, containing several good harbors, great depth of water, and surrounded by a fertile and finely wooded country. About thirty miles from the mouth of the bay, and on the southeast side, is a high point, upon which the Presidio is built. Behind this point is the little harbor, or bight, called Yerba Buena, in which trading-vessels anchor, and, near it, the Mission of Dolorés. There was no other habitation on this side of the Bay, except a shanty of rough boards put up by a man named Richardson, who was doing a little trading between the vessels and the Indians.

Here, at anchor, and the only vessel, was a brig under Russian colors, from Sitka, in Russian America, which had come down to winter and to take in a supply of tallow and grain, great quantities of which latter article are raised in the Missions at the head of the bay. The second day after our arrival we went on board the brig, it being Sunday, as a matter of curiosity; and there was enough there to gratify it. Though no larger than the Pilgrim, she had five or six officers, and a crew of between twenty and thirty; and such a stupid and greasy-looking set, I never saw before. Although it was quite comfortable weather and we had nothing on but straw hats, shirts, and duck trousers, and were barefooted, they had, every man of them, double-soled boots, coming up to the knees, and well greased; thick woollen trousers, frocks*, waistcoats, pea-jackets, woollen caps, and every-thing in true Nova Zembla rig; and in the warmest days they made no change. The clothing of one of these men would weigh nearly as much as that of half our crew. They had brutish faces, looked like the an-tipodes of sailors, and apparently dealt in nothing but grease. They lived upon grease; ate it, drank it, slept in the midst of it, and their clothes were covered with it. To a Russian, grease is the greatest luxury. They looked with greedy eyes upon the tallow-bags as they were taken into the vessel, and, no doubt, would have eaten one up whole, had not the officer kept watch over it. The grease appeared to fill their pores, and to come out in their hair and on their faces. It seems as if it were this saturation which makes them stand cold and rain so well. If they were to go into a warm climate, they would melt and die of the scurvy.

The vessel was no better than the crew. Everything was in the oldest and most inconvenient fashion possible: running trusses and lifts on the yards, and large hawser cables, coiled all over the decks, and served and parcelled in all directions. The topmasts, top-gallant-masts, and studding-sail booms were nearly black for want of scraping, and the decks would have turned the stomach of a man-of-war's-man. The galley was down in the forecastle; and there the crew lived, in the midst of the steam and grease of the cooking, in a place as hot as an oven, and apparently never cleaned out. Five minutes in the forecastle was enough for us, and we were glad to get into the open air.

We made some trade with them, buying Indian curiosities, of which they had a great number; such as bead-work, feathers of birds, fur moccasins, &c. I purchased a large robe, made of the skins of some animal, dried and sewed nicely together, and covered all over on the outside with thick downy feathers, taken from the breasts of various birds, and arranged with their different colors so as to make a brilliant show.

A few days after our arrival the rainy season set in, and for three weeks it rained almost every hour, without cessation. This was bad for our trade, for the collecting of hides is managed differently in this port from what it is in any other on the coast. The Mission of Dolorés, near the anchorage, has no trade at all; but those of San José, Santa

* Woolen sweaters.

Clara, and others situated on the large creeks or rivers, which run into the bay, and distant between fifteen and forty miles from the anchorage, do a greater business in hides than any in California. Large boats, or launches, manned by Indians, and capable of carrying from five to six hundred hides apiece, are attached to the Missions, and sent down to the vessels with hides, to bring away goods in return. Some of the crews of the vessels are obliged to go and come in the boats, to look out for the hides and goods. These are favorite expeditions with the sailors in fine weather; but now, to be gone three or four days, in open boats, in constant rain, without any shelter, and with cold food, was hard service.

Two of our men went up to Santa Clara in one of these boats, and were gone three days, during all which time they had a constant rain, and did not sleep a wink, but passed three long nights walking fore and aft the boat, in the open air. When they got on board they were completely exhausted, and took a watch below of twelve hours. All the hides, too, that came down in the boats were soaked with water, and unfit to put below, so that we were obliged to trice them up to dry, in the intervals of sunshine or wind, upon all parts of the vessel. We got our tricing-lines from the jib-boom-end to each arm of the fore yard, and thence to the main and cross-jack yard-arms. Between the tops, too, and the mast-heads, from the fore to the main swifters, and thence to the mizzen rigging, and in all directions athwartships, trice-lines were run, and strung with hides. The head stays and guys, and the spritsail yard were lined, and, having still more, we got out the swinging-booms, and strung them and the forward and after guys with hides. The rail, fore and aft, the windlass, capstan, the sides of the ship, and every vacant place on deck, were covered with wet hides, on the least sign of an interval for drying. Our ship was nothing but a mass of hides, from the cat-hairpins to the water's edge, and from the jib-boom-end to the taffrail.

One cold, rainy evening, about eight o'clock, I received orders to get ready to start for San José at four the next morning, in one of these Indian boats, with four days' provisions. I got my oil-cloth clothes, southwester, and thick boots ready, and turned into my hammock early, determined to get some sleep in advance, as the boat was to be alongside before daybreak. I slept on till all hands were called in the morning; for, fortunately for me, the Indians, intentionally, or from mistaking their orders, had gone off alone in the night, and were far out of sight. Thus I escaped three or four days of very uncomfortable service.

Four of our men, a few days afterwards, went up in one of the quarter-boats to Santa Clara, to carry the agent, and remained out all night in a drenching rain, in the small boat, in which there was no room for them to turn round; the agent having gone up to the Mission and left the men to their fate, making no provision for their accommodation, and not even sending them anything to eat. After this they had to pull thirty miles, and when they got on board were so stiff that they could not come up the gangway ladder. This filled up the measure of the agent's unpopularity, and never after this could he get anything done for him by the crew; and many a delay and vexation, and many a good ducking in the surf, did he get to pay up old scores, or "square the yards with the bloody quill-driver."*

Having collected nearly all the hides that were to be procured, we began our preparations for taking in a supply of wood and water, for both of which San Francisco is the best place on the coast. A small island, about two leagues from the anchorage, called by us "Wood Island," and by the Mexicans "Isla de los Angeles," was covered with trees to the water's edge; and to this two of our crew, who were Kennebec men, and could handle an axe like a plaything, were sent every morning to cut wood, with two boys to pile it up for them. In about a week they had cut enough to last us a year, and the third mate, with myself and three others, were sent over in a large, schooner-rigged, open launch, which we had hired of the Mission, to take in the wood, and bring it to the ship. We left the ship about noon, but owing to a strong head wind, and a tide which here runs four or five knots, did not get into the harbor, formed by two points of the island, where the boats lie, until sundown. No sooner had we come-to, than a strong southeaster, which had been threatening us all day, set in, with heavy rain and a chilly air. We were in rather a bad situation: an open boat, a heavy rain, and a long night; for in winter, in this latitude, it was dark nearly fifteen hours.

Taking a small skiff which we had brought with us, we went ashore but discovered no shelter, for everything was open to the rain;

---

* "get even with the pen-pusher." (See Glossary.)

and, collecting a little wood, which we found by lifting up the leaves and brush, and a few mussels, we put aboard again, and made the best preparations in our power for passing the night. We unbent the main-sail, and formed an awning with it over the after part of the boat, made a bed of wet logs of wood, and, with our jackets on, lay down, about six o'clock, to sleep.

Finding the rain running down upon us, and our jackets getting wet through, and the rough, knotty logs rather indifferent couches, we turned out; and, taking an iron pan which we brought with us, we wiped it out dry, put some stones around it, cut the wet bark from some sticks, and, striking a light, made a small fire in the pan. Keeping some sticks near to dry, and covering the whole over with a roof of boards, we kept up a small fire, by which we cooked our mussels, and ate them, rather for an occupation than from hunger. Still it was not ten o'clock, and the night was long before us, when one of the party produced an old pack of Spanish cards from his monkey-jacket pock-et, which we hailed as a great windfall; and, keeping a dim, flickering light by our fagots, we played game after game, till one or two o'clock, when, becoming really tired, we went to our logs again, one sitting up at a time, in turn, to keep watch over the fire.

Toward morning the rain ceased, and the air became sensibly colder, so that we found sleep impossible, and sat up, watching for daybreak. No sooner was it light than we went ashore, and began our preparations for loading our vessel. We were not mistaken in the coldness of the weather, for a white frost was on the ground—a thing we had never seen before in California—and one or two little puddles of fresh water were skimmed over with a thin coat of ice. In this state of the weather, and before sunrise, in the gray of the morning, we had to wade off, nearly up to our hips in water, to load the skiff with the wood by armfuls.

The third mate remained on board the launch, two more men stayed in the skiff to load and manage it, and all the water-work, as usual, fell upon the two youngest of us; and there we were with frost on the ground, wading forward and back, from the beach to the boat, with armfuls of wood, barefooted, and our trousers rolled up. When the skiff went off with her load, we could only keep our feet from freezing by racing up and down the beach on the hard sand, as fast as we could go.

We were all day at this work, and toward sundown, having loaded the vessel as deep as she would bear, we hove up our anchor and made sail, beating out of the bay. No sooner had we got into the large bay than we found a strong tide setting us out to seaward, a thick fog which prevented our seeing the ship, and a breeze too light to set us against the tide, for we were as deep as a sand-barge. By the utmost exertions, we saved ourselves from being carried out to sea, and were glad to reach the leewardmost point of the island, where we came-to, and prepared to pass another night more uncomfortable than the first, for we were loaded up to the gunwale, and had only a choice among logs and sticks for a resting-place. The next morning we made sail at slack water, with a fair wind, and got on board by eleven o'clock, when all hands were turned-to to unload and stow away the wood, which took till night.

Having now taken in all our wood, the next morning a water-party was ordered off with all the casks. From this we escaped, having had a pretty good siege with the wooding. The water-party were gone three days, during which time they narrowly escaped being carried out to sea, and passed one day on an island, where one of them shot a deer, great numbers of which overrun the islands and hills of San Francisco Bay.

While not off on these wood and water parties, or up the rivers to the Missions, we had easy times on board the ship. We were moored, stem and stern, within a cable's length of the shore, safe from south-easters, and with little boating to do; and, as it rained nearly all the time, awnings were put over the hatchways, and all hands sent down between decks, where we were at work, day after day, picking oakum, until we got enough to calk the ship all over, and to last the whole voyage. Then we made a whole suit of gaskets for the voyage home, a pair of wheel-ropes from strips of green hide, great quantities of spun-yarn, and everything else that could be made between decks. It being now mid-winter and in high latitude, the nights were very long, so that we were not turned-to until seven in the morning, and were obliged to knock off at five in the evening, when we got supper; which gave us nearly three hours before eight bells, at which time the watch was set.

As we had now been about a year on the coast, it was time to think of the voyage home; and, knowing that the last two or three months of our stay would be very busy ones, and that we should never have so good an opportunity to work for ourselves as the present, we all employed our evenings in making clothes for the passage home, and more especially for Cape Horn. As soon as supper was over and the kids* cleared away, and each man had taken his smoke, we seated ourselves on our chests round the lamp, which swung from a beam, and went to work each in his own way, some making hats, others trousers, others jackets, &c., &c., and no one was idle. The boys who could not sew well enough to make their own clothes laid up grass into sinnet** for the men, who sewed for them in return. Several of us clubbed together and bought a large piece of twilled cotton, which we made into trousers and jackets, and, giving them several coats of linseed oil, laid them by for Cape Horn.

I also sewed and covered a tarpaulin hat, thick and strong enough to sit upon, and made myself a complete suit of flannel underclothing for bad weather. Those who had no southwester caps made them; and several of the crew got up for themselves tarpaulin jackets and trousers, lined on the inside with flannel. Industry was the order of the day, and every one did something for himself; for we knew that as the season advanced, and we went further south, we should have no evenings to work in.

Friday, December 25th. This day was Christmas; and, as it rained all day long, and there was no hides to take in, and nothing especial to do, the captain gave us a holiday (the first we had had, except Sundays, since leaving Boston), and plum-duff for dinner. The Russian brig, following the Old Style, had celebrated their Christmas eleven days before, when they had a grand blowout, and (as our men said) drank, in the forecastle, a barrel of gin, ate up a bag of tallow, and made a soup of the skin.

Sunday, December 27th. We had now finished all our business at this port, and, it being Sunday, we unmoored ship and got under way, firing a salute to the Russian brig, and another to the presidio, which were both answered. The commandante of the presidio, Don Guadalupe Vallejo, a young man, and the most popular, among the Americans and English, of any man in California, was on board when

---

* Tubs for serving food to sailors.
** They wove grass into ropes for the ship's rigging. (See Glossary.)

we got under way. He spoke English very well, and was suspected of being favorably inclined to foreigners.

We sailed down this magnificent bay with a light wind, the tide, which was running out, carrying us at the rate of four or five knots. It was a fine day; the first of entire sunshine we had had for more than a month. We passed directly under the high cliff on which the presidio is built, and stood into the middle of the bay, from whence we could see small bays making up into the interior, large and beautifully wooded islands, and the mouths of several small rivers. If California ever becomes a prosperous country, this bay will be the center of its prosperity. The abundance of wood and water; the extreme fertility of its shores; the excellence of its climate, which is as near to being perfect as any in the world; and its facilities for navigation, affording the best anchoring-grounds in the whole western coast of America,—all fit it for a place of great importance.

The tide leaving us, we came to anchor near the mouth of the bay, under a high and beautifully sloping hill, upon which herds of hundreds and hundreds of red deer, and the stag, with his high branching antlers, were bounding about, looking at us for a moment, and then starting off, affrighted at the noises which we made for the purpose of seeing the variety of their beautiful attitudes and motions.

At midnight, the tide having turned, we hove up our anchor and stood out of the bay, with a fine starry heaven above us,—the first we had seen for many weeks.

The high cliff on which Dana saw the presidio no longer exists. The Spanish called it *Punta del Cantil Blanco*—White Cliff Point—and on top of it they built an adobe fort, *Castillo de San Joaquin*. In 1853-1854 the cliff was leveled to make way for Fort Point, which today sits snugly beneath a steel arch of the Golden Gate Bridge.

The *Alert* was not the only ship to take trees from Angel Island. The practice was so prevalent that by 1850 the island was stripped almost bare of native coast live oak, buckeye, bay laurel, and madrone trees. Australian eucalyptus was planted in their place, but today 90 percent of these are being removed to make way for a new crop of native trees.

White Cliff Point before it was leveled to make way for Fort Point. Today, the
Golden Gate Bridge spans the strait.

The "shanty of rough boards" that Dana saw when he sailed into the bay was San Francisco's first private dwelling. It was erected in June 1835, near the beach of Yerba Buena, a cove which came up to where Montgomery Street is today, and for several months it was the home of the Richardson family— William Richardson (a former English sailor), his Spanish wife, Maria Antonia (daughter of the Presidio *comandante*, Ignacio Martínez), and their three small children, Mariana, Esteban, and Francisco. Later, the shanty was replaced by the more substantial adobe home which Esteban recalls in this brief excerpt from his memoirs, *The Days of the Dons*. These memoirs appeared under the name Steve Richardson in the San Francisco *Bulletin* between April 22 and June 8, 1918. He was about 30 when this daguerreotype was made.

Bears, wolves, and coyotes

ONE THING ABOUT THE COVE OF YERBA BUENA, or San Francisco, as it very soon came to be called, was the great number of good-sized fish that swam close in shore and were stranded by the out-going tide. These were the natural food of all sorts of predacious animals, which existed in enormous numbers and, being little interfered with by man, were for that reason indifferent to his presence. I often used to sit on the veranda of my father's house and watch bears, wolves and coyotes quarreling over their prey along what is now Montgomery street. These wild animals were perfectly harmless, only it was not wise to have too much fun with an old bear with cubs.

I have no recollection of the time when I could not ride. When I was 5 or 6 years old I often galloped as far as the Mission Dolores and even further to visit my chums at the neighboring ranches. I often passed bears and wolves so close that I could have thrown a lariat over them. So far as danger went, they never interfered with me in the least.

But, as my father had anticipated, the cove of Yerba Buena at once began to grow. First one settler came, then another. The name was changed officially from Yerba Buena to San Francisco, for now we had the beginning of local government; an alcalde, who was a sort of mayor and overlord, frequently combining the duties of justice of the peace; and an ayuntamiento, or town council. To show how expansive things were in those days, my grandfather, who lived in Martinez, was the second alcalde of San Francisco in the year 1837.

The authority of the alcalde was represented by a "barra," or iron rod, which was the emblem of authority, somewhat the same as a policeman's star. Everything was done in the name of "la barra." Stripped of this emblem, the alcalde descended from the realms of power to plain Carlos or Jose. Once my grandfather came from Martinez to adjust some matter of local importance. But he had left his barra at home and the people made a josh of him. So my father had to make a flying trip to Martinez and bring back the all-important barra. With this, the people were perfectly content and submissive.

.   .   .

In 1841, with everything on an edge in San Francisco (my father) sold his big house and moved bodily to Sausalito. As I recollect, San Francisco contained then from fifty to sixty houses.

Indeed, my father believed that two cities would spring up on each side of the Golden Gate and he preferred to cast his lot where he owned everything. But his hopes were never realized. When he died San Francisco had risen to the rank of a great commercial city, while Sausalito embraced only a pitiful collection of ramshackle huts. That, of course, excepts the great adobe hacienda of the Rancho Sausalito, or the Richardson Ranch, as it came to be named. The ranch was stocked with cattle, and it was my business to learn the ways of the rancho. When I was fifteen years old, one year after the American occupation, I was given full charge of this great property with its thousands of head of cattle, and continued to manage it until it passed into other hands.

My father did not, however, entirely sever his connection with San Francisco. He was appointed the harbor captain of the port at Yerba Buena, later designated as San Francisco, and remained so until the Americans took the job off his hands. For acting in this capacity, the Mexican government, always short of cash, but liberal in land, granted my father a vast concession—thirty leagues frontage along the shore line of the Pacific Ocean, from the mouth of the Gualala river, to the mouth of the Rio Grande river, now called Big river, in Mendocino county. I forget how many leagues deep it extended into the interior. But my ancestor always sniffed at this gift, worth countless millions today, and never took the pains to take the simple steps to insure his title. Solely because he had slept at the switch and overlooked a few technicalities the Richardson title to this principality was finally rejected by the United States government.

.   .   .

If the plain truth must be told, the cove of Yerba Buena was a dismal thing to look on in those early days. The beach was right enough, but to the westward stretched a wilderness of desolate, forbidding sand dunes, often shifting their positions overnight. When one considers that many of them were 100 or more feet high, one can realize the uncertainties of the landscape. When the trade wind blew in fresh from the ocean, it carried with it an almost incredible burden of both fine and coarse sand that got into clothes, eyes, nose, mouth—anything that was open in short—besides penetrating the innermost recesses of a household. Only sound lungs were proof against the accumulation of sharp, gritty material daily inhaled. In fact the place long had a reputation for unhealthfulness, not entirely undeserved, until the levelling of the dunes and the reclamation of the park tract checked the shifting sands for good.

I really believe the misery this caused my mother, who was a notable housekeeper, occasioned, in the end, the family's removal to Sausalito. Add to this, while there were good springs in the neighborhood—one on what is Clay street, near Kearny, the cove was many miles from running water.

Nevertheless, nothing was ever able to keep population and commerce away from it, though it has received thumps enough to kill any other ambitious town that ever happened. The instincts of the people are often far wiser than the master minds. From the very time that we set up house, Yerba Buena cove began to grow, and pitiful little beginnings of business commenced to lift their heads. Everyone had something mean to say about the cove. Still, they stayed. To tell the truth, they had no other place to go. The Presidio had been abandoned. Little remained of it but fast crumbling walls and rusty guns. The Mission building was deserted and lapsing into decay, the last human evidence of its former greatness being an encampment or rancheria, of half-civilized Indians on what is now Sixteenth Street, not far from Dolores.

Before coming overland to California in 1845, Englishman John Henry Brown was a sailor and a fur trader. He was one of the earliest settlers in Yerba Buena and, as a bartender and hotel manager during the town's formative years of 1846-1850, was in a unique position to observe the lives and times of his fellow pioneers. His *Reminiscences and Incidents of the Early Days of San Francisco (1845-1850)*, published in 1886, recalls those days with a fascinating attention to detail which most other accounts lack.

In this excerpt, the first of five included here, he tells of the Bear Flag Revolt—an ill-conceived attempt by a handful of American settlers to establish an independent Republic of California. When the revolutionaries raised their homemade flag at Sonoma they had not heard the news that the United States was already at war with Mexico. The republic lasted only one month, from June 14 to July 9, 1846, and fizzled when Commodore John Sloat raised the American flag at Monterey.

Brown wrote his reminiscences more than 40 years after the events occurred. Although historians accept almost all of the manuscript as accurate, there are a few errors that need to be corrected. Most of these concern names which he spelled as they sounded to him; a few involve dates. (See "Resource notes" at back of this volume for corrections.)

JOHN HENRY BROWN (1810-1905)

Revolt, occupation, and foreign intrigue

W HEN I FIRST CAME TO THE CITY, there was only one vessel in the harbor, the bark "Emma" of London, England. I cannot recall the Captain's name; but the First Officer was Mr. Pritchard, the Second, Mr. Norris. They were on a whaling trip and stopped at Yerba Buena for supplies, etc.

The only pay the City officials received for their services, was that raised by fines, most of which was taken from sailors, who would remain on shore after sunset. The fine for this offense was usually five or ten dollars, as the case might be, and the money thus received was equally divided between the authorities. Captains and First officers were permitted to remain on shore as long as they pleased.

As stated elsewhere I was in the employ of [John] Finch and [John] Thompson, having charge of the bar, and also keeping the accounts. Mr. Finch was a man of but little education; in fact, he could neither read nor write and he had a peculiar way of his own in keeping accounts. He had an excellent memory for names and was in the habit of noting any peculiarity about a person as regards his dress and general appearance. Captain Hinckley wore brass buttons on his coat and was represented on the books by a drawing of a button. A certain sawyer in the place was represented by a drawing of the top saws of a saw pit, and many others were thus represented according to their various characteristics or callings. Many of the drawings showed considerable ingenuity and originality. I remained with Finch about three weeks, during that time I became acquainted with Robert T. Ridley the proprietor of a liquor and billiard saloon [Vioget's House, which Ridley was leasing from Jean Jacques Vioget, the man who had drawn up the first map of Yerba Buena]. He made me an offer of fifty dollars per month to take charge of his place. I accepted the offer and commenced my work there in the early part of February, 1846.

The bark "Sterling" of Boston, Captain Vincent, Master; and William Smith, Super Cargo; arrived in port in February, with a full cargo. Ridley had made some large purchases of wines and liquors from Mr. Smith. The billiard-room was at that time the head-quarters for all strangers in the city, both foreigners and Californians. All persons wishing to purchase lots would apply to Ridley: as the first map of surveyed land was kept in the bar-room, the names of those who had lots granted were written on the map. The map was so much soiled and torn from the rough usage it received, that Captain Hinckley volunteered to make a new one. He tried several times; but, being very nervous he could not succeed in making the lines straight, so he got me to do the work, according to his instructions. The original map was put away for safe keeping. The maps were left in the bar-room, until after the raising of the American Flag, when they were demanded of me by Washington A. Bartlett, of the United States Ship Portsmouth, by order of Captain Montgomery.

Things went on as usual in the city until the latter part of May, when a report reached the city, that trouble was expected. A party at Sutter's Fort were raising a company to take possession of the upper part of California. In the early part of June, a boat arrived from Martinez, with the news that Sonoma was taken, and a proclamation, with Mr. Hyde's signature, was posted in a prominent place which announced that General Vallejo and Timothy Murphy, of San Rafael, with many others, were taken prisoners. A few days after, a party of fourteen Californians came to Saucelito, and wanted to hire Captain Richardson's boat, to take them across to Yerba Buena. As they were all well armed with pistols, rifles and guns and were very much excited and badly frightened, Richardson inquired what the trouble was, they told him that a party of four armed men were pursuing them, and that they were afraid they would be shot. As they were fourteen against four, Captain Richardson asked why they did not stand their ground, and fight the men. They said they had been fighting the past four days, but had not succeeded as yet in frightening the party away; and as the men appeared to be very determined, and bent upon injuring them, they had decided that "discretion was the better part of valor," and consequently took to their heels. A few days after, General Castro [José Castro, the Mexican military commander for California] issued a proclamation, commanding all Mexican citizens to meet him at Santa Clara for orders. The only foreigners who left the city for Santa Clara, were Captain William Hinckley and Robert T. Ridley. [See comment.] They were ordered to stop all boats and prevent all persons from landing in Yerba Buena. On their return home, Hinckley was taken sick and died, on Burnell's Ranch, and was buried in the church at Mission Dolores.

Robert T. Ridley returned to the city to carry out the orders of General Castro, but could not find anyone to assist him, as there was not one Mexican citizen to be found in Yerba Buena, and the few foreigners who were here, were in favor of the "Bear Flag," as it was called. This flag was made at Sutter's Fort, of bunting, and had the picture of a grizzly bear painted in the center, as the parties making the flag had no paint on hand, they used some blackberry juice, which answered the purpose very well. But they did not take up arms until the American Flag was raised.

A few days after the return of Ridley, a boat landed with two men, named Edge Path and Dr. Sample; Edge Path remained to guard the boat, and Sample came to the billiard-room and inquired for Mr. Ridley. He was in the house at the time and I went to call him, and when I returned with Ridley to the billiard-room, Sample drew his pistol and commanded Ridley to stand still, saying: "If you make a move, or attempt to escape, you will be a dead man." Ridley wished to return to his room for some clothing, Dr. Sample refused, and told me to go and get the clothing he wanted. When I returned with the clothing, Ridley took some money, and two bottles of liquor, and then left with Sample, without communicating with his wife or family. He then bid me good-bye, telling me to take charge of things, and do the best I could for him. A few days later the "Portsmouth" came into port, anchored in front of the town, and lay there for several months. The officers and crew would come ashore daily, and I got well acquainted with them.

In the latter part of June, a gentleman by the name of Gillespie, an officer, arrived in San Francisco, on his way to Sutter's Fort, to recall Fremont, who was about leaving California. We were daily expecting to hear of the Declaration of War between the United States and Mexico; and, about this time I received a letter from Ridley, asking me to call on Captain Montgomery, and inform him that he was a prisoner; and to ascertain whether he could in any way, be instrumental in securing his release. I made inquiries of some of the officers, and also of Captain Montgomery, of the Portsmouth, who informed me that he had no power to act, until he received the news of the Declaration of War between the United States and Mexico. When this announcement was received, all persons who had been taken prisoners, under the Bear Flag would be released. ...

In the early part of July there were some false reports started; one of which was to the effect, that an English Man of War was coming in to hoist the English Flag. It was the wish of most Californians to be under the English Government. One morning in July, while we were eating breakfast; there was a heavy gun fired, and in about five minutes, the long roll was beat aboard the United States Ship Portsmouth. All the port holes were thrown open and every man was at his post, and the few people who were in town, came down to Clay and Kearny streets, expecting to see an engagement in the harbor between the English and American ships.

Another report started, was that Alexander Forbes, the English Counsul, had sent a messenger to Massack Land for an English vessel to come and take charge of the city. Every precaution was taken and every movement watched by the officers of the Portsmouth, so that if the English vessel had made the least move, she would certainly have been sunk in the harbor.

The English vessel came into the harbor, rounded too, and came to anchor, right abreast of the Portsmouth. The cannon was fired for Captain Richardson and Captain Able as they were the only pilots in the harbor, and both resided at Saucelito. No one was permitted to leave the Portsmouth that day or the next, to go ashore. After 12 A.M. some eight officers and a boat crew, came ashore on liberty, from the English vessel. The Captain in full uniform walked through the town, and called on the English Consul, and then returned to his ship. Among the officers who came ashore, was a young Midshipman, named Elliot; his father was the owner of a large hotel in Davenport, Devenshire, England. We were old school-mates, and he was much surprised to find anyone he knew so far from home, and in such a lonely country. I asked him if he thought there was any truth in the report about the hoisting of the English Flag, in this town. He said: "Not any, as far as I know." He said they were out on a surveying expedition for the Government, and were bound for Oregon, and expected to be gone for three years.

The next day, at evening tide, the pilots went on board, and the vessel left for Oregon.

.   .   .

At the time Ridley was made a prisoner, he only kept a billiard-room and saloon; but, as there were a large number of officers coming ashore daily, besides many other persons who wanted accommodations, a good lodging-house and restaurant was badly needed. I was persuaded by my friends to furnish the necessary accommodations. Shortly after this a whaler arrived in port, and discharged three of its crew, two Englishmen and one American. One of them, Tom Smith, by name, I hired as cook and steward, while Charlie, as the other was called, joined Captain Fremont's company. While in his service he was reprimanded by the Captain for disobedience of orders, and he became so angry that he wanted to fight a duel with Fremont. ...

I will give a true account of the reading, for the first time, of the Declaration of Independence, in this city, July 4th, 1846: On the morning of July 4th, Captain Leidsoff asked me if I was an American; I told him I was a white-washed one and had been naturalized. He invited me to come to his house, corner of Clay and Kearny streets, fronting Portsmouth Square, (afterwards known as the City Hotel) where Captain Montgomery was to read the Declaration of Independence. There were present: Captain Leidsoff, Captain Montgomery and two sons, John Fuller, a Midshipman, from Portsmouth, and myself (John H. Brown). I have been particular in naming all the persons present on this occasion, as I have both read and heard, many reports in regard to the rejoicing of the first fourth of July in this city, which were incorrect.

The next year, 1847, the Declaration was again read, at the same house, on the verandah, by Dr. Sample and at the same place in 1848, by Joseph Thompson, while Dr. Sample delivered an address.

I will not mention the celebration of later years, as there are many persons now living in this city who can remember events, as well as myself, and will, no doubt, be proud to speak of them.

The first Fourth of July celebration was held at Jacob Leese's house.

Business in the city was improving, and Yerba Buena was rapidly becoming quite a place of note. In July 1846, a young man named Fisher arrived in this city from Monterey, with dispatches for Captain Montgomery, bringing the glorious news that the flag had at last been hoisted, and that the stars and stripes were waving over the city of Monterey.

On the following day, shortly before noon, we heard the fife and the beating of the drum. There was great rejoicing by the few who were in the city, and that small and faithful band were united as brothers; and their hearts swelled with pure pride and patriotism at the thought of being under the protection of the flag of their own country. The first person who made his appearance was Captain Watson of the marines, with his company of soldiers. The next in command was the First Lieutenant of the Portsmouth, whom everybody called by the nickname of "Mushroom" for lack of a better. He was followed by Lieutenant Revere's two Midshipmen, and about a dozen sailors. They all marched up Clay street to Kearny, and thence to the old Mexican flag pole in front of the Adobe House, used as a Custom-House.

This being an important event in the History of San Francisco, I will give the names of those who witnessed the hoisting of the American Flag. Captain Leidsoff, John Finch, Joseph Thompson, Mrs. Robert T. Ridley, Mrs. Andrew Hepner, Mrs. Captain Voight, "Richard the Third," and John H. Brown.

Captain Montgomery and his men of the *Portsmouth* raise the flag.

Hinkley was born in Massachusetts and Ridley was born in London, but both married Mexican women and became Mexican citizens. Both were opposed to the Bear Flag revolt.

Castro Street was named for General José Castro.

One of the *Portsmouth* sailors mentioned by Brown was Joseph Downey. It was he who wrote the following account of the historic flag raising.

In 1853, a series of reminiscences appeared in the *Golden Era*, a San Francisco literary weekly, under the pseudonym "Filings." More than a hundred years later, in 1955, Yale University Library received the handwritten journal of a crew member who had served on the *Portsmouth* when that ship took part in the American occupation of California in July 1846. The journal was signed "Fore Peak" and had the title *Odds and Ends or Incidents of a Cruise in the Pacific In the U.S. Ship Portsmouth from January 1845 to May 1848*. After extensive research, Fred Blackburn Rogers determined that the journal and the "Filings" pieces had been written by Joseph T. Downey, a yeoman on the *Portsmouth*.

The *Golden Era* pieces were later edited by Colonel Rogers and published in 1956 as a book entitled *Filings From an Old Saw*. The journal was edited by Howard R. Lamar and published by Yale University Press in 1958 as *The Cruise of the Portsmouth*.

The following is excerpted from the original "Filings" item that appeared in the *Golden Era* on Sunday, February 27, 1853.

JOSEPH T. DOWNEY (b.1820)

Raising the flag

T HE MORNING OF 9TH OF JULY BROKE bright and beautiful, and long before the sun rose the crew of the Portsmouth were
roused from their hammocks, and contrary to the usual custom, the
decks were left to their own fate for the nonce,* for far more important affairs were on the *tapis*** than the mere cleaning of decks and
scouring of brass work. Breakfast was served at 6 A.M., and the word
passed for all hands to clean in white frocks, blue pants, black hats
and shoes and prepare for muster. Breakfast was soon despatched, for
every body was too much interested in the crowding events of the day
to have much appetite, and long before the sound of the drum called
us to muster the boys might be seen each in his respective station
around the guns.

Precisely at eight the drum beat to quarters, and the Captain
[John Montgomery] made a speech of (as one of the fore-topmen
called it) 11 or 8 words, which conveyed to us the idea that he, in
obedience to orders from the Commodore [John Sloat], should hoist
the stars and stripes in the public square that day, and take possession
in the name of the United States of America. The First Lieut. then
called over a list of the carbineers, who were for the nonce to become
soldiers and form a part of the escort. The Marines under the command of Lieut. Watson, were in full dress and every officer of the ship
save two, who remained on board to fire a national salute, were to

* For the time being.
** Under consideration. (See Glossary.)

accompany the party. As soon as retreat was beaten the boats were ordered alongside, and the marines and carbineers filed into them. We were landed on what is now Clark's Point, and when all were on shore, formed in sections, and to the soul-inspiring air of Yankee Doodle from our band, consisting of one drum and fife, with an occasional put in from a stray dog or disconsolate jackass on the line of march, trudged proudly up through Montgomery street to Clay, up Clay to the plaza, and formed a solid square, around a flag staff which stood some 50 yards north of where the present one now is, though nearly in the same line. Here we rested on our arms, while the Aids of the Commander-in-Chief disseminated themselves through town, and by entreaties, menaces and promises at last gathered together some 30 or 40 persons of all nations, colors and languages and having penned them in the square formed by the soldier sailors, the Captain putting on all his peculiar dignity, walked up to the flag staff and gave a majestic nod to his second in command; the First Lieutenant gave a similar nod to one of our Quarter-Masters, who came forward, flag in hand and bent it on the halyards.

This was an eventful moment—something was about to be done that could not be easily undone, and as I gazed upon that crowd of manly faces, I fancied I could read a settled determination to do or die in defence of the act of this day, should it become necessary. Capt. M. had a proclamation all ready prepared, and our First Lieutenant now read it to the assembled crowd, and when he had finished gave the signal, and in a moment, amid a roar of cannon from the ship, and the hurrahs of the ship's company, the *vivas* of the Californians, the cheers of the Dutchmen, the barking of dogs, braying of jackasses and a general confusion of sounds from every living thing within hearing, that flag floated proudly up, which has never yet been cowered to mortal foe.

When the ceremony was over and the Captain had proclaimed himself Governor of the northern portion of Upper California, he constituted the aforesaid Lieutenant Watson of the Marines, Military Commandante of the town of Yerba Buena, and giving him a garrison of 24 rank and file marines, installed him into the Adobe Custom House, which from thenceforth assumed the name of the barracks, and made him at once from a poor Lieutenant of Marines, the great and noble potentate of the village.

The "Jacks," whose imbibing propensities are so well known to the whole world, were not permitted to stroll about, but were marched at once down to the landing, where, notwithstanding various and sundry wistful looks and longings were cast toward the several rummeries, they were embarked, and before noon were again on board ship. "Filings" was one of those who was detailed for shore duty, and consequently had an opportunity to see the end of the fun.

As soon as the "Jacks" had marched away, a guard was placed at the foot of the flag staff, and the assembled crowd of the free and enlightened citizens of Mexico, at last forced into their brains that they had by some magical proceeding suddenly been metamorphosed into citizens of the U. States, and unanimously voted to go where liquor could be had, and drink a health and long life to that flag. The Indians consequently rushed frantically to one pulperee,* Capt. Leidesdorff and the aristocracy to Bob Ridley's bar-room, and the second class and the Dutch to Tinker's [John Finch's saloon]. These houses being on three of the four corners of the square, one in the door of the barracks could see the manoeuvres in each of them.

For the first hour things went quiet enough, but soon the strong water began to work, and such a confusion of sounds could never have been heard since the Babel Tower arrangement, as came from these three corners. First would be heard a drunken *viva* from an Indian who would come out of Pulperee No. 1, gaze up at the flag and over he would go at full length upon the grass, for reader there was grass on the square then. Then the aristocrats would raise a hip, hip, hip and a cheering, "three times three," then from Tinker's a strange jumble of words, in which hurrah, viva, hip, pah and Got verdam, were only too plainly distinguishable. This Pandemonium lasted for some hours, in fact until sundown, when the Commandante sent a guard to warn the revellers that as the town was now under martial law, they must cease their orgies and retire to their respective homes. But few, however were able to do so, and the greater part of them either slept in Tinker's alley or on the grass in the plaza, and only woke with the morning's first beams, to wonder what was the cause of yesterday's spree.

* (Pulpería) A store selling food and liquor. (Spanish)

When Downey wrote this piece for *Golden Era* (April 3, 1853), he hid behind his pseudonym, "Filings." This enabled him to write about "a wild, harum-scarum blade [named] Joe Downey" who had an "irresistible thirst for mischief." He would have been about 26 years old at this point. Apart from revealing his own personality, Downey here gives us several fascinating details about the *Brooklyn's* arrival with 238 Mormon colonists, the appointment of the first American officials, the town's first court case, and the first election.

The Mormons, and Sam Brannan

THE ARRIVAL OF MORMONS IN YERBA BUENA, a sect of whom we had heard so much, was an event which caused great surprise and no little share of excitement in our little colony. Curiosity was raised to the highest pitch, and surmises ran rife among all the inhabitants. The stories of their adventures in Illinois and Missouri had preceded them, and a vague idea seemed to predominate in the minds of all that they were a sort of wild, desperate people, and that trouble would soon arise from their arrival. Captain M., however, was a man equal to any emergency, and with him to will was to do, consequently he at once decided upon a plan to curb them if hostile, or to foster them if they came in peace. Our boat was again despatched to the Brooklyn, and soon returned, having on board their leader, a man who has since won himself an enviable name and a princely fortune, viz: SAMUEL BRANNAN, and two or three of his coadjutors, who were designated as Elders, and being ushered into the recesses of the private cabin of the Portsmouth, the views and plans of the new comers were at once explained, preliminaries arranged, the harmony so necessary to good government concerted, and the parties departed for their own ship again.

The next day being the Sabbath, no work could be done, but as before stated, our Captain being of a truly Christian turn, in default of a chaplain, always mustered the crew for church and read the service of the Episcopal persuasion, and afterwards a printed sermon, of which he had a copious supply on hand. This Sunday was to be a memorable one to us, for we were to have strangers on board. The new comers, male and female, were to visit us, and anxiety to see and examine the female portion of this strange sect, was apparent on the faces of all. At the appointed hour the quarter-deck was cleared, the awnings spread, and the chairs from the ward room and cabin placed for the ladies, the capstan-bars ranged as seats for the men, and the boats called away to bring visitors.

When on their return with their live cargoes they hauled along-side the gangway, the whole ship's company was collected on the larboard side of the spar deck, and every eye was fixed on the ladder, anxious to get a first peep at that portion of the human family which is generally denominated the better half of man. Over they came, and as they followed one after another, curiosity appeared to fade away, and ere the last had seated herself in the chair appropriated for her, a long drawn sigh of disappointment escaped from that large crowd, and a dilapidated specimen of a Quarter-Gunner growled out, in no very sweet tones, "D-mnation, why they are just like other women." And so they were; sect, creed or religion had not changed the human form divine, and they sat as meek and smiling as though they had no religion at all. Service over, they one and all partook of a lunch with the Captain and Lieutenants, inspected the ship all over, and then took their leave, having created a most favorable impression among the hardy Tars of the good ship Portsmouth.

There arrived also in the Brooklyn, several other passengers, but none who ever created much sensation in the country save Frank Ward, a jolly, good hearted, enterprising young man, who, imbued with a strong love of adventure, had laid in a small but very select and valuable lot of goods, and came to this almost unknown land to try his fortune here. Frank was one of those choice spirits who are welcome everywhere, and he soon made himself a pet with the officers and men.

On Monday morning, all the boats of the ship were despatched to aid in disembarking the Mormons and their plunder, and before night they were all snugly on shore, and their white tents were pitched in the lot bounded by Kearny, Montgomery, Clay and Washington streets, directly opposite the Barracks, and presented to the eye quite a military appearance. Indeed, to a stranger, ignorant of the majority of the sex in occupation, it would have seemed that a large force was concentrated here, and that Uncle Sam had determined that the Army of Occupation of the Northern District should be strong enough to defy all attempts of the doughty Mexicans to dislodge them.

The cargo of the Brooklyn consisted of the most heterogeneous mass of materials ever crowded together; in fact, it seemed as if, like the ship of Noah, it contained a representative for every mortal thing the mind of man had ever conceived. Agricultural, mechanical and manufacturing tools were in profuse abundance; dry goods, groceries and hardware, were dug out from the lower depths of the hold, and speedily transferred on shore, our men working with a will which showed the good feeling they bore for the parties to whom they belonged.

A Printing Press and all its appurtenances, next came along, and last though not least, three beautiful pieces of brass cannon, six pounders, mounted in the style of light artillery, with the necessary complement of powder and shot, round, fixed and grape, gave token to the reflecting mind of what would or might have been done, had the flag of Mexico, instead of our own, waved over the port of Yerba Buena upon their arrival. These cannon were pressed into the service of the United States, and all the immense supplies of ammunition transferred to the powder house, which was erected in the Square, under the special guard of the sentry who paced beneath the Flag Staff.

The men, too, were formed during the passage into military companies, and armed with the Yager of the style formerly in use in Florida, were drilled day after day, and made a most respectable appearance on parade. They were all enlisted in the service of our government, and though not required to do day duty, yet a detail was regularly made out and they served as a night patrol and each and every one was ordered, under severe penalties, to muster at the Barracks at given signals and armed and equipped for duty. Our little garrison was now in complete order, and we thought ourselves competent to defy even the devil himself.

Another of the passengers by the Brooklyn whom we had nearly overlooked, was a Mr. [George] Hyde, who afterwards sprung himself into immense notoriety in the country by his connection with the Alcaldeship, and the quantities of land he granted away. Now, Mr. Hyde was a lawyer by profession, and in order to recruit* his health,

---

* Refresh; reinvigorate.

which was failing him at home in consequence, as he said, of too intense application to his business, had joined the U.S. frigate Congress, bearing the broad pennant of Com. R. F. Stockton, in the capacity of clerk to the Commander-in-Chief. Arriving in the Sandwich Islands, and having recruited sufficiently, he left her and came to Yerba Buena in the Brooklyn, determined to carve a name and fortune from the sterile rocks of California.

It is an old maxim and true one, that where there is a lawyer, that lawyer must live, and if he cannot find business ready made, he will always make business for himself—consequently as we had now a real live lawyer, we must have some law, and as to have law we must have a head in the person of a Judge, Capt. M. wisely concluded that in order to meet the growing wants of his little Kingdom, he would appoint from among his own officers the most erudite, and to all outward show, the most learned, to assume temporarily the ermine, and dispense justice right and left, until he could with fitting dignity call an election for the office of Alcalde.

He was the more induced to this step so prematurely, for the reason that some of the male portion of the disciples of Joe Smith [Joseph Smith, founder of the Mormon faith], disappointed in their cherished hopes of founding a colony of their own, and raising a Tree Flag, and with ready hand grasping the lands and cattle of the old Rancheros of California, had become much discontented with the prospect before them, and wished to withdraw from the league which bound them together and start business on their own hook. But Samuel, the smart, acute and far-seeing Samuel, had with his eagle business eye foreseen the possibility of such a state of affairs, and guarded well against such a proceeding.

When the expedition was projected, each and every one of the faithful who desired to go to the far-off land of Paradise was required to contribute not only a part, but the whole of his or her means, to defray the expense, and purchase the necessary articles for the outfit and to serve for three years from the date of embarkation. This was cheerfully done, and the whole became common stock, each owning equal shares in the property so purchased. The between-decks of the ship were comfortably fitted up, and the privates and lesser lights of the great Prophet, occupied this portion of the ship, while the Elder and his Staff of Councillors occupied the cabin. Although separated by a partition of boards, all were to be on an equality; none were to enjoy luxuries which were not allowed to others, and the freedom of the quarter-deck was to be open to all. After being a few days at sea, Capt. [A. W.] Richardson, the old salt who commanded the ship, began to exhibit decided objections to the Plebeians or steerage passengers promenading and encumbering his quarter-deck, and of course made his complaint to the Elder [who] forthwith called his councillors together and in solemn conclave laid his views before them. He foresaw that to draw the reins tight just now might prove a very disastrous thing to the whole scheme, but in order to obviate any difficulty, smooth the way and restrain any who might be inclined to rebel, proposed that a fair scheme should be drawn up, and each and every member be induced by persuasive means to sign it, in which they solemnly bound themselves to remain banded together in the bonds of brotherly love for the space of three years, working for the common good, depositing their worldly gains with the Elder and his Staff, to be invested as he and they might see fit, thus forming a grand Sinking Fund, which at the expiration of said three years should be divided equally among the survivors or their heirs.

This all looked fair—but following was one small codicil, which provided that should any one of the League prove refractory, refuse to obey the mandates of the council, or to comply strictly with all laws made or hereafter to be made, he should be tried by said council, and if found guilty, he should be expelled. Also, if any one should be expelled, or voluntarily leave the league, they should forfeit all right and title to the property of the company, and be sent forth to start anew in the world without a claim upon them. If all but the council should stray away, then the whole was to devolve to them; and if they, too, proved refractory, all became the property of the elder. This contract or bond was signed by all, and then the reins were drawn taut. Restricted to certain parts of the ship, and fed upon food of inferior quality, denied the luxuries, they saw going every day under their noses to gratify the palates of their leaders—their complaints unheard, and their remonstrances treated with disdain—no wonder they became indignant and tried to right themselves. As long as they were on shipboard, they could be kept under subjection through fear of the Captain, but now they had arrived in a port where there could be law gotten—law they would have.

The *Brooklyn* brought Sam Brannan and the Mormons to San Francisco.

Mr. Hyde during his passage from the Islands made himself acquainted with all the circumstances, urged them on, and induced them to send the petition to Capt. M., which prompted him to create a court of justice in Yerba Buena. Lieut. Washington A. Bartlett, a name which afterwards became somewhat famous in many ways in California, was the individual whom he selected as the representative of Justice; and having by virtue of the authority vested in him, commissioned him as Alcalde, he was forthwith detached from naval and attached to civil duty, and ordered on shore, to hear, adjudge and decide upon all cases which might be brought before him. Now, in order to have an imposing court, he must "per se" have a clerk for said court—and as the fees of said court did not, from appearances promise to be too heavy for him to carry off, he must have a clerk, who would require none of the said fees, ergo, said clerk must be chosen from the ship's company.

Now, among said ship's company was a wild, harum-scarum blade yclept* Joe Downey, who had passed through many a grade on board said ship, from yeoman to confidential clerk to the executive officer, down to one of the after guard and steady sweeper on the quarter-deck. His love of change and irresistible thirst for mischief preventing him from holding any one place long at a time. Joe was good enough in his way, but his was a bad one for a man of war, and this way, bad as it was, he seemed determined to have, despite of law, gospel, or that stringent argument, the *cat*, a large quantity of which latter alternative he had at various and sundry times backed off, with the greatest of humor.

Joe was a favorite with the crew, and didn't care a d—m for the officers, and his fate though a checkered one, suited him well enough and he was happy. A good scholar, an apt penman, and well versed in the Spanish language, he was the very man for the Alcalde. Consequently when he was selected, the lst Lieut. was delighted at the thought of getting (for a time at least) rid of his "John Jones," gave a glad consent, and Joe *nil hi nil hi*,** was transported from steady sweeper to Clerk of the Supreme Court of Appeals and Admiralty of the Northern District of California.

* Called; named; known as. (Often used as an affectation.)
** Whether he wanted to or not. (See Glossary.)

Behold them then opening the court on Monday morning, with all the pomposity imaginary, and calling the cases as they appeared on the docket. There was no lack of business for a week, Mormon after Mormon cited the immaculate Samuel and councillors to answer; cords of evidence were taken and committed to paper, fact after fact was proven, but the fate of all was decided by the production of that same contract, and verdict for defendants was tacked to the tail of every case, until the plaintiffs in sheer despair, gave up the job. The councillors came out with flying colors, and the plebeians, after mature consideration and deep deliberation, came to the conclusion that they had made pretty considerably d—d fools of themselves, and with this consolation returned to their first love, and adhered to the contract.

These cases had occupied a whole week, costs on paper had run up to a large sum, of which sum the amount of $2.75 was one day mysteriously collected by the aforesaid Joe, the Clerk, and instantly deposited in the bar till of John Brown, of the Portsmouth House, in exchange for certain and sundry toddies, thus more effectually diddling the representative of the majesty of the law out of his rights and dues. The effect of said toddies was so very palpable on Joe, that the Alcalde was fain to enquire where he had obtained the pesos, to pay for liquor, and having satisfied his mind on that head, he in the violence of his rage, dispatched poor Joe on board ship, where at seven bells the next morning he squared the account with a round dozen [lashes], and came on shore again to assume the duties of his office.

The prisoners who had been taken by the Bear Flag and sent to Fort Sutter, were now released and returned to their homes, and again Bob Ridley figured in the streets of Yerba Buena. But alas, now shorn of honors. He no longer held office of trust or emolument, and it was death to him to see himself, the original potentate outpotentated, by a stranger, and he inwardly vowed he would not stand it. He procured a petition signed by a majority of the old standbys, and not a few of the Mormons, who disliked the decisions of the Alcalde, and sent it to Capt. M., praying for an election to be ordered, wherein the people should decide by the ballot box who should rule over them. The petition was duly considered, an election ordered, and the two candidates, Bartlett and Bob Ridley, laid their several merits before the sovereign people.

Here the genius of Joe shone out again. His influence was courted by both parties, to each he gave heed, pocketed the dimes, drinked, stump-speeched and advocated the claims of both, acted as clerk of the election, and strange to say when the returns were counted, out of 64 votes polled, Joe Downey had received 38, and was per force of circumstances elected Alcalde of the Northern District of California. Following the footsteps of all winning candidates, he got very drunk on the night of the election, and the next morning found himself on board the good ship Portsmouth, charged with tampering with the purity of elections. At 7 bells he appeared at the gangway, was disgraced from his office, settled the drunken charge in the usual way, and went on shore in the afternoon rejoicing. A new election was ordered, but this time Joe was not clerk. Bartlett won, and Joe resumed his old station. It mattered but little to him, he had played off his joke, had a glorious spree, been triumphantly elected first Alcalde, and bore his misfortune with becoming fortitude, laughing heartily whenever the subject was broached to him.

In 1853 the *Golden Era* published a series of articles entitled "Judges and Criminals; or—Shadows of the Past." The writer, using the pseudonym "Juris Consult," accused Downey of having erased the candidates' names from the tickets and substituting with his own. For this, the young seaman was "instantly disrobed of his mantle of office, and received a ration from the 'cat o'-nine-tails'."

Just a month after the American flag was raised, the entire community was roused from its sleep one night by what was perceived to be an enemy attack. The incident is referred to in several eyewitness accounts, but it is Downey's version that zeros in on the absurdity of it all. A recollection he wrote several years later for the *Golden Era* lacks the punch and immediacy that makes this one so delightful. This is from his journal, *The Cruise of the Portsmouth*.

JOSEPH T. DOWNEY (b.1820)

The night they cried "To arms!"

O N THE NIGHT OF 12TH AUG. AN INCIDENT occurred at once laughable, and showing to what a pitch of discipline these defenders of a conquered territory were brought, and what our resources were in a state of revolt. First let us premise, that Soldiers as well as Sailors love liquor, and will drink whenever chance offers. Also that Soldier Officers, and ours in particular, are very fond of Ardent. Secondly, there was lots in town, for those who knew how to procure, and our Jollies* had their skins well saturated the major part of the time while their valorous Commander [Watson] had never less than 15 or 16 inches of raw Brandy imprisoned under his Jacket. Having established this fact, the reader will be prepared to understand more fully what follows.

On the night above mentioned, many of the soldiers were well corned, more especially those who were detailed for Post on that eventful occasion. The Gallant Captain [Watson] had swallowed his accustomed quantity, and in staggering across the square to regain his quarters, suddenly comes to a halt and peers sagely into the Darkness—what is it that he sees? Something, which bodes no good to the peace and harmony of Yerba Buena. With his eyes, blinking and twinkling like glowworms, he sees right before him, and bearing directly down upon the spot where he stands a band of Horsemen, armed "cap a pie." His soul burns with valor, or Aguadiente** (most probably the

* Marines.
** (Aguardiente) Firewater (brandy). (Spanish)

latter). He shouts to the sentry on Post— "Fire— Fire— God-d--n you—dont you see the enemy?"

The Sentry [Philip McGowan], like a good soldier, fires when he hears the stentorian voice of his commander ordering him—the garrison is aroused—Hurry, skurry—every one jumps to his feet—drunk and sober, are armed at once—What is the matter? bursts from every lip—no one can tell. At last, in rushes the valiant officer, breathless, and *fatigued*. By G-d, here's a pretty state of affairs—100 mounted Mexicans in the very square, and no alarm. Turn out—to arms—to arms—keep within the shade of the house—give me my carbine— Burns—Burns! Sir? says Burns—Take charge of the artillery—McG-- [owan] assist Burns. Where's the Dog? His last question caused a laugh, the dog mentioned was a little Californian puppy he had adopted, and a shrewd wag not having the fear of the cats before his eyes, suggested that perhaps the reason he asked for him, was, he was afraid the dog might turn *traitor*.

All was breathless silence for a few moments—still the expected attack came not. After a lapse of a quarter of an hour, all Hands retired to their Beds again—they had not lain long however when Bang went another gun—the same farce was enacted. All hands were called. Burns and Mc ordered to stand by the Artillery and the Dog again enquired for. The Corporal visited the Sentry who had fired, and came back with a report that he (the Sentry) had seen a Body of Horsemen and fired at them. Still the attack did not commence.

Our Old Commander [Montgomery] who lodged on shore now appeared, his cloak streaming behind him, and carbine in hand, he charged upon the Barracks. He said it was evident that the Enemy was concentrating his force, and that it was "highly important" to be on the alert, yet not wishing to fatigue the troops, he suggested that they should lie down on their arms, and thus be ready for any emergency. This suggestion was acted upon, and for a short time the Barracks were again silent—presently the report of a third gun is heard—to arms—to arms, resounds through the House, Burns and Mc fly to the Artillery, and the Dog is searched for. This time the sentry saw both Horses and Men plainly, and counted 80 or more. The time has arrived for action. We must have reinforcements from the Ship, says the Commander, Yes, says the Soldier Officer, make the signal, Fiz, Fiz, Fiz goes a Sky Rocket, a blue light is burned.

We will now step on board the *Portsmouth*. No sooner was the signal made and reported, than all was Hurrah Boys on board. The alarm was given on the Berth Deck—Hurrah Hurrah. Turn out—the Mexicans are charging on the town—up you go—trowsers or no trowsers—sang out the *Tool* [Henry Osborne, ship's corporal], Legs [John Morgan, Master at Arms] and his aid. Such another mess. The Old Gunner and his crew running hither and thither. Bring the Carbines here! says one. Bring em here! says another. Where's my musket? Call away a Boat! shouts an officer, Call away all the Boats! says another. Give me a Cutlass! Get off my toes! You've rammed your bayonet in me!—Get out of the way there! Give me some powder! Give me some Balls!—such were some of the cries, amid the confusion that reigned for a few moments.

After a short time they got in the boats, and all armed—but such arms—some had Muskets, and no Bayonets, some Bayonets and no Muskets, some had Cutlasses, Powder and Balls, and some carbines and no ammunition—one man had a musket with no lock—while another had his lock tied on to a cutlass, and one fellow, a wild rollicking Irishman, having run fore and aft the decks to get a shooting iron, in vain, at last seized a quilgee* handle and jumped in the Boat, twisting it by the middle and exclaiming, "By J---s I will fight them Irish fashion."

The debarkation was a difficult affair; the water was low and the boats could not get close to the shore. However this was no stay, overboard they went and fell into a sort of line as they reached the shore—Fall in! says one—I've lost my powder, says another—My cartridge Box has capsized and spilt my caps and balls!—Never mind, fall in!—and they did fall in, and marched up, falling out with each other every step of the way.

One party was marched down to where the enemy had been last seen—and made a grand charge up a pile of shavings; another party charged on a little house and found the *enemy* there in the shape of certain barrels of wine. Oh, how brave they were; they rushed in, fell to hand and hand conflict with him, and soon his destruction, if not total defeat, was certain. The destruction came, but the defeat was on the other side altogether, for no sooner was he imbibed than he

---

* Probably intended to be *squilgee*—a nautical term for a mop.

assumed the mastery, and Poor Jack, arms and all, was completely at his mercy. Nor was the enemy slow in taking advantage of this mastery for he threw him on his back completely "hors de combat" and played all sorts of antics with him.

As soon as the first fright of the attack was over and our Autocrat who was in command of a party, ascertained how matters stood, he pronounced the whole affair a humbug, and after detailing a small party to remain on shore, ordered the remainder to return on board. As luck would have it, the party detailed to remain were those who had made the aforementioned assault on the Liquid Enemy, and consequently their deplorable condition was not discovered by his *Majesty*. Foremost among this valorous gang was Legs, who as has been before stated, was a very Christian Like Man and *Loved* all his *Enemies*, particularly that *Arch Enemy*, Alcohol and all his *satelites*. Such was his love for this Gentleman, that it almost amounted to *Idolatry*, and yet such was his strict regard for duty that animal passion could never overcome it. He well knew it was wrong for the Jacks to get hold of the stimulant, and consequently when he found the insiduous gentleman was roaming at large, he strove to fulfill the trust confided in him by putting him out of sight as soon as possible, and not being able to find any more secure place for him, out of pure zeal for the service, he stowed away an immense quantity under his Jacket. Of course he was but a man, and Stimulants showed as soon on him as on other men, and the next morning when he and his gang came on board they looked to use the expression of one of our Old Salts "as if they had been dragged through hell and beat with a soot bag." This was the end of the tremendous night attack upon the town of Yerba Buena.

The affair was wrapped in mystery for some days, but at length like all other mysteries it was solved, and turned out to be this: a gang of stray horses and wild mares, not having the fear of the Laws, Civil or military, which then ruled the environs, before their eyes, had chosen this eventful night to have a ramble and a race round the town. The Soldier Officer had first started the idea that they were mounted, and the Sentries, half drunk and half asleep, had seen double, fired at them, and thus caused all this row and trouble. This was the first and last attempt made during our stay by the Mexicans to regain possession of Yerba Buena.

Commodore Robert F. Stockton.

Commodore Robert F. Stockton of the *Congress* succeeded
Commodore John Sloat as governor of California. After cap-
turing Los Angeles without a fight, he proclaimed California
to be U.S. territory. On October 5, 1846, he was given a grand
reception at Yerba Buena—and our friend Downey accompanied the civic dignitaries who greeted him. Here is how
Downey described the occasion in *Golden Era*, March 27, 1853.

When the governor came to town

THE COMMODORE DETERMINED TO VISIT Yerba Buena, and see how matters stood in that quarter. Accordingly, upon his arrival at Monterey he sent an express to the Commander of the Northern District notifying him that the Frigate Congress, having on board His Excellency, Robert F. Stockton, Governor of California and Commander of the Land and Naval Forces of the Pacific, would enter the harbor of San Francisco on the 28th day of September, 1846.

Here was a chance for a large display of patriotism; here was an opportunity to dazzle the eyes, and astonish the comprehensions of the rancheros of California, and well was it taken advantage of. The Alcalde, or as he was now dubbed, Mayor Bartlett, called instanter* a public meeting at the Great Hall in Leidesdorff's adobe house, where, after an elaborate preamble, he offered a set of resolutions, decreeing a grand procession, ball, and jollification necessary for the auspicious occasion, which resolutions were adopted unanimously.

Committees of arrangements, finance and reception were appointed. Sam Brannan, who had now got his press in operation, was commissioned to print the Programmes, which were got up in a magnificent style (on paper). The Commodore-Governor was to be received at the landing, corner of Clay and Montgomery streets, on a splendid staging (constructed of empty casks, and stray logs of wood) by the Mayor and corporate authorities, (consisting of Bartlett and Joe his clerk) dressed in their best, and wearing white cotton scarfs, silk not

---

* At once; immediately.

being come-at-able. The procession was to be formed on Montgomery street, composed of all the marines of the Congress and Portsmouth, all the militia of the Mormon Battalion, and the *elite* of Yerba Buena, at alternate intervals. As soon as his Highness popped his head above the bank, the band was to strike up "See the Conquering Hero Comes," then they were to sound the trumpets, and whang the drums, the military were to present arms, the cannon on the Plaza and on board the ship were to blaze away, and a general "devil to pay" was to be kicked up.

It is not very necessary to state here that the sun rose on that day, for the simple reason that the sun has been in the habit of rising every day, but we may state that contrary to his usual custom on gala days, he rose bright and blooming on that eventful day, and soon succeeded in dissipating one of those delightful fogs, which even to this day are in the habit of paying our magnificent bay a passing tribute of cold and damp. At an early hour every one on board and on shore was astir, and as the hour for the landing of his Excellency was fixed at 11 o'clock A.M., of course at 9 boats were called away, and with their crews all dressed in holiday costume, and the boats bedecked with flags, were engaged in transporting on shore such as were to participate in the coming festivities. Bandsmen, marines, companies A and B, and sailor-soldiers from the *Congress*, were landed at Clark's Point. The artillery company was quartered in Fort Montgomery. Every steward, cook and wardroom boy that could be spared was sent on shore, to arrange and attend to the grand dinner, and divers and sundry boxes similar to those which contained "Old Otard,"* and baskets yclept Champaigne, which by their weight were filled with something more than wash-cloths, were passed down the side of the Frigate and walked away from the landing on the shoulders of sturdy "Jacks," toward the house of Capt. Leidesdorff.

The Mayor and his staff, consisting of Joe and Sergent Miller of the Marines, who (for want of a better) officiated as constable of the court, were on hand at peep of day, hurrying here and there, and there and here, up one lane and down two streets, coaxing one and bullying another, in the vain attempt to make all hands as respectable and happy as possible. At 10 precisely, a desperate assault was made by the

* A brand of whiskey.

body corporate on all the rum mills, and customers and proprietors were ruthlessly dragged forth, to fall in the procession, whether they would or no, and if any one dared to prove refractory, he was threatened with a file of marines and the guard house. At 30 minutes past 10, a crowd consisting of 200 (marines music and all) were collected and got in a straight line, which proceeding was no sooner finished than a telegraphic despatch was sent to the ship announcing that all was ready. But the Commodore-Governor obstinately refused to start until five minutes before eleven, consequently the crowd got dry, and *bust* up to have a drink, which ungentlemanly conduct kept the Mayor, Joe and Miller on a continual trot to hunt them up. Joe got tight and so did Miller, but not awfully so. The mayor was so puffed up with the gas of importance that liquor would have no effect upon him.

At length the barque of State shoved off, every body made a desperate rush to get in place. The Mayor, with Joe on his right and Miller on his left for body guards, took their stations on the temporary landing. The Governor's august foot touched the plank; the Mayor grasped him by the hand; they mounted the bank hand in hand, Joe and Miller following. As soon as seen, the artillery bang, banged; the music too, tooed; the soldiers presented arms; the rag, tag, and bobtail hurrahed; and down the whole length of the line marched the Governor, his Aids, the Mayor and his Aids, each and every one acknowledging the compliment as if he thought it was meant for himself.

The Mayor then in a very flowery speech, welcomed the Governor to Yerba Buena, and said he would have presented the freedom of what he knew would be a future city, only he could not procure in time a proper box, the only one at hand being his own blacking box, and that was not yet empty. The Governor gave 'em a stumper, told them that he slept with a rifle under his pillow every night (which was a mark of bravery, because there were four 32-pounders in the same cabin), how he had marched to Los Angeles, how Castro had fled at sight of the glistening bayonets of his gallant marines, and ended by proclaiming that death alone should separate him from his gallant companions in arms. Then the band played another tune—then every body hurrahed again—then the Governor and his staff and the Mayor and his staff mounted their steeds. The soldiers wheeled into sections; rag, tag and bob-tail fell in pell-mell; and round town we went on an exploring expedition, but did not find any thing until we brought up all standing in front of Leidesdorff's, where the assembled female beauty of Yerba Buena were gathered, waiting to greet the hero.

How he and his staff and the Mayor and his staff dismounted from their war steeds, how the ladies waved their handkerchiefs, how the Governor marched in, how he kissed the pretty ones, how he shook hands with the old and ugly ones, how his staff and the Mayor and his staff wanted to do so too, how the ladies wouldn't let 'em (that is all of 'em), how they all drank wine and eat lunch, while the soldiers were peeping in the door, how some folks got tight and some folks didn't, are matters easier imagined than described. Suffice it to say, such was the case. After all this, the Governor again reviewed the troops and praised them highly. When they were dismissed, the steeds were again brought up, the Governor again mounted, and with a body guard of devoted hearts, made a desperate foray of 3 miles into the heart of the enemy's country, and saw a fierce bull. He returned without a scar, sat down to supper, and at 9 P.M. opened the ball with the belle of Yerba Buena.

The ball was like any other ball—lots of dancing and lots of laughing. Plenty to eat, and gallons to drink, every body got happy, and sometime in the early hours of the morning—"Filings" don't know when, by reason of a-sort-of-a-kind-of a leave of absence which his senses took of him—they all cleared out. But judging from the size of the heads of the male portion of the populace, next day at 2 P.M., there had been lots of "bricks" toted about in the course of the preceding night.

Thus ended the first visit of the Governor of all the Californias to Yerba Buena. He had intended to have given several more entertainments of the same kind, with "entire change of performances," but unluckily the next day a courier arrived from below, with the news that the rancheros had risen, hauled down the flag at Los Angeles and San Diego, and drove the garrisons out. All was now bustle. The Frigate Savannah was sent down to punish them, and the Commodore promised soon to follow.

PUBLIC RECEPTION
OF HIS EXCELLENCY
ROBERT F. STOCKTON,
GOVERNOR, AND COMMANDER-IN-CHIEF
OF CALIFORNIA, &C., &C.

The Citizens of the District of San Francisco and vicinity, having, united for the purpose of giving a public reception to His Excellency, ROBERT F STOCKTON. on the occasion of his landing, on Monday, Oct. 5th, 1846; The following is the

ORDER OF THE DAY.

1st The citizens will assemble in "Portsmouth Square" at 8, A. M. and form in procession in the following order

CHIEF MARSHALL
AID.   AID.

MUSIC

MILITARY ESCORT. under command of
Capt. J. Zeilin, U. S. M. C.
CAPT. JOHN B MONTGOMERY, U. S. N.,
(Commanding the Northern District of California)
and SUITE.
OFFICERS, U. S. N.,
CAPTAIN JOHN PATY,
Senior Captain of the Hawaiian Navy.
Lieut. Commanding BONNET,—French Navy.
Lieut. Commanding RUDACOFF,—Russian Navy.
The MAGISTRACY OF THE DISTRICT,
and the
ORATOR OF THE DAY.
FOREIGN CONSULS.
THOS. O. LARKIN, and WM. A. LEIDESDORFF, Esqs,
(Late U. S. Consuls for California.)
U. S. Navy Agent,
and the
U. S. Collector of the District.
Gentlemen who held Civil or Military Comissions
under the late Government.
STRANGERS OF DISTINCTION.
COMMITTEE OF ARRANGEMENTS.
MASTERS OF SHIPS IN PORT.
CITIZENS GENERALLY.

2d. The procession will move at half past eight o'clock. to take up a position to receive His Excellency at the point of landing.

3d. The Governor and Suite will land at 9 A. M. under a salute of seventeen guns.

4th. The Governor will be received by His Honor WASH'N A. BARTLETT; Magistrate of the District, attended by the Corporation,

5th. The Governor will be addressed by Col. WM. H. RUSSELL, Orator of the day.

6th The procession will then move through the principal streets to the residence of WM A. LEIDESDORFF Esq where the LADIES will be presented to His Excellency; after which a cavalcade will be formed to escort him on his tour of inspection,

7th. On returning from the tour a collation will be served up at the residence of WM. A. LEIDESDORFF Esq.

8th. The following gentleman will be known as AIDS to the Marshall viz: C. E. PICKETT, WM. H. DAVIS, FREDRICK TESCHMAKER, and J. K. WILSON Esqrs; the Aids will appear in uniform

FRANK WARD, Marshall

Yerba Buena, October 5th., 1846.
(S. Brannan, Printer.····San Francisco.)

Schedule for the governor's visit, printed by Sam Brannan.

In his 1853 *Golden Era* account Downey said that the governor's ball was "like any other ball." Yet when he first recorded the event in his journal he said there had been nothing else like it "since Noah first landed from the ark," and then he went on to describe it as a bacchanalia. This final excerpt is from his journal, published as *The Cruise of the Portsmouth*.

JOSEPH T. DOWNEY (b.1820)

The governor's brawl

 T ALK OF YOUR DIGNITY BALLS, your Ball en masque, your
Fancy Balls, and your 4th of July Balls—Pshaw. There never was a Ball
given since Noah first landed from the ark that could compare in all
its details with the "Reception Ball" at Yerba Buena. The Large Dining
Room of the largest house in the city was most brilliantly illuminated,
and shone forth in all the blaze and brilliancy of 100 Spermacitte*
Candles, which reflected from some 30 or 40 mirrors. The resplen-
dant countenances of all the assembled beauty of the District of San
Francisco. There was the fine open countenance of the Russian Brunette,
which seemed to say, "love me if you dare," there was the happy
round smiling face of the Dutch Frow of the Cigar Maker, which said
"I know you like me" and there was the pretty faces of all our Yankee
Mormons, blushing and blooming like full blown peonies, and there
was also a decent and rather numerous sprinkling of the dark hued
daughters of California, who would dance no matter who feed the
Fiddler.

These were the occupants of the Dancing Room, and hovering
round them were the Beaux, from Dancing S--l, the most graceful
performer upon the heel and toe principle, I ever saw, down down a
long row from the grave citizen to the Lace and Epaulette bedizzened
Officer of the Navy and winding up with Old Chips, with his beautiful
teeth and snow white pants who stood at the door, grinning from ear
to ear.

---

* Spermaceti: fat from the sperm whale, formerly used in candle making.

In the next room however were the sterling attractions of the evening. The first sight that struck the eye upon entering was the long table, spread over with an abundant quantity of the good things of this life—and then immediately in the rear was the *Bar*; not the Bar of the Law, but the Bar of the Law's particular Friend—Mr. Alcohol. Here he lived in all his splendor with all his multifarious names and cognomens. And the old round, chubby faced decanters stood so loving-ly side by side, seeming to invite the bystanders to partake, and hard indeed must have been the heart of any one who could have withstood the temptation. Certain am I, that few if any of that crowd, stood immaculate on that eventful night.

When the Ball first opened, all was joy and merriment, but as Alcohol began to obtain the mastery, strong symptoms of pugnacity showed themselves. Some old grudge had existed between our Purser and one of the Dignitaries of the Town and high words ensued, but suddenly, slap, bang, went a blow and down went the dig. Now then all was hubbub, noise and confusion—"Struck, in my own house," says the Dig, "Give me my pistols." "Pistols be d--d," growled the pugnacious man, "if you stir from that spot I'll brain you." "Peace—Peace or order Gent—Gentlemen," hiccupped the Soldier Officer [Watson], who had on this occasion raised his dose from 20 to 24 inches—"I demand, and command silence," sung out a short, fat red faced Lieut. from the Flag Ship. "Silence yourself," muttered the Sol-dier, "I am Commanding Officer here—you be d---d if you open your mouth again." "Well sir, what then?" "Why I'll sew it up for you, that's all!"

Bottles, tumblers, canes, and all sorts of missiles were flying about the room. Old Chips was in the thickest of the fight, striving as he in his drunken mood thought, to preserve the peace, or the Liquor (most likely the latter) until at last he found himself most unceremoniously pitched out the window, and landed on a dung heap in the back yard. Being nearly overcome with his exertions during the day, and finding his bed a soft one, he at once resigned himself to the arms of Mor-pheus, nor did he again open his peepers till the hogs rooted him out, and he found it was broad daylight.

Meanwhile the Row within doors was carried on in full force, and there was a fair chance for murder till some one who had not lost his wits ran to the Commodore with the news, and his appearance and commanding voice put a stop to all belligerent proceedings. By dint of loud talking, some small cussing and lots of knocking on his own part, he at last arrived at the merits of the affair, and having consigned some of the most unruly to durance vile, in the Calaboose, and sending others on board their own Ships, he at last restored order, and at an early hour in the morning the Ball broke up, and the Belles retired to dream of conquests made, while the major portion of the Beaux if they slept at all, awoke with such awful feelings in their heads as would cause them to remember for some time the Reception Ball at Yerba Buena, the latter part of which was not announced in the Programme.

Initial attempts to rout the Mexicans from Los Angeles failed and, on December 5, the *Portsmouth* sailed for southern California. Downey was one of the men who marched 160 miles from San Diego to Los Angeles in 13 days, and his accounts of the battles that lead to the recapture of that town on January 10, 1847, have provided historians with a number of significant and amusing insights.

The ship remained eight months on the California coast—including a return visit to San Francisco for two weeks in August—and then it sailed for Boston where, in May 1848, Downey signed off. Little is known of him after that, other than that he was in San Francisco in 1853 when the "Filings" pieces appeared in the *Golden Era*.

Howard R. Lamar, who edited Downey's journal, wrote in the introduction to *The Cruise of the Portsmouth*: "By 1853, Downey, still seeking fun and companionship—and perhaps audiences as well—caroused nightly in the rooms of a set of friends whom he dubbed the 'jolly sort' of San Francisco. What happened to this convivial young sketcher after that year can only be surmised. 'Peak,' 'Filings,' and Downey disappeared forever after this last hearty flourish of the pen."

One of those "Yankee Mormons, blushing and blooming like full blown peonies" whom Downey saw at the governor's ball may have been 25-year-old Mary Holland Sparks, who had arrived on the *Brooklyn* with her mother (Mary Hamilton), her husband (Quartus Strong Sparks), and their infant son. On November 15, 1846, she wrote to her sisters Maria and Holly Clark, describing the voyage and her life in the new land. This excerpt begins with the ship's departure from the Sandwich Islands (as the Hawaiian Islands then were called)—a regular stopover for ships sailing to California and Oregon from the East Coast. In true Victorian style, she refers to her husband as "Mr. Sparks."

Mormons at the Mission Dolores

W E THEN SET SAIL [FROM HAWAII] for California. Was about five weeks from Sandwich Islands and then we came in sight of the shores of California. Sailed up the Francisco Bay until we came in sight of a beautiful village on the shore where we landed.

All things safe; nothing broke or injured much. Some of us found houses to move into and the rest pitched tents. I lived in our tent a few weeks. We then moved to a place called the mission—into the old castles we used to read about so much in the *Children of the Abby*. It looks as though it had been a convent. There is no windows in the room except at the top of the doors—although mother and I have two little rooms where we live very comfortable. We live among the Spaniards. But they are very kind to us. They often send us a quarter of beef at a time and milk and vegetables, fruit etc. They come to see us—some of them—almost every day. I can talk with them some. They call beef— carny, milk—leche, man—ombre, yes—si, cow—vaca. No more Spanish this time. There is a Roman Catholic Church a few doors from where we live. They have an Indian priest that stays here part of the time.

The news has just come that the Mexicans have had a battle with the Americans. Seven Americans killed and one hundred and ten Mexicans. The battle was fought about six hundred miles from here. We believe there is to be wars and rumors of wars in order to fulfill prophecy and that peace is taken from the earth for the present.

We believe in *Mormonism* yet, although we are poor samples of Mormonism. Mr. Sparks and some others have gone off taking up their lands, sowing wheat, building houses, where we expect to move in the spring. The soil is very fertile. Beautiful fields—no stones, some hills, and the climate is very healthy. We never enjoyed better health than we do now and if you were all here, we should be perfectly contented. No danger of starving here; if we can work half as hard as we did in the states. Business is pretty lively here. Most all kinds of wages are very high—money plenty. Mother has earned four dollars per week some of the time. But goods and groceries are pretty high on account of so many people emigrating here. Most all kinds of goods are brought in; but we have not had to buy anything as yet. We brought plenty with us for the present. Maria if I could only see you and the children, Clarissa and her children, I could tell you more than I can write. And I hope that we shall meet before many years but I cannot tell when or where. We want to see you all so much.

Wild horses and cattle are very plentiful here. But if we are as smart as the Spaniards are, we can catch them and tame them. Beef is very cheap here—only two cents a pound. We have not starved yet. There is plenty of wheat here for 75 cents per bushel. Mother cannot speak of you without crying. Her health has been remarkably good since we left home. She wants to tell Hugh, if she could see him now that she could tell him plenty of stories about the bears and wolves and Indians—for there are plenty here. Tell Adeline that Granny cannot forget her baby. Tell Elizabeth that there is a little girl here that we love because she looks just like her. Tell Dwight and Mary Jane that little Quartus can throw the lasso and call mamy and papa and is as full of mischief as he can be—running from place to place.

I must hurry and close my letter for it is most time to send it on board ship. You must give our love to all our brothers and sisters, uncles and Aunts, and Southworh [?] and her husband. Tell her to write. There is ships coming and going all the time from New York to Sandwich Islands and from Sandwich Islands here. You must take pains to send up a letter. We want to hear from you so very very much. One more thing, I thought I would tell you the name of the ship we came on is called the Brooklyn commanded by Capt. Pritchardson [A. W. Richardson]. Sophia Clark is here keeping house for Mr. Goodwin—his wife died on the ship. I have no time to write all this time but intend to write every opportunity I have of sending to you. Mr. Sparks has written once or twice and sent paper from the

Sandwich Islands. Tell Clarissa and Ely to write also. This is from you[r?] sister and mother.

Mary H. Sparks M.H.

[A new page is added:]

When we arrived here the American man-of-war called the Portsmouth commanded by Capt. Montgomery lay at anchor in the harbor. They had taken possession of the place about three weeks before we came. Had hoisted the American flag before the barracks. Soon after the Congress came in another man-of-war. They fired a gun salute, was immediately answered by four cannons from the Portsmouth and four from the fort on the hill, which made the ground tremble; which sounded like war. The American officers were so pleased to see so many immigrants, only 240, that they gave a festival at the tavern. Invited us all to attend. A great number attended plenty of cakes and wine, music, and Spanish dancing. I wish you could see them dance what they called a Spandango. If you write you can send your letters to New York or Boston which will be sent in the first ship that goes out. Direct your letters to Yerba Buena, Francisco Bay, California. Give my love to all inquiring friends.

Yours MHS

> Yes my native land I love thee
> All thy scenes I love them well
> Friends, connections, happy country
> Can I bid you all farewell
> > Can I leave thee
> For in distant lands to dwell.

The Sparks were only one of several Mormon families billeted at the secularized Mission Dolores buildings. Quartus Sparks was sent with a group of about 20 other men to the San Joaquin Valley to construct the town of New Hope, in preparation for the arrival of Brigham Young and the Mormons who were coming overland. However, Young decided to settle in the Salt Lake area, and the New Hope project was abandoned.

This is one of the few accounts known to exist that tells of early San Francisco from a child's point of view. James Horace Skinner was four years old when he and his parents arrived on the *Brooklyn*, and he was 12 when they left the Bay Area to join the Mormon colony in southern California. Although he was 73 when he set down these reminiscences, it is obvious that he still felt close to those days when he helped his mother sift wheat and took part in a huge patriotic parade.

The whereabouts of the original 40 sheets on which Skinner wrote this are not known. What follows is an excerpt from a photocopy in the archives of the Church of Jesus Christ of Latter-day Saints in Salt Lake City, Utah. Although most of the manuscript was written in a clear, round handwriting, several of the passages are almost illegible. Errors and inconsistencies of spelling and punctuation remain as in the original, except in a few cases where corrections have been made for clarity's sake.

Through the eyes of a child

At last we reached our destination and Haven of safety, after a long and tedious voyage of six months, buffited by wind and waves. Thanking Our Hevenly Father for His watchfull care, and mercy, in bringing us safely through our many trials and dangers, and unseen.

We arrived in what is now known as San Francisco California, then known as Yerba Buena (Good Herb) on the last day of July 1846, to find our country then at war with Mexico, a country barren and dreary: not like the California of today. As I remember where San Francisco now stands, was coverd with chaparrall manzanetta, poison ivery etc, miscetos etc with very little fresh water.

Before we had time to get settled, or any way fixed to live, Father, and Mr Austin, with most of the men of our company was called to go up the secromento River to load the ship with Red wood, Hides and Tallow for her return trip home to New York. While they were gone their families were to draw rations from the stock that was brought with them from home. But what they got was something scandelous: Not enough to hardly keep life in their bodies, [There was] plenty for all, But the (Big Fish) got it as they most allways will—and still do.

The President of the co. Sam Brannan, him and his family lived high at the expence of poor and needy, the widows and orphens, what he dident need, sold which laid the foundation for wealth that he afterwords accumulated. But tribulation and sorrow overtook him in after years For he lost his Fortune, Family, and Friends, and at last Died a miserable death without a friendly white person to comfort him in his last hours. He died at Guaymas in Old Mexico—as I read in the papers—in an old adobe hut, with dirt ruff and floor, no one to help or comfort him but an Indian squaw: so perish all such. I will not tell more, the above is enough: The readers can fill out the balance: a miserable old sinner, forsaken by God and man.

Soon after Father and Bro Austin left, Mother and sister Austin, with their Families, with what Food they could get, moved to the Mission Delorus, some 3 miles from San Francisco. And to try and help make a living for themselves and children, with what they had or could get in the way of food, [they] opened a small eating house. The Spanish women helped them what they could, with milk, beef, chickens, Eggs, onions, Beans etc, after they got aquainted with them, and found that the Mormons were Friends, not enimies.

You must remember the United States was at war with Spain (Mexico). We were right in the midest of war, but as providence would have it, there was peace arround where we were, for which we were very thankfull.

One day I remember a company of sholders and marens passed our place going out to fight the Spaniards who were posted on a bluff, with cannen trained ready for battle. For our troops to attack them, it was nessesary to cross a soft piece of ground—or bog. The enemy awaited their comming.

In attemting to cross this bog they mired their horses, cannen, and men. They had a terrable time. in the menetime the enemy did not fire a shot, but looked and laughed. After wallerring arround in the mud and slush all day, they returned at night tired and sore. Marched out in the morning with banners flying and in high spyrits. Marched back at night dejected. A sorry lot of Troops. Such is war.

Mother and Mrs Austin some way got hold of a busher or more wheat that had been thrashed with horses on the ground. They cleaned and washed and dried it good, Then took it to be ground. The Spaniards had riged up a pair of burros (Spanish) that they used by hitching a mule to a sweep, or pole.

The women took me along to feed the mill, ... [words illegible] The 2 women turned, and hard work it was you better believe. There were 2 very tired women when the job was done, but they had some good Flour after it was sived and made in to Bread. It would have been much better if there had been less grit mixed with it.

While living here, (Doloris) I witnessed 4 or 5 Bull Fights; In fact the ring was in front of where we were living. One fight as I well remember, The Bull broke out just in front of our door. The path was packed with men, women and children. They opened a path for him to pass through. he passed clost enough to me that I could have touched him. He passed through that crowd without hurting a person, but as soon as he reached the street he began to hook every person that he could get at. he was soon caught and brought back to finish his work, which was to kill a horse or two, or perchance kill an Indian or two, who had been made drunk for that special purpose. Blood was what they wanted to see flow. Nothing else would satisfy them. a Bull fight without blood and death was not a fight. They are a crual, treatchus people. Be good to your Face, and stick a dager in your Back at the first good chance.

A Mr. [blank] a native of Russia, and a very wealthy man for those days, owning lots of property in San Francisco. Among the rest was the Big Hotell, called the City Hotell. He used to come out often to the Mission with his Friends, and would allways stop and order Lunch. he was a great spender. He took quite a liking to Father and Mother—Father had returned from loading the ship—and offerd them a good salary to take charge of the Hotell and run it for him. They accepted his offer and moved back again to the City, which had grown like a musroom by this time.

While takeing charge of the Hotel Father bought a lot on Clay st, and comensed to clear it off and preparing to build Father was badly poisened by poison ivory. He built us a 4 or 5 room house which we occupied untill we sold when we moved to San Jose.

While we were living in the Hotel I took a hardy Feaver. was out of my head most all the time so the nurse said. They would not let me have one drop of water.—This *I* remember well enough—I was dieing for a drink, but No it would kill him, so the Doctor said. Oh how fullish. It took them a long time to learn. Many have died for the want of water in Better Feavers.

The nurse left me for a short time. At the foot of the bed stood a bucket of water. I managed to get out of bed and to the water, and I tell you I drank my fill, but was too weak to get in to bed again.—It was the old kind of a bedsteat, tall and stout. When they found me, and what I had done they were scard allmost [to] death. Horace would surely die. but not so. that drink was what saved him, and he soon got well again.

Mothers Brother came from the states soon after we got our house finished and moved in. He remained with us, as one of the Family, untill we moved to Utah in 1868. He and Father worked together as pardners. Not long before our coming to Utah, he married Miss E. A. Guy, who had arrived only a few months from Austrila.

My first schooling was had in San Francisco. The first and only time I ever plaid hooky was here. In going back to school after dinner I ran across a man with a hand organ and a monkey. That afternoon I forget all about school in following the man and monkey arround.

.   .   .

I remember well when peace was signed between the United States and Mixico, as I was one of the Boys that repsented the 29 states. We were all dressed in uniforms and each carried a banner, suposed to repsent the state that each was born in. Oh, it was one of the grandest sights that a person will see in a lifetime, and once seen never to be Forgotten. The first white girl born in California was our Goddess and carried the stars and stripes. We were all in a float some 10 feet from the ground drawn by six white horses. All crafts and trades was repsented in the parade. We led the prossesion, and we were back at the starting point before the last had left. After the march was over we were taken to a Banquet, where we were waited upon as if we were the Lord Mayor of London. We were given our costume and banners. I kept mine and brought it to Utah with me when I came.

The booming of cannen snaping of fire crackers and the shouting of the people was something long to be remembered.

Not long after uncles arrival Father sold out and all moved to San Jose where they bought a farm of an hundred and twenty acres. I attended school again.

The school house was about two miles from home, out on the open plain. When there were no wild cattles in the way, I could make it all right, but when they were between our place and the school-house I had to follow fences and under a steep bank untill I got within some 30 or 40 rods then make a run for it. There was thousands of wild cattle when we first moved to San Jose valley.

Many times in going to school, a fighting cow or bull would be on one side of a wire fence, and I on the other, Hooking and bellowing, and trying to reach me. I tell you it made my hair pull more than once. Sometimes the men or Father would take me on a horse.

We had a beautiful place here. Our Farm borded on a fresh water lake—or as it was called La Genes—Ducks and Geese by the Thousands. I knew of one man who killed 21 ducks at one shot, as I helped to pick them up with the boat. Many got away that was wounded. Wings broken.

Oh, what fun I used to have in the boat on the lake. I have caught many a Duck that had had his wing broken, and not able to fly. They would dive a few times, get out of breath. I would hit them over the head with the oar, then it was mine. OK. Then after another. What fun. Often the Goodwing Boys or the Switchers Boys would come over and spend the day with us. Then wouldent we have a fine day of it: oh no?

This is a most lovely country—a Gods country—to live in. Neither too hot or too cold. a live plain for miles coverd with grass, and not a brush or shrub could ... [word illegible] for miles. Grass to your knees with Flowers of all colors by the thousands, as far as the eye could see. I used to pick a Bouquet for Mother every morning early while the due was still on. In the year of 1854 we sold our Farm and moved to San Bernardino.

Skinner's comments about the "crual, treatchus people" were probably induced by the general hostility that many Americans felt for all foreigners, particularly Spanish-speaking, during the Gold Rush years.

Samuel Brannan died in Escondido, near San Diego, not in Guaymas, as stated above. The unnamed "native of Russia" could only have been William Leidesdorff, although he was born in the Virgin Islands of a Danish father and a black mother. It was he who built and owned the City Hotel. Mr. and Mrs. Skinner took charge of the hotel's catering from John Henry Brown briefly in October 1847.

The question of whether the parade celebrated peace with Mexico (1848) or—more likely—California's acceptance into the union (1850) is discussed in "A city is born."

By the time John Henry Brown sat down in 1885 to write his
Reminiscences and Incidents, the town and its people had
changed dramatically. In this excerpt he looks back with nos-
talgia on the pioneer days of the 1840s and recalls a time of
"open heart and hand."

JOHN HENRY BROWN (1810-1905)

A *different*
class of people

I HAVE OFTEN HEARD IT REMARKED "If I had come to California in early days, I would have been worth millions." The persons who were here in early days, and those who came when gold was first discovered, were a different class of people altogether from those of the present day [1885]. Money was of little if any value to them, and they were always ready with open heart and hand to help their fellow men, especially a friend, in a most liberal manner.

I will here mention a few things that happened to my certain knowledge: In the first place, as far as I was concerned myself, I never allowed any person to want for a meal, and many a time I have fed them for weeks together without pay, or even expecting to be paid. I will name one instance: A young man came here from New York, who informed me that he would give me anything he had, if I would keep him at the hotel for a few days, and give him something to do that would enable him to go to the mines and try his luck. I could see by his behavior that he was well brought up. I did not like to offer him money for fear it might be a temptation to lead him astray, so I offered him something to do that enabled him to make enough in a few days to take him out of the city.

When I went to pay him for what work he had done, I informed Parker and John Owens of my intention, and they each gave me ten dollars to swell the amount. I heard of his death sometime afterwards at Stockton, and have received two letters from his mother, thanking me for my kindness; also making some inquiries as to what had become of his effects.

There were three persons residing in the city, doing a good business, whose names were as follows: John Owen, Richard Ross and Captain Robert Harly. These persons were well known by all who came here from Texas, most of whom were usually "dead broke." As soon as they could find either of the above mentioned parties, they would receive what assistance they needed. John Owens informed me that inside of ten months he had given away over six thousand dollars. I know Dick Ross must have given away that amount, if not more. Another man I knew, from Indiana, gave away thousands for charitable purposes, out of pure generosity of heart. I know of one person, belonging to Indiana, who went to the mines, where he was not at all successful. He returned to the city and applied to George McDougal for assistance. The man was pretty well along in years; Mr. McDougal gave him a slug,* and told him to call again in about three days. When he came back, McDougal had bought him a cabin passage on the steamer, and also gave him five hundred dollars, so that he might go home to his family.

Another of McDougal's good deeds occurred as late as the year '51: He wanted me to take a ride with him out to the race course. On passing through Kearny street, on our way to the stables, to obtain a horse and buggy, McDougal suddenly came to a full stop, and looking very attentively at a man who was laboring, repairing the street; he said to me: "I know that man's face well; I must find out, who he is," and going up to the man, he accosted him and asked if his name was not ——— , from Indiana. He said it was; McDougal told him to throw down the shovel, and come with him to the hotel. He hired a room for the man, and engaged his board. He then got him a suit of clothes at Cronin and Markley's, and gave him means to go to the mines.

I will now speak of another person, who, when possessed of means, had a heart equal to half a dozen such men as you will find nowadays. No person ever asked him for a loan or any thing he had, but he would give with a good free heart. This man's name was Robert A. Parker. I will mention one circumstance that happened about this time: I was in debt to a firm, and owed a balance of three hundred and sixty dollars. As Parker was going down the street in that direction, I gave him the amount, and asked him to please call and settle it for me;

* Could be either a gold nugget or a gold coin.

it was in gold dust. I did not hear anything concerning it for about three weeks, when one day a collector for Ward and Smith, by the name of Craner, presented the bill for payment. I informed him that it had been paid already, by Robert A. Parker. Thinking there must have been some mistake to whom they gave the credit for that amount, I went and called Parker into the office, and informed him in regard to the matter. Parker smiled, and said he never thought of telling me, that there were two poor fellows whom he met on his way to the store, whose parents he had known in Boston, and being informed that they were dead broke, and having no other money with him, except what I had given him, he gave them the loan of it instead of paying the debt. They told Parker that they got to gambling and lost all, and as they were anxious to go to the mines, Parker took this means of helping them out.

After making this explanation, Parker called Crane into his office and paid the debt. The parties who received the loan were very careful never to pay it back again. I have known of this same Parker helping many persons, and he has often borrowed money of me for the purpose. I do believe if Parker had had a ship load of gold dust, any person from Boston, particularly, if they chanced to be acquainted with his father, could get all they wanted, by simply asking for it.

There were many men who became wealthy through what they got out of Parker. I will mention one more person who did much good by his generosity of heart. The man's name was Jack Hays. During the time he was Sheriff, there was an execution handed him to serve. He gave it to one of his deputies, who went to serve it. He found the man in a dying condition, and the family, which consisted of a wife and five children, very needy. The deputy returned the writ to Jack, saying he could not serve it, under the circumstances. The parties for whom the money was to be collected, sent to Hays, to know if the amount had been received. The next day Hays called, not for the purpose of serving the execution; but to ascertain for himself the true state of affairs. He found things in a much worse condition than he anticipated. He put his hand in his pocket, and gave the woman what money he had with him, promising to assist them farther. He then sent to the man's relief, Dr. Nelson, one of the most noted physicians then in the city. When Jack returned to his office, he told the parties to send and get their pay. He made out a receipt, and by the side of it he placed thirty dollars. He informed the parties in regard to the straightened circumstances of the family, who were without a dime in the house. The reply was, "that they could not afford to lose their money in that way." Jack told the man to sign the receipt, and that there was the thirty dollars, which he would pay out of his own pocket but, if he took the money, he would get the worst whipping he ever had, if it cost him a thousand dollars. The party signed the receipt in full, but was very careful not to take the money, as he thought Jack was a little more than he cared to handle.

Miners & gamblers
1848-1849

Ann Eliza Brannan was the wife of Samuel Brannan, leader of the *Brooklyn* Mormons. This letter is not unlike many others written by the early settlers, who praised the healthy environment but insisted they would leave as soon as they had made their fortunes. At the time she wrote this, her husband was well on his way to becoming the town's first millionaire, thanks to his various property dealings and the exorbitant prices he was charging miners for picks, pans, and other essentials. The letter was sent to Mary Brannan, wife of Sam's brother, John.

ANN ELIZA BRANNAN (1823?-1916)

"Now is the time for making money"

San Francisco Sept 2 1848

Dear Mary

I now commence to write you a long letter, and you must excuse it if it looks as though it had been wrote in a great hurry; for perhaps I shall be three or four days at it just as I have time now and then. We received your letter, and was happy to hear of the good health of you all. also to know that we had not passed entirely away from your minds.

Our family are all well and enjoying good health. little Samuel has grown very much and is another S. Brannan over again. he is quite tall, but rather slender, he will be three years old the 17th of next month. he knows his letters and is beginning to spell quite rapidly.

We are living in one of the most healthy places in the world, and I am quite contented and happy for the time being; that is, untill we make our fortunes, but we would never think of setling here for life, and I rather think that too or three years will find us in *New York* or some wheres there abouts where we can enjoy life. that is, if we have good luck as at present: but now is the time for making money.

Mary if you and John had come out hear when we did you would now of been independent for John could of made five dollars a day the year round, from the time we came here, and now it is much better; for the Gold mines yeald abundance for all, and you by sewing could of made three times what John does now, besides doing your work. You will hardly believe me when I tell you that this summer that in little more than three months I have cleared five hundred dollars by making and getting made cheap clothing. pants and shirts, such as you would get in N.Y. 25 cents for making I am given $1,50 cents and they have only one pocket in them as women can make five and six pair a day.

tis true I have a good cook and also have had a good girl which I brought from N.Y. with me but she has lately married and left, and I don't know but my cook will go to the Gold mines soon to work and then I shall be without help. I would like if you come out here that you would bring a girl for me and I will pay her expenses. If you come bring every garmant to last you a year or so that is clothing, and a plenty of dried fruit of every discription and I will buy all you don't want yourselves.

I send by Mr Mellus three rings which we got made of the gold from the mines, one for your self, and one for Jane, Daniel wife, and one for Mary Ann Badlam. you must deliver them with my love and best wishes for their welfair and hapiness. I would write to them both if I knew where to direct them, you must give Mr Mellus directions where Jane lives so that he can call and see her, and tell Jane I shall expect a letter from her without fail if it is no more than three lines for she will have a good chance to send by the vessel that Mellus sends here from N.Y. And the same to Mary Ann if you see her, as for your self I shall say nothing for a word to the wise is suffiscent. Samuel says he wishes that Daniel was here with his family to; and I wish you all was here for we have a pleasant place and good health also doing well and with these you could not fail to be contented for a year or too.

I think of you often and of N.Y. also for that is the place of my child hood and I look forward with a joyous heart to the time when I shall return. There is many things I would like to write of if I had time. I will send a little of Samuels hair to you all. And I hope this will find you in the enjoyment of good health.

Yours with love and respect

A. L. Brannan

These miniatures were made circa 1856 while the Brannan family was in Europe. L-R: Ann Eliza, Fanny, Samuel, Samuel Jr., Lisa, and Adelaide. Not shown is Don Francisco, who died of cholera while a child.

Although her name was Ann Eliza, she signed this letter—and also a power of attorney when her husband opened the Brannan Bank—with an "L" as her middle initial. Paul Bailey, in his fictionalized biography of Samuel Brannan, *The Gay Saint*, said she changed her name to Ann Lisa "in keeping with her new queenly estate." The wealthier the Brannans became, the more she detested San Francisco, which she considered coarse and uncultured. She insisted that her children be educated in Europe, and she lived with them in Paris while they were there. In 1870 she divorced the then hard-drinking Samuel, demanding settlement in cash, which hastened the decline of his financial empire. Samuel died penniless in 1889. Ann returned to San Francisco, where she died in December 1916, at the age of 93.

With the discovery of gold, San Francisco became the stopover point for thousands of prospectors who poured in from all corners of the world on their way to the mines. When winter rains flooded the diggings, those prospectors returned to San Francisco to while away their time and to spend their hard-earned findings. By the winter of 1849, John Henry Brown, now established as California's foremost hotel manager, was again in charge of catering at the City Hotel and was also a part owner—with Robert A. Parker—of the Parker House. To him fell the task of finding sufficient food to feed his guests. Meanwhile, large portions of the Parker House were being rented out as gambling dens. This is from his *Reminiscences and Incidents.*

JOHN HENRY BROWN (1810-1905)

Food and faro

I FOUND IT VERY DIFFICULT TO KEEP UP the boarding department in the City Hotel, and would have failed entirely had it not been for the fact that I was personally acquainted with the captains of vessels, and consequently had an opportunity of procuring from them a portion of what they had for the use of their ships. Although they were charging me enormous prices, I still considered that they were doing me a great favor by letting me have such provisions, as I really needed them and could not well do without.

By every vessel that left for Oregon I would send for such articles as butter, onions, pickled tripe, hams, bacon, eggs or anything I could obtain in the way of provisions in the Oregon market. Fresh meats, such as beef and mutton were very reasonable, much cheaper than they are now [1885]; pork was very dear. I will name the highest prices I had to pay at that time when purchasing provisions in the city: onions were one dollar per pound; potatoes, seventy five cents per pound; fresh butter, one dollar and fifty cents per pound; eggs, I once paid nine dollars a dozen for, but the common price was six dollars per dozen; for a small roasting pig, I twice paid fifteen dollars; the common price was ten dollars. An old gentleman by the name of Herman, supplied the hotel with vegetables, such as lettuce, cabbage, turnips, radishes, carrots and other small articles for the use of the table. These he brought daily; I had to pay him from fifteen to twenty dollars per day. Such articles as tea, coffee, sugar, spices, etc., were very reasonable, and there were plenty in the market. Another item of considerable expense to me, was the hiring of two hunters and a whale boat to go off up the creeks after game; they would make two trips per week, and were usually very successful. If I had been compelled to purchase in this city every thing I needed in the way of provisions for the table, I would have lost every day, at least, one hundred dollars. Had it not been for the large amount of wine that was generally consumed at the dinner-table, I could never have stood the losses made in the boarding department. Many times it has taken over a thousand dollars worth of wine for one dinner-table; but when I obtained my provisions from Oregon it would be less by one-half than the California prices.

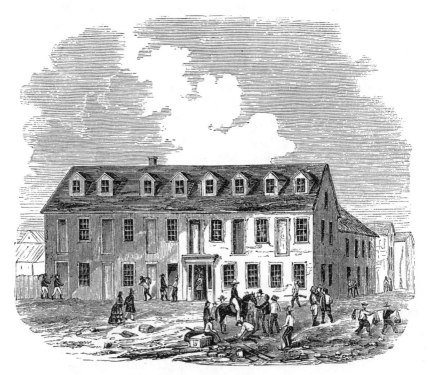

The Parker House when it first opened.

At the opening of the Parker House, there was a grand ball given, followed by a bountiful supper, which was free to all. In expectation of this event, I had been saving a great many delicacies, which could not be obtained except from foreign ports. The invitations were general in those days, there was no distinction as regards persons, Jack was considered as good as his master. After this event the Parker House was in full blast. There were two billiard-rooms, with two tables in each room. There were two bar-rooms. One billiard-room was in the second story, one on the first floor, and one in the cellar. There was a large amount of liquors, wines, and other things on hand, sufficient nowadays to fit out a wholesale establishment.

The lower floor, called the billiard-room, was short-lived, as Mr. Parker had an offer of ten thousand dollars per month for the gambling privileges alone. In this room there were seven gambling tables: three for faro, two for monte, and one for rolette; the other was used for general purposes, and these tables made a good business for the bar. The dealer of the table would always treat all at his table, usually, every hour, and if he had a good game, oftener. There was another gambling room back of the bar, which paid three thousand five hundred dollars per month. On the second floor, there were three rooms, which rented for three thousand five hundred dollars per month. There were two other rooms hired for gambling purposes. These were private, and were only engaged for the game of poker. In those rooms the biggest bet I know of, was a one thousand dollar blind.

The extravagant rents paid for the use of these rooms, will show how I was enabled to pay one dollar per foot for lumber. These monte banks generally had in coin on their tables from ten to twenty-five thousand dollars. These large amounts, were for the purpose of keeping any person from tapping their banks. The dealers would usually have no percentage on anything of that kind. I know of one person, who said they had in their bank over forty thousand dollars in gold and silver coin.

As gambling fever took hold of San Francisco, billiard tables were replaced by faro, monte, and roulette tables. And gold was often rejected as currency because there was so much of it about, causing people to fear depreciation, as Brown tells us in this third excerpt from his *Reminiscences and Incidents*.

JOHN HENRY BROWN (1810-1905)

Gold at $6 an ounce

W HEN GOLD WAS FIRST BROUGHT TO Yerba Buena I had
no idea of what its real value was, and most people had an idea that
gold dust would depreciate in value, judging from the quantity which
was brought to the city; consequently, I would pay out the gold dust
as fast as possible, fearing I might lose by keeping it; selling it often at
the rate of ten to twelve dollars per ounce. Cash seemed to be money,
but gold dust was looked at more in the light of merchandise. I have
often purchased it for six dollars per ounce. In the Fall of 1847 the
miners began to come to Yerba Buena for the purpose of spending the
winter, and they continued to come until the latter part of December.
In those days there were no towns or houses at the mines, and the
only place that afforded any shelter was at Sutter's Fort, which afforded room for only a small number, however, I think I can say with
safety, that there were that winter between eighty and ninety boarding
and lodging at the City Hotel.

At the commencement of the winter the miners would pass the
time away by playing billiards; but they soon tired of that, and wished
me to take the billiard-table out and turn it into a gambling saloon.
They said they would pay me two hundred dollars per day; or pay five
dollars an hour after six o'clock up to twelve at night; later than that,
they would pay ten dollars per hour. The size of this room was thirty
feet by twenty-four. I got eight tables made for this room, and before
the tables were finished they were all taken. One man was so afraid he
would not be able to obtain one that he gave me one hundred dollars
in advance to secure one. When it was in full blast, we found that

there were not tables enough to accommodate all who wished to join in the games. I could have rented, in the same room a dozen tables; but the room was not large enough. I had three more tables made and placed them in an adjoining room. All three rooms were used for gambling purposes; such games as Monte, Faro, Rolette and others being played. Most of these tables were spoken for in advance; sometimes they were engaged by the week, and I could then have rented as many more if I had had room for them. There were two other rooms used for gambling purposes, in the back of the hotel. I remember one instance where a gambler gave five hundred dollars premium for a room with a lease on it for three months. I feel almost ashamed to put in print some of the things which happened in those early days, as they seem almost incredible, and still it is the truth.

At this time gold dust was only worth eight dollars per ounce, and the gamblers would not play for it. Those having no coin were obliged to come to the bar and sell the dust for eight dollars per ounce; and when I was short of cash I would only pay six dollars per ounce. All persons that were boarding in the hotel, also, those running bar bills, on making payments we would buy their gold dust at the rate of eight dollars per ounce.

The first shipment which I made was with Captain Newell, of the schooner Honolulu, which was going to the Sandwich Islands for goods. I remember giving Newell twenty pounds of gold dust in bottles, with which to purchase goods for me, and he was to sell the balance of the dust and bring back what cash remained after purchasing the goods. The next was Captain John Young, who, later on had charge of the Alameda Quicksilver Mines. He had a charter for Mazatlan. He had only half a cargo. I gave him a gallon pickle bottle full of gold dust; just how much it weighed I could not tell. On his return I received a large amount of coin, more than the first cost of the gold dust; also, all the goods I had sent for. Commodore John Patey would take gold dust for me on every trip, and would return to me such goods as I would order from him, and the balance in money. These Captains would charge me ten per cent on all money they brought back, and also ten per cent and freight for all the goods they purchased for me.

The City Hotel stood on the corner of Kearny and Clay streets.

Chileans were the earliest and—next to the Mexicans—the second-largest group of foreigners in San Francisco during the first Gold Rush summer. They flooded in, bringing not only their own equipment but also a firsthand knowledge of mining that would soon ensure their success. Vicente Pérez Rosales was already 41 years old when he arrived with three of his half-brothers and two indentured servants. He had been educated in France and had met and dealt with leaders in art, literature, and politics. His bewilderment with this "new and unusual town" is quite apparent in this excerpt from his 1878 book, *Diario de un Viaje a California*, part of which was first published in English in *We Were 49ers* (Ward Ritchie Press, 1976), translated and edited by Edwin A. Beilharz and Carlos U. López. The entry is dated February 9, 1849.

VICENTE PÉREZ ROSALES (1807-1886)

Noise and confusion

IT WAS SIX O'CLOCK THE NEXT MORNING. Each one was up and gathering his belongings and equipment to be ready to spring on shore. While that was going on, my companions and I climbed up onto the poop so we could quietly study the place where we were about to land. It is the port of Yerbas Buenas, or the port of San Francisco, one of the numberless inlets that form the irregular southern coast of the bay of San Francisco. In spite of its being inland, very strong winds blow there, strong enough to cause a good deal of trouble in fall and spring.

The city, or rather the small village at the port, lies upon the slopes of some hills. These are treeless, but covered with bushes, wild strawberries, and colorful flowers. The population of the town is rather small, about five thousand. The houses are of one-story, many of them made of adobe in the Spanish style, some of a more modern look, along with a great number of tents and cabins. At the moment they represent the beginnings of a new and unusual town.

All of it conveys the impression of a large camp. There are twenty-five ships in the port if you include the squadron.

Our ship is an object of interest to many. It has been, all of a sudden, surrounded by boats and launches, some looking for passengers, some looking for business, and some for news of Chile. All was noise and confusion. Those who had recently arrived confirmed the stories of gold. Most of them had some of the precious metal to show. Wrapped in rags were nuggets as big as walnuts, and gold dust like lentils.

What a pleasant surprise it was to be surrounded suddenly by people we knew—though one had to look hard to recognize the dandy of Valparaíso or the fashionable gentleman from Santiago in ragged pants and huge pea jacket, with calloused hands and tar-blackened face. Young Hamilton, now a sailor and the operator of a boat in partnership with a Negro who owned the solitary bed in which they slept, was waiting in oilcloth hat and soggy woolen shirt for a passenger to carry ashore. Manuel Price, fat and rosy, with pants rolled up and shoes full of mud, fired questions at us to find out what we had brought, and answered our flood of questions with tales of wonders.

Rosa's friend, Nisser, together with Sánchez, Cross, Pinet, and others called me by name, though we had never met, and swarmed into the cabin. Each of these adventurers was clad in clothing so wild and odd that Dumas, the mulatto, would have found material for ten novels just by looking at them. It was not curiosity that brought this bustling band of men on board. There is no time to waste on curiosity here. Each one had business in mind. They knew everything on the ship could be sold in California at fantastic prices, and they wanted to make deals before the passengers had time in town to discover this. Chileans are not all that stupid, but they are not accustomed to Yankee methods.

Cross, who is making a lot of money here, was trying to bargain with someone for the windows of the poop when another man rushed by on another deal, collided with him, and knocked his hat into the water. Neither one noticed it. Cross kept on bargaining and the man kept on running. A little later Cross left, wearing a tattered sailor's cap as jauntily as though it was a papal tiara.

To avoid the uproar and expense, we decided not to go ashore that day. We will let the small fry go to the lie-factory while we pay our respects to the port captain who has just come on board. He is a tall Yankee, portly and bright of eye—or rather in one of them; the other is black and blue from a blow someone gave him last night. He is also rather run-down and smells of alcohol.

Along with him there is a customs officer who is to stay on board until the cargo has been landed. On entering the cabin the captain hailed us in a loud jovial voice:

"Welcome, gentlemen, to the land of gold. Lots of gold. Lots of gold."

Our captain, who did not understand English, thought he wanted the passports, and immediately produced them. You should have beheld the Yankee's face when he saw the passports and the official stamps. It was as though we had insulted the stars and stripes. You remember that one of the causes of the American Revolution was the Stamp Act.

Our fine Yankee, tearing his one good eye away from the thing that disturbed him so, said to us:

"Forget all those stamps and passports. You are now in the United States, and here we don't put up with the stupid tyranny of passports and the robbery of having to buy stamps for documents. I only came to congratulate you on your happy arrival in this rich land, and to give this customs official my authorization here on the ship to receive and put through the permit you need from the government to unload your cargo."

We offered him wines or liqueurs. He replied that he drank only champagne. He was given a generous dose, and wound up his visit to the satisfaction of all.

You may be surprised at the lack of curiosity we showed by remaining on board ship that way. The truth is we were a bit stunned. Besides we had to write letters to Chile to go by the *Anamakin*, which was ready to sail. As we had to write at once, we decided to content ourselves with what we had seen and heard, and with what we had been told by the port captain. He was a respectable official, even though he had not been respected by the drunkard who had struck him. They had probably been drinking together.

Rosita had outfitted herself for business with a magnificent silk dress, a cape, and a cap or hat as they call it nowadays. She had won the good will of everyone on board. I do not know what kind of card or letter of recommendation she carried, but everyone on board had had dealings with her, and she with them.

All except us, that is. We alone were virtuous, chaste; or finicky and choosy. The truth is, one would have to come to this country and spend days and nights seeing men and only men before he could find the sight of this charming siren tolerable. That is why she has the eyes and attention, now, of everyone who happens to see her. But let us say goodbye and Godspeed to Madam Rosita. May she go conquering, and being conquered, as is the norm and custom in these calamitous times.

As soon as the captain left, our newly arrived dandies fixed and fitted themselves up as if for a ball, and went ashore looking as if they had just stepped out of a band box. You should have seen what they looked like when they got back! It was as if they had been rolled in the mud. They returned happy, but full of contradictory tales about the mines, and cursing the mud that made up the streets-to-be of this extraordinary town.

As we had been able to get no very clear idea about the mines, their distance away, the weather there, or the best way to travel, we decided to send a reconnaissance party ashore next day.

What you see and hear in California is so odd and unexpected, so different from the natural order of human affairs, and everything goes by so quickly, it is only by writing things down as they happen, and later looking at the account in your own handwriting, that you can convince yourself it was not all a dream. You remember we all had laughed derisively in Chile at the first stories we heard about California. I thought it was only natural that the account of its richness would be more and more exaggerated the farther the news travelled; and as Chile was two thousand leagues away, the increase would be on the scale of a funnel: what was the size of the spout would have grown to the size of the upper rim. I believed, though I did not say so then, that California would be only a second edition of Chile's own gold strike. It would be one of those golden dreams with which a man consoles himself when he is maddened with desire for a gold that does not exist.

We came, in the end, because we could not resist the weight of so much testimony and because we felt sure only a lazy man could fail to make money, and we were willing to work hard. But little did we know what we faced. We went on shore, and, after having paid our entry fee per head and sloshing through the muddy slime of low tide, took our way to the hillside slopes that form the dry part of the town.

We had been told the day before that we should go armed, and in pairs. So, like most people in the town, we had pistols and daggers thrust under our belts.

To reach Price's house we had to pass through a good part of the town. The people look as though they are having a carnival, with their strange costumes, the character of their occupations, and their tongues, which seem more multiplied than those in the Tower of Babel.

Apparently, too, all the women here dress up like men, for there are no skirts to be seen anywhere. At each step we have to move aside to make way for a man in wool shirt and rolled up pants, panting under the weight of a trunk or big sack he is carrying from the beach for pay; or to make room for a more fortunate drayman with a wheelbarrow, pushing it along proudly and exciting the attention and envy of those who do not own such a marvelous vehicle.

Some men are putting up tents; others are dragging timbers. This man is rolling a barrel; that one is struggling with a post, or trying to drive it into the ground with mighty blows of a crowbar. The ones who had managed to get their tents up are already doing business. Through their tent openings you can see open trunks, and ragged clothes one would be ashamed to wear but which are on sale for fabulous prices. Liquor is unbelievably expensive here as compared with Chile. Brandy sells for sixty pesos an *arroba*,* champagne for half an *onza*** per bottle. Goods have whatever value the seller wants to set; because the buyer, aware that in California time is money, will buy at sight whatever he needs, without bothering to shop around.

Gold dust is the money used, and the ease with which it is exchanged in buying and selling suggests that one has little difficulty in acquiring it. The streets are strewn with broken bottles; and among the many little buildings that have sprung up like magic—or rather like mushrooms in the first rains of May—there are many saloons and gambling houses.

Near the beach and about in the middle of the town an elegant brick and stone house is going up. It belongs to a certain Mr. Hassar, yesterday a common sailor but today a millionaire. On the plaza they are building at great expense an immense structure that will house a cafe. It belongs to another sailor as rich as the first.

Most people here speak English, good or bad. But you find, at the side of a lean Yankee in tight pants, others recognizable by their clothing or accent. There is a stocky John Bull, a Chinaman, a Hindu, a Russian, and a native Californio,*** all trying to converse. A Chilean and an Oregonian are watching each other suspiciously. A

* Liquid measure, approx. 11.5 kg.
** An ounce (in this instance, an ounce of gold).
***A Spanish or Mexican resident of California before American occupation. (See Glossary.)

Frenchman and an Italian are winking at a Hawaiian girl crowned with flowers and clad in a blue dress and red shoes.

In short, you can find whatever you like in terms of oddities and extravagances in this land of promise. It is like a masquerade ball of gigantic proportions. Not the least strange are those creatures of what some call "the fair sex." Here they are called simply "shes," or, as the Yankees say, "females." What else can you call women who belong to such animals as you find here?

At the end of a slow but entertaining fifteen-minute walk we reach an attractive hotel that belongs to a gringo adventurer of the filibustering army that went down into Mexico. One of the servants (actually a young gentleman clad as a waiter) is ringing a huge Chinese gong to call those nearby to dinner. We found Price and Claro there in the dining room. Claro was making scabbards for daggers for which he was paid two dollars each. These men, and other acquaintances of ours, were getting ready to sit down at the table. It occupied the whole room, and we watched as the most grotesque group of diners imaginable hurriedly took their places.

There were men from all countries in their national dress. Their talk was a real gabble. You could see, sitting shoulder to shoulder, poorly dressed men with fine manners, and boors in fancy clothes. There were very very old men alongside burly lads wolfing their food like so many Heliogabaluses.* Among them all, however, there reigned an air of contentment as if they were partaking of the finest of cuisines.

The Yankee eats three times a day, and always the same things: roast meat, salted salmon, an inferior stew, tea or coffee, and butter. He has breakfast at seven, lunches at noon, and has dinner at six. Despite the fact that we talked to everyone we could reach, none of them was able to tell us exactly what we wanted to know. The men who had been in the mines did not want to talk about it just for the sake of satisfying our curiosity. We had to listen to stories by fellows who knew as little about it as we did; at the same time we were simpleminded enough to accept as true the tales confided to us with an air of mystery by the troop of jokers who take advantage of newcomers.

---

* Heliogabulus was a Roman emperor notorious for debauchery and extravagance.

See what you could have made out of these bits of advice:

—Don't go to Sacramento; there's no gold there. The place is Stanislaus.

—Don't even think about Stanislaus. Sacramento is a better bet. A guy took out several thousand dollars worth in one day.

—The mines are flooded and it's crazy to think you can go there now. A friend of mine has just got back, and he tells me he was wading in water up to his middle.

—What do you mean, water? That place is drier in winter than it is in summer.

—An ox is worth one hundred dollars.

—It's worth five hundred at least.

—Don't believe anything they say. They're fooling you. There are rich farmers around there who will rent oxen to you. Just bring your carts.

—Don't try to carry a cart through those marshes and up the hills. Buy some horses, or break some wild mares that can be bought for fifty dollars.

—Forget about mares, horses, and carts. Whoever advised that has never been to the mines. Get some good boots and a leather bag. You can only find good places by walking.

This was the kind of information we got. As far as distances were concerned, the stories were even more contradictory. We were given estimates of from forty miles up to one hundred and eighty leagues.

Price took me to the house of a friend of his who had just got back from the mines. There, for the first time, I saw a solid nugget of three pounds. He told me he had picked it up while taking a walk before lunch. I also saw some sacks of gold. I returned with my head in a whirl and not knowing what to think. After this we decided to leave our future course up to fate.

New arrivals in town were sometimes the butt of pranksters eager to separate them from their money. This episode is included in Brown's *Reminiscences and Incidents.*

JOHN HENRY BROWN (1810-1905)

A Yankee trick

I KNOW OF ONE INSTANCE WHERE A PARTY, after night, placed on the ground, in a spot where he would know well where to find it, some two or three ounces of gold dust. It happened to be in front of the Parker House, and he took several strangers to show them that gold could be found in the streets.

Some forty or fifty persons followed him to the spot, when he took a pan of dust from the street, and on washing it out he got nearly two ounces of gold dust; this created quite an excitement among all new-comers, who went and purchased tin pans, with which to commence gold washing. One of the party was lucky; he got about twenty cents in his first pan. There were some forty or fifty who worked hard all day; but could not obtain the color of gold. It was afterwards discovered that the parties who had the tin pans for sale, and the parties who washed out the gold dust were in partnership, and they made money by selling all the tin pans they had, for two dollars each. The same can be purchased now for ten cents each. This, they called a Yankee trick.

It sounds almost incredible now, the many stories that are told of the manner in which persons would waste the gold dust in those early times; but it was the truth, nevertheless. In front of Mr. Howard's store, on Montgomery street, from the sweepings of the floor a man got over fifty dollars in one day. Another instance occurred in the City Hotel bar-room. The man who did the sweeping would save the sweepings in a barrel, until full; and on washing it out he obtained over two hundred dollars in gold dust.

This scene may have been played out more than once in those trigger-happy days. It was reported by Vicente Pérez Rosales in his *Diario de un Viaje a California*.

VICENTE PÉREZ ROSALES (1807-1886)

One way to win

EVERY DAY THE SOUND OF MUSIC in some gambling hall, or the beat of a drum or Chinese gong in others, called the compulsive gamblers to the tables amid the intoxication that dancing and drinking produce. And every night someone was wounded, clubbed, or beaten up; and from each gambling hall the losers would sally forth and try to recoup their losses by robbery and assault.

I had occasion to observe a gambling scene in which a crafty Oregonian played a role. He approached the table and without saying a word placed a little sack containing about a pound of gold on one card of the deck. He lost. With the same silence and gravity, he set down another of the same size, and lost again. Then, without losing his calm manner he took from his belt a snake* that must have contained about six pounds of gold. He stacked it on a card, took out his gun, cocked it, and pointed it at the dealer as he waited silently for the result. He won! "With that I won," he remarked sarcastically, gathering up his winnings without a change of expression, "That's certainly lucky." And with that he disappeared. He won because the sensible dealer knew very well *that* card might cost him his life.

* A hollow belt worn by miners to carry their gold.

Gambling is discussed with more fervor than almost any other topic in these personal accounts of early San Francisco. Interestingly enough, in virtually every instance the writers cloak their impressions in a self-righteousness that might suggest they were the only people in town not under the spell of the demon dice!

William Perkins was a Canadian who did his gold prospecting in the Southern Mines around Sonora, in Tuolumne County. His story remained unpublished until 1964, when the University of California Press printed his journal under the title *Three Years in California. William Perkins' Journal of Life at Sonora, 1849-1852*. His description of a gambling saloon is reprinted with permission of the University of California Press.

The Polka Saloon

O<small>F ALL THE VICES WITH WHICH</small> California has been and still is cursed, gambling has been the most fatal. The legislature has been powerless to put a stop to it, and has consequently turned it to account by licensing it, and the ingress to the treasury through this means is quite respectable.

The immense, richly furnished and dazzling gambling saloons form the great attraction, the lions of San Francisco. From a score of such palaces of iniquity, nightly issue strains of the most ravishing music, and the street is inundated with the light of hundreds of lamps.

Let us pay a visit to the "Polka" Saloon, one of the largest and generally most crowded of the City. It is situated in Clay Street, a few steps from the Plaza. To the right on entering one of the numerous doors, is a bar of liquors, with marble counter; gold and silver and rich crystal of every form combining to make it attractive, and as if something more was necessary to induce people to drink, two beautiful girls, elegantly dressed, are behind the counter to serve out the liquor. They are French of course. How can a man resist their smiles? We can't; so we stop and after a compliment or two, ask for a glass of native wine, and with a bow which is answered by a fascinating smile (it could not have been more so, had it been an "adobe" instead of a two real piece I put on the counter) we move on.

The huge saloon is crowded with a motley congregation; well dressed gentlemen, belonging to the City; sailors; miners in red and blue flannel shirts and long boots, ignorant of the existence of blacking; Mexicans in their long brilliantly colored *zarapes*; Chilenos in dark, and Peruvians in light colored *ponchos*; Californians in scolloped and silk worked leather jackets and wide brimmed *sombreros*; some like ourselves strolling about indulging merely their curiosity; but there are very few who do not stop now and then to put down a stake at one of the innumerable tables which crowd the saloon.

Here is a Monte table: let us approach; it is crowded with eager betters. In the center is about a bushel of silver dollars, forming a bulwark around a peck of gold "Adobes," Eagles and half Eagles. Look at the Yankee dealer, and owner perhaps, of the pile of riches in front of him. See him as he slowly and deliberately draws card after card from the pack. He is the personification of Calm Villainy. You can no more detect a transient feeling in that man's face than you might from one chiselled out of marble. He may lose or win ten thousand dollars, staked at this moment on his table, but he will be the same, impassible, cold and silent. The practice of his trade has petrified his human nature. Look at these young men, these boys, staking fifty, a hundred dollars upon a card! Some of these will go home tonight, ruined, and from industrious sober men will, at one plunge, change to professional blacklegs and ruffians. There is a merchant, a rich merchant of the City, betting a thousand dollars. He is an old hand and remains calm under his losses; not so with that young sinner who has apparently lost his last coin; he is drinking madly of the liquor that is furnished at the table gratis, and savage imprecations are grinding through his hard set teeth. No one bestows a thought on him as he scowlingly watches the game, until impatient at not being able to join in, he rushes out of the house perhaps to beg, borrow or steal another stake.

Cowper must have had a prophetic idea of California when he wrote the following lines:

> The wings that waft our riches out of sight
> Grow on the gamester's elbows; and the alert
> And nimble motion of those restless joints
> That never tire, soon fans them all away

The spacious saloon is thickly sprinkled with *Monte*, Roulette and Lansquenet tables, round each of which is a crowd of votaries. The Lansquenet tables are presided over by handsome, brilliantly dressed women, and their sparkling eyes are continually on the look-out to intice the young men to join the game. See, there is one pretty woman beckoning us to her side. I knew her in Sonora. What a bewitching smile she vouchsafes us as we shake hands with her! She does not ask us to play, and for a few minutes seems to forget her game. We will not detain her impatient customers.

"Je suis si content de vous avoir vu!"*

"Good bye."

Don't look back; be satisfied with the beaming smile of adieu which gave an angel's expression to her handsome countenance. One minute later perhaps, and you may trace the passions of Hell in that face!

I have so often spoken of these fascinating votaresses of the Devil, that it would be repeating a thrice told tale, describing the dozens of beauties in the Saloons of the "Polka." Many of the gamblers have one by their side to serve the glasses of liquor to the players, and to chat and flirt with them, while the dealer fleeces their pockets.

At the further end of the Saloon are several well lighted rooms partitioned off from the body of the hall. You might imagine them to be refreshment rooms. Not so. It is here the Genius of the establishment resides. Here the *serious* business of gambling is carried on. Here nought is heard save the *clacking* of ivory counters. Here you have the princes of the profession assembled. These chambers receive the adventurous class who profess to "fight the Tiger." Here are the Pharo banks, and men will walk out of these dens fifty, a hundred, two hundred thousand dollars richer or poorer than they entered. Not a night passes that fortunes are not squandered in these places. This is the game that the master gamblers play amongst themselves; and many a blackleg has brought down a fortune from the mines, the proceeds of his iniquitous industry in the diggings, and lost it in a single night at a Pharo bank. The princes of the gambling profession seldom go out of San Francisco; they leave the inner towns to be gleaned by less ambitious rogues, and are content to fleece these same rogues on their arrival at the metropolis. Sometimes one of the "bigwigs" will also find himself ruined some fine night. In this case he quietly packs up his trunks, and makes the provincial tour himself.

It seems an extraordinary fact, and looks like a wise dispensation, that no gambler can hoard money. He can't give up playing and retire from business. An irresistible impulse still pushes him on, and

* "I am so happy to have seen you." (French)

[149]

whatever may be his winnings, he invariably loses every thing at one time or other. Out of the thousands and thousands of blacklegs who have "exercised their profession" in California, there are not probably a hundred who have not been at one or various times, in the possession of a fortune. Some in San Francisco have been worth as much as half a million of dollars. But there is apparently a curse to their winnings. Like the gold of the Magician in the Arabian Nights Entertainments, after a few hours it turns to dried leaves and rubbish. Were it otherwise the United States would soon have been flooded with millionaire gamblers.

A familiar scene in the gambling saloons of San Francisco.

When I speak of gamblers in California, the word only applies to those who have adopted gaming as a profession; and it is a profession that lawyers, doctors and divines have embraced. The former and the latter are quite numerous in the brotherhood. Methodist parsons and temperance men seem to take very kindly to Monte, and one of the strangest phases of gambling in California is the great number of once respectable and educated men who are found professedly owning and conducting a gaming table. I have known dozens of young men, whose fathers stand among the proudest in the land in the United States, dealing Monte to a lot of dirty drunken Mexicans: one of them, I am sorry to say, being the son of a Canadian gentleman. It appears that as soon as a man loses all he possesses at a gambling table, a reckless impulse impels him to turn gambler himself, as the surest way to retrieve his fortunes; and once in the vortex, he is lost. He becomes vicious and quarrelsome; is continually in rows, and, after shooting, maiming or killing some half dozen, ends by being shot himself, or being strung up to the nearest tree by "Judge Lynch."

Such has been the fate of hundreds of this class. In Sonora at least fifty individuals have been killed in quarrels, by blacklegs, and a great many more wounded and maimed; and of the gamblers, three or four have been hanged and at least a score shot.

In San Francisco the rage for gambling is something fearful. Merchants, Lawyers, Politicians, Judges, Governors, all gamble to a frightful extent. How many failures of rich mercantile houses are due to the Pharo table, and the ill-luck of business to be accounted for by the ill-luck at a gaming table!

In 1881, William F. White published his own book, *A Picture of Pioneer Times in California*, because—he wrote in the introduction—he wanted to "expose the misstatements of itinerant lecturers and thoughtless or vicious writers" who he believed were maligning the memory of the early pioneers. The following excerpt is his attempt to correct any erroneous impressions we may have about the intelligence, attitudes, and morals of the gold miners. White published the book under a pseudonym, "William Grey."

WILLIAM F. WHITE (1829-1891?)

The metamorphosis of a miner

It is true that many lucky miners, coming to San Francisco from the interior, visited gambling saloons, lost their money, and committed excesses against decency and morality; but it is also true that hundreds and hundreds of such, coming from the mines, did their business in the city in a quiet, earnest way, without committing one act of indiscretion or losing one dollar foolishly.

To look at the returned miners in those days in San Francisco the first impression you would get was that they were all of a rough cast of men, uneducated and savage. Their uncut hair, their long beards, their red flannel shirts, with flashy red Chinese scarfs around their waists, the black leather belt beneath the scarf, fastened with a silver buckle, to which hung the handsome six-shooter and bowie-knife, the slouched, wide-brimmed hat, the manly, bold, independent look and gait of the man as he walked along, made each one look the chief of a tribe of men you had no knowledge of before.

Get into conversation with this man, and you will find, to your surprise, in nine cases out of ten, a refined, intelligent, educated American, despising the excesses of the idle and the dissipated. You will find his whole heart on his old home and those he has left there. Look up as he speaks to you of wife and children and draws from beneath his red shirt a photograph of those loved ones, and you will find him brushing away tears that have fallen on his great shaggy beard. Stand behind such a looking man in the long line from the Postoffice window, waiting for his turn to get letters. See; he takes his letters from the clerk at the window, and his whole frame shakes with

[153]

emotion, and, as he looks at the well known handwriting, his hand-kerchief is again on his face. Here are the sort of pioneers the authors of the "Annals" somehow never saw. A circumstance which occurred to myself will show how completely the miner's dress of '49 changed and disguised him.

I was busy selling goods in my store, when a miner, just such as I have described, entered, announcing that he wanted to purchase some clothes. I pointed to a pile of men's clothing and told him to take what he wanted, and when he had made his selections I would tell him what he had to pay. He did as I told him, and I went on with my business. In one part of our store there was a room curtained off, where my partner slept, and occupied as a private apartment. In a few moments the miner turned to me, and asked if he could go into this room to fit the clothes he had selected. I answered "Yes," without even looking at him, or knowing what he had picked out.

Being in one constant rush of business that morning, I com-pletely forgot all about this man after he went into the room. In two or three hours afterwards I stepped from the store to help to unload a wagon bringing in new goods. When I returned I was surprised to find an almost elegantly dressed gentleman standing in the store, waiting for me. I supposed he had just come in, and yet I was puzzled as to how he could have passed me at the store door. He was dressed far better than it was usual for any one to dress in San Francisco at that time. He had on a handsome black coat and brown pants and vest, a handsome white shirt with black necktie, a pair of fine boots, a nice new hat, though not a stovepipe, yet a stylish one compared to the usual miner's slouched hat. He was newly and neatly shaved.

I saluted him with considerable deference, but of course with evident wonderment in my manner, for I was puzzling myself to think where the mischief such a man could come from. The stranger, I thought, half smiled, but answered my salutation and inquiry as to what I could do for him, by saying: "Nothing, thank you; I merely stepped in to ask the way to the Postoffice." "Oh," I said, "I suppose you have just arrived; what ship did you come in? I did not know we had had an arrival this morning." "I came across the plains," said my visitor.

I looked at him from head to foot, but for the life of me I could not make him out. I said to myself: "How on earth did this fellow get into the store, and I not see him;" but, giving it up as a California riddle, I gave him the direction to the Postoffice. He bowed, and thanked me with uncommon cordiality, adding, while he reached out his hand, that he hoped some day to be able to show his sense of the favor I had done him. I took his hand and looked at him, completely mystified.

As he shook my hand he continued, with a laughing expression in his handsome eyes: "Oh, by the way, did you see a rough looking fellow, one of those red-shirted miners, come this way this morning? He wanted to get a new pair of pants. I thought he might have bought them at your store. He is a friend of mine. I must be off to join him; so good-by." And he turned slowly to leave.

For the first time the rough, red-shirted miner I had told to go into the room came into my mind. "Why, yes," I said: "I do recollect now." "Oh, you do recollect such a fellow, then?" "Can it be possible?" said I, as the whole truth flashed on my mind. "Yes, that hat is of our stock. That coat, those pants are ours. That pair of boots are of our extra fine ones." We now both went into a hearty fit of laughing, from which we did not recover for some minutes.

It appeared that while I was engaged in waiting on other customers, this miner had selected a full suit from head to foot, and when he went into the room he found water, soap and razor, all ready to his hand, so he just went to work and completely metamorphosed himself, while I had forgotten him altogether. We went together to the room where he had dressed, and from under his clothes he drew a buckskin sack, containing five thousand dollars in gold-dust. After weighing out the price of his clothes he tied up the sack and deposited it in our safe. I found that he was from the State of Virginia, and that he and his brother had come across the plains some months before, stopped at the first placer mine they had come to, and made this amount. He had come down to San Francisco for his letters from home, and to make some purchases as a matter of speculation in the mines. He was some twenty-three years of age, a perfect gentleman, and well educated. ... We continued fast friends while he remained in the State; that was until 1854, when he returned home with a handsome fortune made in business in the interior.

There were very few American or European women in San
Francisco when Vicente Pérez Rosales arrived in 1849, although
the situation did change slightly during the next few months.
Of the 39,888 immigrants who arrived by sea between April 12,
1849 and January 29, 1850 1,421 were women, according to the
1852-1853 *San Francisco Directory*. What shocked Pérez was how
some of these women paid their boat fares, as he recalls here
in his memoirs which appeared in *We Were 49ers*.

"Pretty dames, fresh from New York"

THE MERCANTILE SPIRIT THAT SPECULATES even with immorality did not lose much time in seeking out substitutes for the fair sex. Paintings of women totally nude and very badly drawn were hung in the best cafes of the city. These nauseating pictures that covered the walls of the saloons would have put the most wanton satyr to flight in any other place; but here, offered along with gambling tables and liquor, they filled the pockets of their lucky owners with gold. With such a precedent to go on, it was only to be expected that the mercantile spirit would not lose much time in procuring the real thing, of flesh and blood, as repulsive as are the painted representations.

The passenger ship from Panama on its first voyage brought two daughters of Eve of the sort called "liberated." Those who went down to watch the steamer come in at the western headland, when they saw the hats and sunshades of women, became so enthusiastic and ran down to the pier so fast that they drew in everyone they passed; so a thousand men were waiting on the beach.

No sooner had the anchor been dropped than there broke out a noisy quarrel between the two damsels and the purser. They wanted to come ashore at once; the purser said the arrangement had been that they would pay their passage as soon as they reached this city. The more spirited of the two Yankee girls, acting on the principle that "time is money," said the purser would be held responsible for damages and losses, plus interest, caused by the delay. Whereupon two of the waiting crowd, tired of marking time, clambered on board the ship, and, throwing a bag of gold at the feet of the greedy purser, came back to land with the girls to a general "Hooray!" from the crowd.

The joyful crowd opened a path, and the girls on the arms of their two deliverers, waving greetings and receiving "hurrahs" in turn, quickly disappeared into the crossroads that led to the cribs, followed at a distance by the lascivious and envious eyes of those who had not given the maxim, time is money, its legitimate importance.

It was to be expected that shipowners, noting the high passage rate feminine merchandise could command on arrival at San Francisco, set out to procure and did procure the embarkation of as much of this kind of merchandise as they could find. On the next voyage seven more arrived, and were received with the same gallantry.

The cafe owners were alarmed by the competition that their badly painted monstrosities had to meet from these real monstrosities who kept on arriving. They planned and carried out the most incredible and obscene projects that human shamelessness can improvise in such situations. They hired these creatures, at a gold peso each, to pose in plastic displays* in the cafe dining halls. They set up platforms on both sides of the room, and on them placed, totally nude and assuming indecent poses, these exemplifications of California modesty and decency.

The doors of the exhibition were opened at eight in the evening to the sound of music. The curious men, who had left a good part of their gold dust at the door, were pushed rapidly through to the exits by those coming on behind them, before they had time to look. They came tumbling out the rear door, cursing like fiends.

I remember that a Chilean of good family, Don J.E., whose name I will not further clarify, said to me, "My friend, the devil tempted me, and then cleaned me out of all the gold I had in my purse, a half-pound! I was pouring onto the scale enough to pay for my entrance when a shove from behind made me dump it all; and then I was pushed on forward so I couldn't get back to recover the extra gold."

This enterprise could be kept going only for a month, though, because the steamers began coming not with a few but with whole cargoes of women on board, all under agreement to pay for their passage before disembarking, or, at least, the next day afterward.

* Tableaux; like statues.

If the scenes described to this point are repugnant, those I will sketch next, before closing this page of my notes, are no less to be wondered at.

At the door of the room each one of these first Messalinas had on arrival, fights with clubs and pistols broke out every night between those who wanted to get in first to meet them. The women knew very well there was no profit to be had from men who were beaten up or dead, so they would rush out to pacify the combatants, using kinds of arguments that shame prevents me from revealing.

The demand for women had slackened somewhat because the ships were bringing in so many; so, to keep profits up, the captains decided to sell the unpaid passage bills at auction. The highest bidder got to carry off his prize, and the captain pocketed whatever he got over the cost of the passage.

The strangest, coarsest scenes developed as a result of this.

The objects to be auctioned off were assembled in the cabin of the poop deck with all their meretricious ornaments. The man who was to conduct the auction would take one of these shameless creatures by the hand, and, after praising her figure, her youth, and beauty, he would call out in a loud voice, "Gentlemen, what are you willing to pay, any one of you, right now, to have this pretty dame, fresh from New York, pay you a special visit?" The bidding began at once, and the highest bidder, as soon as the hammer fell, handed over the gold dust and carried away his property.

But it is time now to turn this page. May the enchanting sex, who make up the more agreeable half of the human race, forgive me if I have had to give to these abject females in skirts the same name with which we designate the angels in our homes. Among the chosen angels of God there was also a Lucifer.

The Port of San Francisco in June 1849. Portsmouth Plaza can be seen at the left, center.

Daily life
1849-1850

In this episode from his *Diario de un Viaje a California*, Pérez turned his scorn on the American judicial system as he witnessed it in Gold Rush California. The great animosity between the Spanish-speaking miners and their American counterparts was the result of the latter's belief that the gold was for Americans only and that foreigners should be excluded. This, even though the U.S.-Mexican peace treaty was not signed until a few days after the discovery at Coloma!

Sentence reversed!

T HE SUPREME AUTHORITY in San Francisco is not an alcalde as many say he is. He is only a Yankee, more or less drunk, whom they call alcalde. His only function, if two Yankees are quarreling, is to smooth things over; if the quarrel is between a Yankee and someone who speaks Spanish, his job is to declare the Spaniard guilty and make him pay the court costs; if the dispute is between two Spaniards, he sees to it that the decision goes against the one who has money enough to pay the costs and the interpreter. A short time ago there was a trial between two of the first named. The courtroom was full, and as both the litigants were Yankees the judge tried to reconcile them as best he could. But the weight of the evidence was so much against one of them that there was nothing for the alcalde to do but sentence him to twenty-five lashes, for that was the minimum sentence possible in such cases. There was an immediate murmur of disapproval in the courtroom. The alcalde thought he was a lost man because he had passed such a light sentence for such serious misdeeds, but while he was getting ready to admit his error and increase the dose, one of the spectators asked to be heard.

"Citizens," he says, "since this alcalde is so free with punishments he passes out, I propose that the fifty strongest men here drive the alcalde three miles out of town, kicking his behind all the way."

"Hooray!" shouted the crowd. The alcalde, not knowing what was happening to him, left his seat and, quicker than a run, dived out of the window, followed by general booing and laughter. The culprit was then let go.

In 1849, barely three years after it was occupied by the United States, San Francisco could be divided into "old town" and "new town"—according to this excerpt from Perkins' *Three Years in California*. And apparently it was a place where pretense was unnecessary—you could just be yourself.

A *dandy transformed*

IN 1849, SAN FRANCISCO PRESENTED a strange aspect. The old town was composed of some scores of poor adobe huts, with four or five houses of a better class. The plaza or square [Portsmouth Plaza], situated at that time within a hundred yards of high water, had on its upper side two old-fashioned buildings, the principal ones in the town. One was the alcalde's house, the other a government building, occupied at the time I am speaking of, as a post office.

Here and there, without much regard to regularity, were scattered the mud houses or rather huts of the natives.

But these were features completely thrown into the shade by what we may call the New town, which, not as yet offering any buildings as solid even as adobe, monopolized notwithstanding the attention, on account of its lightness and gaiety.

Tents of all colors; light wooden structures; deck cabins from the vessels; brush houses lined with cotton cloth, were placed wherever an open space was to be found near the sea.

The slopes of the hills presented the appearance of a military encampment on a spree; the tents pitched without regularity, and piles of merchandise scattered about in all directions.

. . .

The good brig "Johanna and Oluffa" was deserted by passengers and crew within three days of its anchoring in the harbor. Even the worthy captain, a Dane, and a famous cook, who had insisted during the voyage from Mazatlán, as much in feasting his four [fore?] cabin, as in starving his hundred steerage passengers, also deserted his vessel, after taking, it must be said to his credit, every precaution for the safety of his craft; and the security of the little she still contained.

The second day after our arrival we got our traps* ashore and, putting up a tent in a vacant spot near the water, E—, H—, B— and myself separated for good from our three months' companions, the original company having kept together in the best harmony during the entire trip from the United States; a fact which speaks highly for the respectable elements of which it was composed.

Having arranged our traps, I strolled up towards the hills, and had not proceeded far when I heard my name called out in tones of surprise. I turned towards a person standing at the entrance of a large blue tent surrounded with boxes, bales and barrels.

This was evidently the person who had hailed, and now strode rapidly towards me, and grasping me heartily by the hand, dragged me towards his tent. I strove in vain to recognise my new friend. I saw before me a tall, loose-made, bony individual, with an emaciated, yellow complexion, and hair and beard in which white was certainly the predominating colour. He appeared to be a man of about fifty-five years of age.

"Let's have a drink, first of all," said my new friend.

He opened a bottle of liquor and, pouring out its contents into two tin cups, he gave me one.

"Success, old fellow!" said he.

"The same to you, my boy," said I.

I was completely puzzled. I could not remember having seen the man in my life, and he was evidently enjoying my bewilderment.

"And so you do not remember me, P—," said he at last. "Well it is no wonder; I do not recognise myself, when I happen to look into the glass, which is seldom enough, now that I have eschewed that cursed operation of shaving. I am what was once H. C—."

I was thunderstruck. It was not six months since I had seen Mr. C—, a dandy of the first water in one of the Atlantic cities, with rosy complexion, brown waving hair, and with an imposing *embonpoint***, that really made him a handsome fellow of some twenty eight or thirty years of age.

* Personal belongings; baggage.
** Corpulence. (French) (See Glossary.)

[166]

"And is the climate of California so deadly?" I asked.

"No, my dear fellow," returned he; "but I will let you into my secret, that is no secret any longer. For twenty years I have lived the life of a martyr in order to wear the appearance of youth. I kept up the deceit until I arrived at Panamá where a severe sickness prostrated me for two weeks. Since then I have thrown off all disguise, and really feel younger at this moment than I did twenty years ago. Thanks to California, I have broken my chains. I am fifty two this year and I don't care who knows it!"

"And those magnificent rounded legs, and gentlemanlike signs of good feeding about the region of the waist; and the broad well-filled chest?" I enquired.

"Padding, my son, padding. I have made the fortune of half a dozen tailors. I was made up artificially, from the foot to the head."

"And the brown glossy hair, the full rosy cheeks?"

"Hair dye, paint and a gold apparatus inside the cheeks to fill them out," he answered. "Oh, my friend, what tortures I have suffered! What a fool I have been! And how happy am I now!"

I congratulated the pseudo-beau heartily, and after an other tin cup of wine, we parted.

I met Mr. C— several times during my sojourn in California and must say that he appeared to be growing younger every day.

Sleeping accommodations were at a premium during the Gold
Rush years. There were a few hotels, but they were soon fully
booked. Tents and crude shacks sprang up everywhere. Many
people had no alternative but to sleep at lodging houses such
as the one described here by William Shaw, an Englishman
who arrived from Australia in 1849. This account is from his
memoirs, *Golden Dreams and Waking Realities* (London, 1851).

"Creeping things abounded"

THE LODGING-HOUSES IN FRANCISCO are usually long barn-like tenements, but owing to a deficiency of sleeping places, sheds, stabling, and skittle grounds, were called into requisition. The one I sometimes resorted to was about sixty feet long by twenty in width; it had no windows, and the walls, roof, and floor, were formed of planks, through the seams of which the rain dripped through. Along the sides were two rows of 'bunks,' or wooden shelving, and at the end was some boarding, serving as a bar for liquors; here the proprietor slept. From about ten till twelve at night, men flocked in with their blankets round them—for no mattrass or bedding was furnished by this establishment—and a dollar being paid, your sleeping place was pointed out to you.

If early, you had a chance of securing six feet of the top shelf; otherwise, you stretched yourself on the floor. The bunks were decidely preferable; for, sometimes of a wet night, upwards of eighty people would be packed together: Yankees, Africans, Chinamen, and Chilians, all huddled together on the ground. As it was customary to sleep in one's clothes and boots, abominable odours arose, and creeping things abounded.

When coiled up in your blanket, the smoking, chewing, and (as a necessary consequence) random expectoration, often prevented repose. Towards morning the heat and effluvia became intolerable; on some occasions, of a wet night, I have been oppressed with a vomiting sensation, and crept out in a profuse perspiration to inhale fresh air; sometimes I found a greasy cap close under my nose, or awoke sucking a boot. Restless sleepers, or unpleasant dreamers were not desirable neighbours; for a kick in the ribs, or on the head, in such a case, was an unavoidable occurrence. Loaded pistols and other deadly weapons being numerous also, an accidental discharge would have lodged an ounce of lead in the body of those next. On fine nights, therefore, I always preferred the open air to such indiscriminate companionship.

"Restless sleepers, or unpleasant dreamers were not desirable neighbours."

But though the sleeping accommodation—if such a term may be used—was wretched in St. Francisco, there was no lack of places of refreshment. There were eating-houses to suit the tastes and pockets of people of all varieties of means, and of every nation. The table d'hôte at the best taverns was about three dollars, at others a dollar; at the corners of the plaza, and principal streets, were stalls, where coffee, cakes, pies, &c. were vended to those unable to pay the costs of tavern fare. Some eating-houses resembled our English chop-houses; these were decidedly preferable: each person sat at a side table, ordering what he chose from a printed bill of fare; and if at all voracious, or choice in his selection of food, ten dollars were easily expended.

The eating-houses are peculiarly Californian in character; they are long plank buildings in the shape of a booth, having two rows of tables, placed parallel to each other, extending the length of the room. The sides and ceiling are covered with calico, as a substitute for paper, having prints stuck over it, by way of decoration; the bar, for the sale of wines and spirits, is at the end of the room; the kitchen is underneath. The fare is of the most heterogeneous kind; dishes of the most incongruous characters are placed on the table at the same time: boiled and roast meats, fresh and salt, potted meats, curries, stews, fish, rice, cheese, frijolis, and molasses, are served up on small dishes, and ranged indiscriminately on the table; there is a total absence of green vegetables.

At certain hours in the day, the beating of gongs and ringing of bells from all quarters, announce feeding time at the various refectories; at this signal a rush is made to the tables. It is not uncommon to see your neighbour coolly abstract a quid from his jaw, placing it for the time being in his waistcoat pocket, or hat, or sometimes beside his plate, even; then commences, on all sides, a fierce attack on the eatables, and the contents of the dishes rapidly disappear. Lucky is the man who has a quick eye and a long arm; for every one helps himself indiscriminately, and attention is seldom paid to any request. It is perfectly immaterial the nature of the *fixing* (as a viand is called), whichever is nearest, commonly has the preference; and as they generally confine themselves to one dish, it is difficult to get that from their grasp. Molasses is a favourite fixing, and eaten with almost every thing. Some of the less refined neither use fork or spoon, the knife serving to convey to the mouth both liquids and solids, which is done with surprising velocity.

The voracity with which they feed is equal to the rapidity of their movements; ten minutes being the usual time for dinner, frequently less. As it is customary to rise together from the table, this national characteristic of the Americans excites the emulation of foreigners; but is most vexatious to the slow German. Dinner being over, the table is replenished for a second party; whilst the greasy knives are wiped, preparatory to being replaced, it is not unusual to see one of the satiated picking his teeth with a fork. The quid is then resumed, pipes are lighted, and volumes of smoke mingle with the steam of the approaching repast.

The best eating-houses in Francisco are those kept by Celestials,* and conducted Chinese fashion; the dishes are mostly curries, hashes, and fricasees, served up in small dishes, and as they are exceedingly palatable, I was not curious enough to enquire as to the ingredients.

* Chinese.

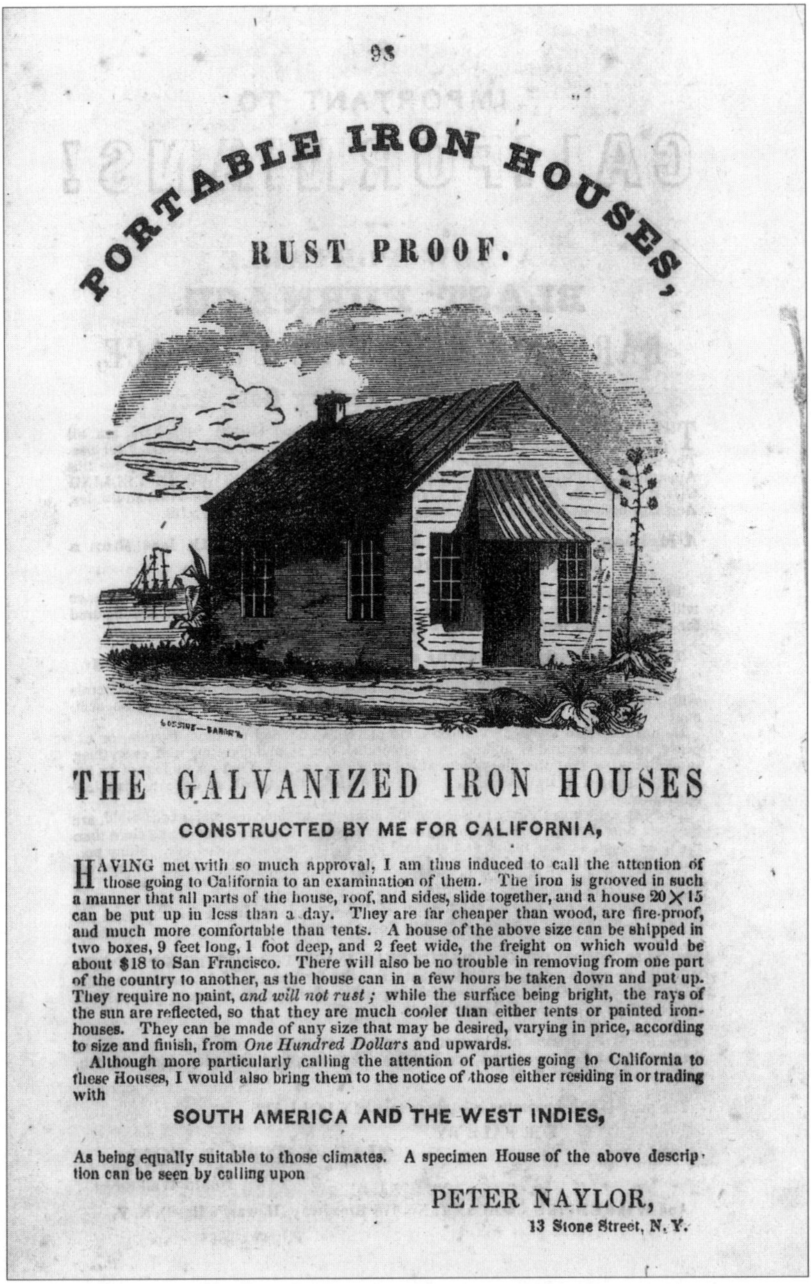

An advertisement in *Pocket Guide to California (1849)*.

It was not unusual for early settlers—whether they came from New York or from Europe—to bring with them a year's supply of canned or dried foods, an abundance of warm clothing, all their furniture, and. . .a house! These houses were carried as kits, to be assembled upon arrival. Although most people brought wooden houses, several brought iron ones, believing them to be fire proof. In his memoirs, *Mountains and Molehills* (New York, 1855), Englishman Frank Marryat tells of his experiences with iron houses. Another excerpt from this fascinating book appears later.

The trouble
with iron houses

Iron HOUSES, UNDER MOST circumstances, are a failure, and I write from experience in the matter. I have sat in churches made of iron, and have been glad to get out of them for that reason. I have thrown down my billiard-cue in disgust in iron club-houses, have paid my bill incontinently and left iron hotels, and have lived in misery in an iron shooting-box of my own, which was supposed to be *very complete.*

I could live comfortably at all times in my little log-hut at the "farm," but never could I endure myself inside my iron house. When the sun shone it was too hot; as night advanced it cooled too suddenly, and at daylight I shivered. When it was too warm, the hot iron, with its anti-corrosive paint, emitted a sickening smell; and when the rain came down on the roof it sounded like a shower of small shot. I lined it with wood throughout; that is to say, I built a *wooden house* inside my iron one, and then it was only bearable. But it would have been cheaper, it seemed to me, to have built the wooden house first, and then have put the iron on if it was wanted, which it was not.

In this age, when so many of our countrymen are emigrating, it becomes almost the duty of a traveler to recount any experience that may tend to the benefit of those who go after him; and, therefore, I trust that in remarks similar to the foregoing, which may or may not affect a peculiar branch of trade, I may be exonerated from any other intention than that of benefiting others by my experience. I have seen so many metal and wooden houses thrown away (I have seen in one heap of rubbish the value of ten thousand pounds), that I would recommend to the emigrant of moderate means not to purchase either the one or the other. If new gold fields are discovered, as most probably they will be, and reports are rife of house-room commanding enormous prices there, never for all that let him take his shell out, snail-like, on his back; let him take the money that would buy the house—the cash will be the scarcest article there, and will find him house-room and a profit too.

Perhaps nowhere has my argument been better proved than in California. Large numbers of iron houses were shipped to that country when first reports arrived of the scarcity of building materials. Had they been capable of resisting fire they would perhaps have been less generally condemned; but of those that were erected, not only did the thin corrugated houses first expand and then collapse, and tumble down with astonishing rapidity before the flames, but in the fire I have just recorded the American iron house of Taeffe and M'Cahill, of which the plates were nearly an inch in thickness, and the castings of apparently unnecessary weight, collapsed like a preserved-meat can, and destroyed six persons, who, believing it be be fire-proof, remained inside. And, in connection with this subject, it is worthy of mention that when these houses arrived in California there was no one to be found who could put them together; not but that the method is very simple, but simple things, as we all know, present great difficulties at times in their solution.

A friend of mine employed a man for a long time at four pounds a day, merely to superintend the erection of an iron hotel; it was completed at last, and although it had a somewhat lopsided appearance, it looked pretty well under the influence of light-green paint; but the fire came, and it "caved in," as the Americans say.

This discussion on iron buildings would have found no place here, had not these cheerless tenements been connected with a speculation into which I was at this time induced to enter: nor would the speculation have been alluded to, particularly as it turned out a failure, were it not again inseparably connected with a peculiar feature of the country. It appeared that the State was looking about at this time for a site on which to erect a capital, where, free from the busy hum of men, the representatives of the people might meet and do their country's work. Upon the condition that General Vallejo would expend a large amount in the erection of public buildings, a part of this gentleman's property was selected by the then Governor as the "seat of government," and upon that, a few scrubby-looking hills that bordered on the bay were surveyed and staked off, and there was your town of "Vallejo."

About this time a store-ship, laden with iron houses, belonging to a friend of mine, sunk at her moorings during a heavy gale. When raised she was so full of mud, clay, and small crabs, that there was no possibility of rendering her cargo fit for sale at San Francisco. The bright idea occurred to me of landing these muddy materials at Vallejo, and, after allowing the tide to clean them, to convert them to some use in assisting to erect this capital that was to be "made to order." Landing my cargo on Vallejo beach at low-water mark, Canute-like, I ordered the tide to complete the very dirty work I had set before it, which it did, and, to finish the story here, in the course of six months I erected a very handsome hotel out of the materials.

I felt rather pleased when it was finished and painted, and handsomely furnished, to think what a butterfly I had turned out of the very dirty grub I had found in the hold of the old hulk. But the moral of the story lies in the fact that at this juncture the government altered their minds relative to the site of the capital, and selected Benicia in preference.

The city "made to order" was then pulled down and sold for old materials, to the great delight, as may be imagined, of myself and the other speculators who had worked so assiduously to raise it, and who had received no compensation. It is quite like the story of the Enchanted City, that was up one day and down the next; but somehow I don't find so much pleasure in recalling the history of Vallejo as I did as a boy in reading the fairy tale.

Mariano Vallejo's grand idea to build a state capital from the ground up proved impractical. When lawmakers arrived in his fledgling town for the 1852 session, they had nowhere to meet and were obliged to accept an invitation to assemble in Sacramento's new courthouse. Another attempt was made in 1853 to convene in Vallejo, but still the facilities were inadequate, causing the legislators to select Benicia as the new "permanent" capital. But Benicia also could not hold the title long, and, in 1854, the California legislature settled in Sacramento.

For Americans, California was the mythical El Dorado—a country of year-round sunshine, towering mountain ranges, immense fertile valleys, and rivers sparkling with nuggets of gold. Bayard Taylor was sent out west by Horace Greeley, editor of the New York *Tribune*, with an assigment to write about whatever he saw. Those reports were later used as a basis for Taylor's best-selling book, *Eldorado*, from which the following is taken. Other excerpts appear later. Taylor was 24 years old when he arrived in San Francisco in mid-August 1849. He left the following January.

Eldorado

At LAST THE VOYAGE IS DRAWING to a close. Fifty-one days have elapsed since leaving New York, in which time we have, in a manner, coasted both sides of the North-American Continent, from the parallel of 40° N. to its termination, within a few degrees of the Equator, over seas once plowed by the keels of Columbus and Balboa, of Grijalva and Sebastian Viscaino. All is excitement on board; the Captain has just taken his noon observation. We are running along the shore, within six or eight miles' distance; the hills are bare and sandy, but loom up finely through the deep blue haze. A brig bound to San Francisco, but fallen off to the leeward of the harbor, is making a new tack on our left, to come up again. The coast trends somewhat more to the westward, and a notch or gap is at last visible in its lofty outline.

An hour later; we are in front of the entrance to San Francisco Bay. The mountains on the northern side are 3,000 feet in height, and come boldly down to the sea. As the view opens through the splendid strait, three or four miles in width, the island rock of Alcatraz appears, gleaming white in the distance. An inward-bound ship follows close on our wake, urged on by wind and tide. There is a small fort perched among the trees on our right, where the strait is narrowest, and a glance at the formation of the hills shows that this pass might be made impregnable as Gibraltar. The town is still concealed behind the promontory around which the Bay turns to the southward, but between Alcatraz and the island of Yerba Buena, now coming into sight, I can see vessels at anchor. High through the vapor in front, and thirty miles distant, rises the peak of Monte Diablo, which overlooks everything between the Sierra Nevada and the Ocean. On our left opens the bight of Sousolito, where the U.S. propeller Massachusetts and several other vessels are at anchor.

At last we are through the Golden Gate—fit name for such a magnifcent portal to the commerce of the Pacific! Yerba Buena Island is in front; southward and westward opens the renowned harbor, crowded with the shipping of the world, mast behind mast and vessel behind vessel, the flags of all nations fluttering in the breeze! Around the curving shore of the Bay and upon the sides of three hills which rise steeply from the water, the middle one receding so as to form a bold amphitheatre, the town is planted and seems scarcely yet to have taken root, for tents, canvas, plank, mud and adobe houses are mingled together with the least apparent attempt at order and durability. But I was not yet on shore. The gun of the Panama has just announced our arrival to the people on land. We glide on with the tide, past the U.S. ship Ohio and opposite the main landing, outside of the forest of masts. A dozen boats are creeping out to us over the water; the signal is given—the anchor drops—our voyage is over.

I left the Panama, in company with Lieut. Beale, in the boat of the U.S. ship Ohio, which brought Lieutenant Ells on board. We first boarded the noble ship, which, even in San Francisco harbor, showed the same admirable order as on our own coast. She had returned from Honolulu a few days previous, after an absence of three months from California. The morning of our arrival, eighteen of her men had contrived to escape, carrying with them one of the boats, under fire from all the Government vessels in the harbor. The officers were eager for news from home, having been two months without a mail, and I was glad that my habit of carrying newspapers in my pockets enabled me to furnish them with a substantial gratification. The Ohio's boat put us ashore at the northern point of the anchorage, at the foot of a steep bank, from which a high pier had been built into the bay. A large vessel lay at the end, discharging her cargo. We scrambled up through piles of luggage, and among the crowd collected to witness our arrival, picked out two Mexicans to carry our trunks to a hotel. The barren side of the hill before us was covered with tents and canvas houses, and nearly in front a large two-story building displayed the sign: "Fremont Family Hotel."

As yet, we were only in the suburbs of the town. Crossing the shoulder of the hill, the view extended around the curve of the bay, and hundreds of tents and houses appeared, scattered all over the heights, and along the shore for more than a mile. A furious wind was blowing down through a gap in the hills, filling the streets with clouds of dust. On every side stood buildings of all kinds, begun or half-finished, and the greater part of them mere canvas sheds, open in front, and covered with all kinds of signs, in all languages. Great quantities of goods were piled up in the open air, for want of a place to store them. The streets were full of people, hurrying to and fro, and of as diverse and bizarre a character as the houses: Yankees of every possible variety, native Californians in sarapes and sombreros, Chileans, Sonorians, Kanakas from Hawaii, Chinese with long tails, Malays armed with their everlasting creeses,* and others in whose embrowned and bearded visages it was impossible to recognize any especial nationality. We came at last into the plaza, now dignified by the name of Portsmouth Square. It lies on the slant side of the hill, and from a high pole in front of a long one-story adobe building used as the Custom House, the American flag was flying. On the lower side stood the Parker House—an ordinary frame house of about sixty feet front—and towards its entrance we directed our course.

Our luggage was deposited on one of the rear porticos, and we discharged the porters, after paying them two dollars each—a sum so immense in comparison to the service rendered that there was no longer any doubt of our having actually landed in California. There were no lodgings to be had at the Parker House—not even a place to unroll our blankets; but one of the proprietors accompanied us across the plaza to the City Hotel, where we obtained a room with two beds at $25 per week, meals being in addition $20 per week. I asked the landlord whether he could send a porter for our trunks. "There is none belonging to the house," said he; "every man is his own porter here." I returned to the Parker House, shouldered a heavy trunk, took a valise in my hand and carried them to my quarters, in the teeth of the wind.

Our room was in a sort of garret over the only story of the hotel; two cots, evidently of California manufacture, and covered only with

* Daggers.

a pair of blankets, two chairs, a rough table and a small looking-glass, constituted the furniture. There was not space enough between the bed and the bare rafters overhead, to sit upright, and I gave myself a severe blow in rising the next morning without proper heed. Through a small roof-window of dim glass, I could see the opposite shore of the bay, then partly hidden by the evening fogs. The wind whistled around the eaves and rattled the tiles with a cold, gusty sound, that would have imparted a dreary character to the place, had I been in a mood to listen.

Many of the passengers began speculation at the moment of landing. The most ingenious and successful operation was made by a gentleman of New York, who took out fifteen hundred copies of The Tribune and other papers, which he disposed of in two hours, at one dollar a-piece! Hearing of this I bethought me of about a dozen papers which I had used to fill up crevices in packing my valise. There was a newspaper merchant at the corner of the City Hotel, and to him I proposed the sale of them, asking him to name a price. "I shall want to make a good profit on the retail price," said he, "and can't give more than ten dollars for the lot." I was satisfied with the wholesale price, which was a gain of just four thousand per cent!

I set out for a walk before dark and climbed a hill back of the town, passing a number of tents pitched in the hollows. The scattered houses spread out below me and the crowded shipping in the harbor, backed by a lofty line of mountains, made an imposing picture. The restless, feverish tide of life in that little spot, and the thought that what I then saw and was yet to see will hereafter fill one of the most marvellous pages of all history, rendered it singularly impressive.

The feeling was not decreased on talking that evening with some of the old residents (that is, of six months' standing) and hearing their several experiences. Every new-comer in San Francisco is overtaken with a sense of complete bewilderment. The mind, however it may be prepared for an astonishing condition of affairs, cannot immediately push aside its old instincts of value and ideas of business, letting all past experiences go for naught and casting all its faculties for action, intercourse with its fellows or advancement in any path of ambition, into shapes which it never before imagined. As in the turn of the dissolving views, there is a period when it wears neither the old nor the new phase, but the vanishing images of the one and the growing perceptions of the other are blended in painful and misty confusion. One knows not whether he is awake or in some wonderful dream. Never have I had so much difficulty in establishing, satisfactorily to my own senses, the reality of what I saw and heard.

I was forced to believe many things, which in my communications to The Tribune I was almost afraid to write, with any hope of their obtaining credence. It may be interesting to give here a few instances of the enormous and unnatural value put upon property at the time of my arrival. The Parker House rented for $110,000 yearly, at least $60,000 of which was paid by gamblers, who held nearly all the second story. Adjoining it on the right was a canvas-tent fifteen by twenty-five feet, called "Eldorado," and occupied likewise by gamblers, which brought $40,000. On the opposite corner of the plaza, a building called the "Miner's Bank," used by Wright & Co., brokers, about half the size of a fire-engine house in New York, was held at a rent of $75,000. A mercantile house paid $40,000 rent for a one-story building of twenty feet front; the United States Hotel, $36,000; the Post-Office, $7,000, and so on to the end of the chapter.

A friend of mine, who wished to find a place for a law-office, was shown a cellar in the earth, about twelve feet square and six deep, which he could have at $250 a month. One of the common soldiers at the battle of San Pasquale was reputed to be among the millionaires of the place, with an income of $50,000 *monthly*. A citizen of San Francisco died insolvent to the amount of $41,000 the previous Autumn. His administrators were delayed in settling his affairs, and his real estate advanced so rapidly in value meantime, that after his debts were paid his heirs had a yearly income of $40,000. These facts were indubitably attested; every one believed them, yet hearing them talked of daily, as matters of course, one at first could not help feeling as if he had been eating of "the insane root."

The prices paid for labor were in proportion to everything else. The carman of Mellus, Howard & Co. had a salary of $6,000 a year, and many others made from $15 to $20 daily. Servants were paid from $100 to $200 a month, but the wages of the rougher kinds of labor had fallen to about $8. Yet, notwithstanding the number of gold-seekers who were returning enfeebled and disheartened from the mines, it was difficult to obtain as many workmen as the forced growth of the city demanded. A gentleman who arrived in April told me he then found but thirty or forty houses; the population was then so scant that not more than twenty-five persons would be seen in the streets at any one time. Now, there were probably five hundred houses, tents and sheds, with a population, fixed and floating, of six thousand. People who had been absent six weeks came back and could scarcely recognize the place. Streets were regularly laid out, and already there were three piers, at which small vessels could discharge. It was calculated that the town increased daily from fifteen to thirty houses; its skirts were rapidly approaching the summits of the three hills on which it is located.

A curious result of the extraordinary abundance of gold and the facility with which fortunes were acquired, struck me at the first glance. All business was transacted on so extensive a scale that the ordinary habits of solicitation and compliance on the one hand and stubborn cheapening on the other, seemed to be entirely forgotten. You enter a shop to buy something; the owner eyes you with perfect indifference, waiting for you to state your want; if you object to the price, you are at liberty to leave, for you need not expect to get it cheaper; he evidently cares little whether you buy it or not. One who has been some time in the country will lay down the money, without wasting words. The only exception I found to this rule was that of a sharp-faced Down-Easter just opening his stock, who was much distressed when his clerk charged me seventy-five cents for a coil of rope, instead of one dollar. This disregard for all the petty arts of money-making was really a refreshing feature of society. Another equally agreeable trait was the punctuality with which debts were paid, and the general confidence which men were obliged to place, perforce, in each other's honesty. Perhaps this latter fact was owing, in part, to the impossibility of protecting wealth, and consequent dependence on an honorable regard for the rights of others.

About the hour of twilight the wind fell; the sound of a gong called us to tea, which was served in the largest room of the hotel. The fare was abundant and of much better quality than we expected—better, in fact, than I was able to find there two months later. The fresh milk, butter and excellent beef of the country were real luxuries after our sea-fare. Thus braced against the fog and raw temperature, we sallied out for a night-view of San Francisco, then even more peculiar than its daylight look. Business was over about the usual hour, and then the harvest-time of the gamblers commenced. Every "hell" in the place, and I did not pretend to number them, was crowded, and immense sums were staked at the monte and faro tables. A boy of fifteen, in one place, won about $500, which he coolly pocketed and carried off. One of the gang we brought in the Panama won $1,500 in the course of the evening, and another lost $2,400. A fortunate miner made himself conspicuous by betting large piles of ounces on a single throw. His last stake of 100 oz. was lost, and I saw him the following morning dashing through the streets, trying to break his own neck or that of the magnificent *garañon* he bestrode.

Walking through the town the next day, I was quite amazed to find a dozen persons busily employed in the street before the United States Hotel, digging up the earth with knives and crumbling it in their hands. They were actual gold-hunters, who obtained in this way about $5 a day. After blowing the fine dirt carefully in their hands, a few specks of gold were left, which they placed in a piece of white paper. A number of children were engaged in the same business, picking out the fine grains by applying to them the head of a pin, moistened in their mouths. I was told of a small boy having taken home $14 as the result of one day's labor. On climbing the hill to the Post Office I observed in places, where the wind had swept away the sand, several glittering dots of the real metal, but, like the Irishman who kicked the dollar out of his way, concluded to wait till I should reach the heap. The presence of gold in the streets was probably occasioned by the leakings from the miners' bags and the sweepings of stores; though it may also be, to a slight extent, native in the earth, particles having been found in the clay thrown up from a deep well.

.   .   .

I could make no thorough acquaintance with San Francisco during this first visit. Lieutenant Beale, who held important Government dispatches for Colonel Frémont, made arrangements to leave for San José on the second morning, and offered me a seat on the back of one of his mules. Our fellow-passenger, Colonel Lyons, of Louisiana, joined us, completing the mystic number which travellers should be careful not to exceed. We made hasty tours through all the shops on Clay, Kearney, Washington and Montgomery streets, on the hunt for the proper equipments. Articles of clothing were cheaper than they had been or were afterwards; tolerable blankets could be had for $6 a pair;

coarse flannel shirts, $3; Chilean spurs, with rowels two inches long, $5, and Mexican sarapes, of coarse texture but gay color, $10. We could find no saddle-bags in the town, and were necessitated to pack one of the mules. Among our camping materials were a large hatchet and plenty of rope for making lariats; in addition to which each of us carried a wicker flask slung over one shoulder. We laid aside our civilized attire, stuck long sheath-knives into our belts, put pistols into our pockets and holsters, and buckled on the immense spurs which jingled as they struck the ground at every step. Our "animals" were already in waiting; an *alazan*, the Californian term for a sorrel horse, a beautiful brown mule, two of a cream color and a dwarfish little fellow whose long forelock and shaggy mane gave him altogether an elfish character of cunning and mischief.

[After a brief visit to San Jose, Taylor and his companions went to Stockton and then to the Mokelumne River, where they spent a few days watching miners panning for gold. They were gone only three weeks, yet they were startled by the vast improvements the town had made in their absence.]

When I had climbed the last sand-hill, riding in towards San Francisco, and the town and harbor and crowded shipping again opened to the view, I could scarcely realize the change that had taken place during my absence of three weeks. The town had not only greatly extended its limits, but seemed actually to have doubled its number of dwellings since I left. High up on the hills, where I had seen only sand and chapparal, stood clusters of houses; streets which had been merely laid out, were hemmed in with buildings and thronged with people; new warehouses had sprung up on the water side, and new piers were creeping out toward the shipping; the forest of masts had greatly thickened; and the noise, motion and bustle of business and labor on all sides were incessant. Verily, the place was itself a marvel. To say that it was daily enlarged by from twenty to thirty houses may not sound very remarkable after all the stories that have been told; yet this, for a country which imported both lumber and houses, and where labor was then $10 a day, is an extraordinary growth. The rapidity with which a ready-made house is put up and inhabited, strikes the stranger in San Francisco as little short of magic. He walks over an open lot in his before-breakfast stroll—the next morning, a house complete, with a family inside, blocks up his way. He goes down to the bay and looks out on the shipping—two or three days afterward a row of storehouses, staring him in the face, intercepts the view.

If Taylor was surprised at San Francisco's rapid growth in three weeks, as related in the previous account, imagine how he might have reacted had he seen the town just three *years* before! His description of a day in September 1849 contrasts greatly with Joseph Downey's reports of the summer of 1846.

A September day in '49

A BETTER IDEA OF SAN FRANCISCO, in the beginning of September, 1849, cannot be given than by the description of a single day. Supposing the visitor to have been long enough in the place to sleep on a hard plank and in spite of the attacks of innumerable fleas, he will be awakened at daylight by the noises of building, with which the hills are all alive. The air is temperate, and the invariable morning fog is just beginning to gather. By sunrise, which gleams hazily over the Coast Mountains across the Bay, the whole populace is up and at work. The wooden buildings unlock their doors, the canvas houses and tents throw back their front curtains; the lighters on the water are warped out from ship to ship; carts and porters are busy along the beach; and only the gaming-tables, thronged all night by the votaries of chance, are idle and deserted. The temperature is so fresh as to inspire an active habit of body, and even without the stimulus of trade and speculation there would be few sluggards at this season.

As early as half-past six the bells begin to sound to breakfast, and for an hour thenceforth, their incessant clang and the braying of immense gongs drown all the hammers that are busy on a hundred roofs. The hotels, restaurants and refectories of all kinds are already as numerous as gaming-tables, and equally various in kind. The tables d'hôte of the first class, (which charge $2 and upwards the meal,) are abundantly supplied. There are others, with more simple and solid fare, frequented by the large class who have their fortunes yet to make. At the United States and California restaurants, on the plaza, you may get an excellent beefsteak, scantily garnished with potatoes, and a cup of good coffee or chocolate, for $1. Fresh beef, bread, potatoes, and all provisions which will bear importation, are plenty; but milk, fruit and vegetables are classed as luxuries, and fresh butter is rarely heard of. On Montgomery street, and the vacant space fronting the water, venders of coffee, cakes and sweetmeats have erected their stands, in order to tempt the appetitie of sailors just arrived in port, or miners coming down from the mountains.

By nine o'clock the town is in the full flow of business. The streets running down to the water, and Montgomery street which fronts the Bay, are crowded with people, all in a hurried motion. The variety of characters and costumes is remarkable. Our own countrymen seem to lose their local peculiarities in such a crowd, and it is by chance epithets rather than by manner, that the New-Yorker is distinguished from the Kentuckian, the Carolinian from the Down-Easter, the Virginian from the Texan. The German and Frenchman are more easily recognized. Peruvians and Chilians go by in their brown ponchos, and the sober Chinese, cool and impassive in the midst of excitement, look out of the oblique corners of their long eyes at the bustle, but are never tempted to venture from their own line of business.

The eastern side of the plaza, in front of the Parker House and a canvas hell* called the Eldorado, are the general rendezvous of business and amusement—combining 'change, park, club-room and promenade all in one. There, everybody not constantly employed in one spot, may be seen at some time of the day. The character of the groups scattered along the plaza is oftentimes very interesting. In one place are three or four speculators bargaining for lots, buying and selling "fifty varas square"** in towns, some of which are canvas and some only paper; in another, a company of miners, brown as leather, and rugged in features as in dress; in a third, perhaps, three or four naval officers speculating on the next cruise, or a knot of genteel gamblers, talking over the last night's operations.

The day advances. The mist which after sunrise hung low and heavy for an hour or two, has risen above the hills, and there will be two hours of pleasant sunshine before the wind sets in from the sea. The crowd in the streets is now wholly alive. Men dart hither and

*   An archaic word for a gambling house.
** 137.5 square feet (1 vara = 33").

thither, as if possessed with a never-resting spirit. You speak to an acquaintance—a merchant, perhaps. He utters a few hurried words of greeting, while his eyes send keen glances on all sides of you; suddenly he catches sight of somebody in the crowd; he is off, and in the next five minutes has bought up half a cargo, sold a town lot at treble the sum he gave, and taken a share in some new and imposing speculation. It is impossible to witness this excess and dissipation of business, without feeling something of its influence. The very air is pregnant with the magnetism of bold, spirited, unwearied action, and he who but ventures into the outer circle of the whirlpool, is spinning, ere he has time for thought, in its dizzy vortex.

But see! the groups in the plaza suddenly scatter; the city surveyor jerks his pole out of the ground and leaps on a pile of boards; the venders of cakes and sweetmeats follow his example, and the place is cleared, just as a wild bull which has been racing down Kearney street makes his appearance. Two vaqueros, shouting and swinging their lariats, follow at a hot gallop; the dust flies as they dash across the plaza. One of them, in mid-career, hurls his lariat in the air. Mark how deftly the coil unwinds in its flying curve, and with what precision the noose falls over the bull's horns! The horse wheels as if on a pivot, and shoots off in an opposite line. He knows the length of the lariat to a hair, and the instant it is drawn taught, plants his feet firmly for the shock and throws his body forward. The bull is "brought up" with such force as to throw him off his legs. He lies stunned a moment, and then, rising heavily, makes another charge. But by this time the second vaquero has thrown a lariat around one of his hind legs, and thus checked on both sides, he is dragged off to slaughter.

The plaza is refilled as quickly as it was emptied, and the course of business is resumed. About twelve o'clock, a wind begins to blow from the north-west, sweeping with most violence through a gap between the hills, opening towards the Golden Gate. The bells and gongs begin to sound for dinner, and these two causes tend to lessen the crowd in the street for an hour or two. Two o'clock is the usual dinner-time for business men, but some of the old and successful merchants have adopted the fashionable hour of five.

Where shall we dine today? The restaurants display their signs invitingly on all sides; we have choice of the United States, Tortoni's, the Alhambra, and many other equally classic resorts, but

Delmonico's, like its distinguished original in New York, has the highest prices and the greatest variety of dishes. We go down Kearney street to a two-story wooden house on the corner of Jackson. The lower story is a market; the walls are garnished with quarters of beef and mutton; a huge pile of Sandwich Island squashes fills one corner, and several cabbage-heads, valued at $2 each, show themselves in the window. We enter a little door at the end of the building, ascend a dark, narrow flight of steps and find ourselves in a long, low room, with ceiling and walls of white muslin and a floor covered with oil-cloth.

There are about twenty tables disposed in two rows, all of them so well filled that we have some difficulty in finding places. Taking up the written bill of fare, we find such items as the following:

SOUPS.		ENTREES.	
Mock Turtle	$0 75	Fillet of Beef, mushroom	
St. Julien	1 00	sauce	$1 75
FISH.		Veal Cutlets, breaded	1 00
Boiled Salmon Trout,		Mutton Chop	1 00
Anchovy sauce	1 75	Lobster Salad	2 00
BOILED.		Sirloin of Venison	1 50
Leg Mutton, caper sauce	1 00	Baked Maccaroni	0 75
Corned Beef, Cabbage	1 00	Beef Tongue, sauce piquante	1 00
Ham and Tongues	0 75		

So that, with but a moderate appetite, the dinner will cost us $5, if we are at all epicurean in our tastes. There are cries of "steward!" from all parts of the room—the word "waiter" is not considered sufficiently respectful, seeing that the waiter may have been a lawyer or merchant's clerk a few months before. The dishes look very small as they are placed on the table, but they are skilfully cooked and very palatable to men that have ridden in from the diggings. The appetite one acquires in California is something remarkable. For two months after my arrival, my sensations were like those of a famished wolf.

In the matter of dining, the tastes of all nations can be gratified here. There are French restaurants on the plaza and on Dupont street; an extensive German establishment on Pacific street, the Fonda Peruana; the Italian Confectionary; and three Chinese houses, denoted by their long three-cornered flags of yellow silk. The latter are much frequented by Americans, on account of their excellent cookery, and the fact that meals are $1 each, without regard to quantity. Kong-Sung's house is near the water; Whang-Tong's in Sacramento street, and Tong-Ling's in Jackson street. There the grave Celestials serve up their chow-chow and curry, besides many genuine English dishes; their tea and coffee cannot be surpassed.

The afternoon is less noisy and active than the forenoon. Merchants keep within-doors, and the gambling-rooms are crowded with persons who step in to escape the wind and dust. The sky takes a cold gray cast, and the hills over the bay are hardly visible in the dense, dusty air. Now and then a watcher, who has been stationed on the hill above Fort Montgomery, comes down and reports an inward-bound vessel, which occasions a little excitement among the boatmen and the merchants who are awaiting consignments. Towards sunset, the plaza is nearly deserted; the wind is merciless in its force, and a heavy overcoat is not found unpleasantly warm. As it grows dark, there is a lull, though occasional gusts blow down the hill and carry the dust of the city out among the shipping.

The appearance of San Francisco at night, from the water, is unlike anything I ever beheld. The houses are mostly of canvas, which is made transparent by the lamps within, and transforms them, in the darkness, to dwellings of solid light. Seated on the slopes of its three hills, the tents pitched among the chapparal to the very summits, it gleams like an amphitheatre of fire. Here and there shine out brilliant points, from the decoy-lamps of the gaming-houses; and through the indistinct murmur of the streets comes by fits the sound of music from their hot and crowded precincts. The picture has in it something unreal and fantastic; it impresses one like the cities of the magic lantern, which a motion of the hand can build or annihilate.

The only objects left for us to visit are the gaming-tables, whose day has just fairly dawned. We need not wander far in search of one. Denison's Exchange, the Parker House and Eldorado stand side by side; across the way are the Verandah and Aguila de Oro; higher up the plaza the St. Charles and Bella Union; while dozens of second-rate establishments are scattered through the less frequented streets. The greatest crowd is about the Eldorado; we find it difficult to effect an entrance. There are about eight tables in the room, all of which are thronged; copper-hued Kanakas, Mexicans rolled in their sarapes, and

Peruvians thrust through their ponchos stand shoulder to shoulder with the brown and bearded American miners. The stakes are generally small, though when the bettor gets into "a streak of luck," as it is called, they are allowed to double until all is lost or the bank breaks. Along the end of the room is a spacious bar, supplied with all kinds of bad liquors, and in a sort of gallery, suspended under the ceiling, a female violinist tasks her talent and strength of muscle to minister to the excitement of play.

The Verandah, opposite, is smaller, but boasts an equal attraction in a musician who has a set of Pandean pipes fastened at his chin, a drum on his back, which he beats with sticks at his elbows, and cymbals in his hands. The piles of coin on the monte tables clink merrily to his playing, and the throng of spectators, jammed together in a sweltering mass, walk up to the bar between the tunes and drink out of sympathy with his dry and breathless throat. At the Aguila de Oro there is a full band of Ethiopian serenaders, and at the other hells, violins, guitars or wheezy accordeons, as the case may be. The atmosphere of these places is rank with tobacco-smoke, and filled with a feverish, stifling heat, which communicates an unhealthy glow to the faces of the players.

We shall not be deterred from entering by the heat and smoke, or the motley characters into whose company we shall be thrown. There are rare chances here for seeing human nature in one of its most dark and exciting phases. Note the variety of expression in the faces gathered around this table! They are playing monte, the favorite game in California, since the chances are considered more equal and the opportunity of false play very slight. The dealer throws out his cards with a cool, nonchalant air; indeed, the gradual increase of the hollow square of dollars at his left hand is not calculated to disturb his equanimity. The two Mexicans in front, muffled in their dirty sarapes, put down their half-dollars and dollars and see them lost, without changing a muscle. Gambling is a born habit with them, and they would lose thousands with the same indifference. Very different is the demeanor of the Americans who are playing; their good or ill luck is betrayed at once by involuntary exclamations and changes of countenance, unless the stake should be very large and absorbing, when their anxiety, though silent, may be read with no less certainty. They have no power to resist the fascination of the game. Now counting their winnings by thousands, now dependent on the kindness of a friend for a few dollars to commence anew, they pass hour after hour in those hot, unwholesome dens. There is no appearance of arms, but let one of the players, impatient with his losses and maddened by the poisonous fluids he has drank, threaten one of the profession, and there will be no scarcity of knives and revolvers.

There are other places where gaming is carried on privately and to a more ruinous extent—rooms in the rear of the Parker House, in the City Hotel and other places, frequented only by the initiated. Here the stakes are almost unlimited, the players being men of wealth and apparent respectability. Frequently, in the absorbing interest of some desperate game the night goes by unheeded and morning breaks upon haggard faces and reckless hearts. Here are lost, in a few turns of a card or rolls of a ball, the product of fortunate ventures by sea or months of racking labor on land. How many men, maddened by continual losses, might exclaim in their blind vehemence of passion, on leaving these hells:

> Out, out, thou strumpet, Fortune! All you gods,
> In general synod, take away her power;
> Break all the spokes and fellies from her wheel,
> And bowl the round nave down the hill of heaven,
> As low as to the fiends!

Taylor gained fame and fortune as a travel writer, but he wanted to be remembered as a poet. He reveled in being called "Poet Laureate of the Gilded Age," and he often decried his own prose. However, little is known today of his volumes of verse, while his *Eldorado* is still considered one of the most perceptive books about San Francisco and the Gold Rush era.

In October 1849, another young newspaperman arrived in San Francisco. Born in Scotland, raised in New York, and trained on the St. Louis *Republican*, James J. Ayers became one of the founders—and the first editor—of the San Francisco *Daily Morning Call*. In his memoirs, *Gold and Sunshine* (Boston, 1922), he recalled how the town looked when he first saw it.

A *heterogeneous* population

W<small>E LANDED AT A POINT SOMEWHERE</small> near where Powell street strikes the bay, and started over the north decline of Telegraph hill towards the city. We passed more than one sportsman with gun hunting small game on the hill before we emerged at the Briones ranch, now Filbert and Powell streets, where we saw some native Californians, in an adobe shed weaving riatas.* When we reached the heart of the town, it presented a scene of wild and picturesque activity. The centre of attraction was Portsmouth Square, fronted on Washington, Kearney and part of Clay streets by great canvas houses principally devoted to gambling. The Parker House was the only building constructed of wood and of architectural regularity.

On the southwest corner of Kearney and Clay streets was a large adobe that had been turned into a hotel. Gambling seemed to be the principal business in this part of the town. Tables, covered with stacks of Mexican dollars and doubloons, forming a coin rampart around a lacquered box into which the gold dust of the losers was dumped, were crowded with men eager to place their money on the turn of a card. Monte was the favorite game, and although there was a goodly sprinkling of Americans wooing the fickle Goddess, the most numerous and persistent gamblers at the tables were Mexicans of the Sonoranian variety. Many of them had evidently just come down from the mines, and hauled out of their bosoms plethoric bags of gold dust to back them in playing their favorite game. Arms were carried openly by

* Lariats.

nearly every one you met. In every gambling hall, a band of music enlivened the play, and in one great saloon called the Bella Union a complete band of negro minstrels delighted the crowds that flocked there.

The streets, or rather roadways, were alive with all sorts of people. The canvas stores were filled with goods and crowded with purchasers. Everybody seemed in a rush, and those who had not just returned from the mines were getting ready to go to them. The business centre was for a few blocks on Washington and Montgomery streets, to which latter street the bay came, and formed a half moon from Clark's Point to Rincon Hill. Tents of all sizes and shapes were planted everywhere, and the population was composed of all races. The best restaurants—at least that was my experience—were kept by Chinese, and the poorest and dearest by Americans.

The day of my arrival was the 5th of October, 1849. I had just been eight months and three days in making the trip from St. Louis. This seems strange in view of the rapid transit of the present day [1922], when one can step on a train in San Francisco and land in Chicago three days afterwards.

When one looks back and recalls the topographical features of San Francisco at that time, he is amazed at its selection as a site for a great city. It had, indeed, nothing to recommend it for that purpose except its magnificent harbor. There was absolutely no level ground beyond the narrow rim that formed the crescent beach against which the tides rose and fell. Where it was not shut in by almost precipitous and rugged acclivities it was obstructed by formidable sand hills. There was here and there a little sheltered valley, but immense sand dunes covered what is now the fairest part of the city. At the intersection of Bush and Kearney streets was a sand hill that rose to a height of forty or fifty feet. There was another on the block where the Lick House now stands. On Market street near Third, and reaching half way to Fourth, was another great sand mountain.

The southwest corner of Geary and Stockton streets was crowned with a great sand hill, one side of which reached to Market and Fourth. Saint Anne's valley, beginning at Dupont street (now Grant Avenue), was buttressed by a chain of these hills leading to Leavenworth street and beyond on the north side, flanked on the south side by a range of low hills which separated it from Hayes Valley. Indeed sand hills large and small covered all the site of San Francisco from the rim of the bay to the chain of mountains that forms a half circle from the Presidio to the Mission and from Rincon Point to Russian Hill. Fronting the city, from Rincon Hill to Clark's Point, was a mud flat upon which the tide rose and fell. The ships anchored well out in the stream, and all the goods landed had to be brought over this marsh in lighters. The tide came up to Clay and Montgomery streets, and that point seemed to be the general dumping place for the business part of the city.

Whilst I was standing at this point musing upon my situation and wondering what part I should take in the activities now opening before me, I heard my name called out, and was warmly greeted by a couple of sailors I had befriended in Realejo. They had shipped on the *Feliz* and been several months in San Francisco. I asked them what they were doing, and they told me they were working for Captain Noyes, who had taken the contract to float the old whaling bark *Niantic* over the mud flat and place her on a corner water lot.

"There she is," said one of my new-found friends, "at the end of this foot-bridge. We are going on board, and you had better come with us."

I accepted the invitation. A temporary foot-bridge had been laid from Montgomery street to the vessel, and passing over it, we climbed on board the *Niantic*. The hulk was snugly in place, at the northeast corner of Clay and Sansome streets. My friends told me all about how they had floated the *Niantic* over the shallow flat. They lashed the empty oil casks, with which she was abundantly supplied, to her bottom, and thus floated her by slow stages when the tide was high into the berth she was destined to occupy. The "boys" told me their job was finished, and that they intended to go to the mines. We agreed to form a company and go together. That day I ran across Captain Hammond, and he said he had bought the interests of the others in the *José Castro* and would take a load of passengers in her to Stockton in a few days. Our company agreed to take passage in her, and at once entered upon the task of purchasing the necessary outfit. Our "Sailor boys" made a strong capacious tent out of some of the *Niantic's* sails, and we started for Stockton in fine shape to pass the winter in the mines.

.   .   .

The dressiest people in San Francisco at that time were the gamblers. Indeed they were the capitalist bankers of the town. Their saloons were all provided with large cafés, and when a merchant required an immediate accommodation, the boss gamblers were the men applied to. Ready money flowed in upon them in great quantities, and through them the wheels of commerce were liberally greased.

The hurry and skurry in the streets was a source of never-ending interest. But few persons wore coats, and the general costume consisted of a heavy woolen shirt, trousers held up by a sash or belt around the waist, and the legs inserted in a pair of high-legged boots. A slouch hat covered the head, and the handle of a pistol or a knife generally protruded from the sash or belt. If occasionally an individual who had been lucky enough to arrive with a complete wardrobe appeared with a white shirt and a silk hat, he soon found that he had made a mistake, and with battered "stove-pipe" hurried off to his tent to don a less esthetic costume. Ladies were almost an unkown quantity in that heterogeneous population. Now and then one would meet a Mexican or a South American woman, dressed from head to foot in loud colors with face "painted an inch thick." Her outfit and tournure* both proclaimed her calling. Native Californians rode into town on fine, high-spirited horses, some of them superbly equipped with costly saddles and silver-mounted headstalls and bridles.

The riders presented a picturesque appearance with their embroidered jackets, broad-brimmed and high-crowned sombreros, calconeros slashed down the legs and a line of gold buttons placed close together the whole length. Some of them wore leggings and carried dangerous-looking knives stuck into the place below the knee where the leggings were fastened. When they dismounted the jingle of their enormous spurs sounded like the rattling of chains. These gentry came in from the ranches with plenty of money to sport with, for at that time cattle were selling at the mines for five ounces a head. The gambling tables formed an irresistible attraction to them, and many a gay don came in from his ranch with a well-filled purse and went home penniless, even having parted with his horse and its costly trappings for money to try his luck with to the end.

At night the gambling saloons were a blaze of light and filled with a dense mass of people. They were the centre of attraction for all classes, and miners, merchants, lawyers, laborers, rancheros and mariners

* The contour or shape of a body; also, a bustle.

mingled together at these places on a common plane. The tables were going full blast, and occasionally a misunderstanding would arise between a dealer and a bettor. A few loud words would be followed by a pistol shot. The saloon would be cleared in a minute, and the only sign of life visible in that vast hall would be the shooter coolly placing his smoking pistol in its holster and a couple of attendants bearing away the dead body of his victim. Yet these episodes were not of such frequent occurrence as one would suppose. The fact is that, as everybody carried arms, men were slow to quarrel because they realized that it would end with a duel to the death. The effect was to keep men cool, and the desperadoes seldom went out of their own class to seek a fight, as the public temper was such that if they did they might expect a short shrift and a quick rope.

San Francisco—and particularly its weather—had detractors then as it does today. Eliza Woodson Farnham shows her disdain in this excerpt from her 1856 book, *California, In-doors and Out*. She was an advocate of women's rights and prison reform in New York when her husband, Thomas Jefferson Farnham, a prominent lawyer and author, died in San Francisco. To settle his estate, she sailed to California with her two small sons. After just two months in San Francisco, she moved to a farm in Santa Cruz and visited the city only when necessary. The trip described here took place in the spring of 1850.

ELIZA W. FARNHAM (1815-1864)

That wretched place, San Francisco!

W E HAD BEEN BUT LITTLE MORE THAN a month settled before it became necessary for me to go to San Francisco, on which journey Mr. Anderson very obligingly undertook to be my escort. Miss S. was to remain in charge of affairs at home, and especially to take care of Eddie, the great object of anxiety to us all, as his health seemed to have failed since we had been at Santa Cruz. The journey was to be made on horseback, and the road for the first day lies across the range of mountains that skirts the coast. We set out with formidable preparations of lunch, fire-arms, etc., Mr. A. carrying two revolvers, and each of our horses having a satchel of provisions in addition to those of clothing. A habit-skirt, which I was assured I could not wear through the mountains, was packed conveniently, that it might be put on when we reached the inhabited regions on the other side. The road across these mountains is stern and solitary in the extreme. Portions of them are heavily wooded with the enormous red wood which abounds here. One tree especially is pointed out by the cicerone,* which is said to be 403 feet high. The valleys and many of the gentle slopes are fertile, and produce the wild oat and some varieties of clover in abundance, but immediately succeeding them we get precipitous cliffs of shale, in which the mule-path is so deep that rider and horse are swallowed up, and so narrow that there is only room to ride through without brushing the sides of the chasm. On either hand you have heather wastes intermingled with flowering

---

* A guide. (Italian)

shrubs, many of which, in their seasons, are very beautiful. At this time all the more productive regions were sparkling with the flowers common to the country, chief among them the eshcholtzia, purple and blue lupin, columbine, white and variegated convolvuli, fleur de lis, white lily, and innumerable smaller flowers of exquisite beauty, with whose names, being no botanist, I am unacquainted.

Something more than midway across, after all sorts of scramblings up and down rocky stairs, and through brush that has nearly torn your hat from your head, and certainly your spectacles from your face, you are quite surprised to find your horse treading a wagon-track, and riding further on, you find in a large valley shut in by high hills, partly wooded and partly covered with oats and grass, a house and saw-mill. The proprietor of this valuable property is an emigrant from Ohio, who brought his family across the plains three or four years ago. He started with a company for Oregon, and says that when he reached the point where the California trail diverged, he let his oxen choose which they would take. They turned southward, and the consequence is that he is now the owner of one of the finest timber ranches in the country, whose wealth his children's children cannot exhaust. So inadequate and fantastical are sometimes the influences that produce to us the most grave results.

From the first summit eastward in this range, you get a magnificent view of the coast-table, the bay of Monterey, and the ocean; from the last you behold a portion of the bay of San Francisco, and the great valley of the Puebla de San José, lying spread as it were at your very feet—one of the most beautiful views conceivable. And as the eye dwells upon the fertile plains, in some parts thickly dotted with the ancient and picturesque live-oak, its branches laden with gray, trailing mosses, in others sparsely set with the same, and still others open and smooth as a shaven lawn, one readily imagines that the time is not long distant when from this mountain-top the famous pine-orchard view shall be rivaled. Cover the bay with sails and steamers, variegate the uniform green of the fertile plain with grain-fields, orchards, gardens, farm-yards, and houses; dot the sunny slopes with vineyards, and let the church-spires be seen pointing heavenward from among occasional groups of dwellings, and I know not what would be wanting to complete the picture, and make it one on which the heart and eye could dwell with equal delight. The valley itself, when you descend into it, though very pleasing by its smooth and open surface, is less beautiful to my taste than our own little rougher and brisker Santa Cruz. Advance a few miles from the foot of the mountain, and you have a monotonous level that lacks extent to give it grandeur—variety of any sort to give it everyday interest.

From the Puebla to San Francisco, a distance of sixty miles, almost the entire road is over a surface so level that you see the broad bay, that puts up between you and El Contra Costa, only as a belt of water. An occasional sail seems to be gliding along in the grass over the top of which you look. Yet a ride through the valley is one of the most charming in the country, so fertile is it—so adorned with the orchard-like trees that take on new forms in their groupings from every point of view by which you approach or recede from them. It only begins to be disagreeable when you reach the hills some ten or twelve miles from San Francisco, and grows constantly more so till you reach the same point on your return. Here the San Francisco winds meet you face to face, and search you like an officer of the customs. They grow more unpleasant till you enter the city, by which time you are thoroughly chilled and dampened by the humidity with which they have been charged. Your eyes, ears, nostrils, and mouth are filled with the sand they have hurled at you, and you just begin to remember that out of Santa Cruz one must expect to encounter many disagreeable things that one has entirely forgotten the existence of in that delightful spot.

San Francisco, I believe, has the most disagreeable climate and locality of any city on the globe. If the winter be not unusually wet, there is some delightful weather to be enjoyed. If it be, you are flooded, and the rainy season closes to give place to what is miscalled summer—a season so cold that you require more clothing than you did in January; so damp with fogs and mists, that you are penetrated to the very marrow; so windy, that if you are abroad in the afternoon it is a continual struggle. Your eyes are blinded, your teeth set on edge, and your whole person made so uncomfortable by the sand that has insinuated itself through your clothing, that you could not conceive it possible to feel a sensation of comfort short of a warm bath and shower by way of preliminaries. These, as water is very scarce (and, for the most part, very bad), it is, as yet, impossible to have in dwelling-houses, consequently, you give yourself up to a state of physical wretchedness, your self-respect declines, and you go on from day to day, hoping more and more faintly, on each succeeding one, that your moral nature may withstand these trials of the material, but feeling, if you are possessed of ordinary sensibilities, lively apprehensions that your friends will have cause to deplore the issue.

Something like this has, at least, been my state when I have been compelled to sojourn for a season in that wretched place, and I believe it does not differ greatly from that of a majority of persons with whom I have compared notes. What sort of end the unfortunates, who spend their lives there, can expect under such circumstances, one does not easily foresee.

.   .   .

We spent but a single day in San Francisco, and on that the election for county-officers was held; as stirring a one as ever, I imagine, Gotham, or any of the Atlantic cities, beheld. One of the candidates for sheriff was a professed gambler, and keeper of a hotel on the Plaza, the bar and tables of which had been kept open for three weeks previous to this election. The canvassing for his office cost him $50,000, and he failed at last to get it, by reason, not of any bad odor that attached to him as a gambler, but of the idolatrous affection in which the southern and western men held his antagonist, the famous Jack Hays, of Texas.

I was obliged to pass through the most excited quarters of the city several times during the day, and my serious belief was, that any honors awarded to Mr. Jack Hays after that day would be postumous. No man ever received such treatment at the hands of a friendly mob— now upon their shoulders; now hoisted upon the counter of some public-house; then pulled down, to be borne off somewhere else; now compelled to stop and address a crowd at this corner, and then borne, without ceremony or tenderness, to some other spot; alternately seized by the arm, neck or leg, by men in all stages of drunkenness, and all degrees of popular frenzy—poor Jack Hays seemed to me a man much to be pitied. He triumped, however, politically, and his constitution triumphed, also, over the violence done to it; for he survives to this day to enjoy his hard-earned honors and emoluments.

[Eliza Farnham returned East in 1856, by which time she had apparently changed her attitude toward San Francisco. Near the end of her *California, In-doors and Out* she becomes possessive, referring to the town as "ours":]

As a maritime city it has no peers. ... And no harbor affords a finer picture than ours on a beautiful morning—the tall clipper masts piercing the radiant blue skies; the huge, sullen steamers lying in black silence at the wharves; half a dozen vessels dropping down to the Golden Gate, their white sails bearing them slowly on, as do the half-folded wings of a great sea-bird about to rise from his liquid bed.

When the Reverend William Taylor saw the words CITY HOSPI-
TAL in large red letters outside a building on Clay Street his
first impression was that they had been written with blood.
With trepidation, he went in and asked to be shown around.
The doctors refused, but a patient offered to take him through
the wards. What he saw on that fall day in 1849 was enough to
validate his worst fears. The stench, the filth, the almost total
neglect of the patients shocked him into a determination to
do what he could to comfort these sick and dying men—a task
that was to occupy much of his time during the seven years he
was in San Francisco. When not visiting hospital wards,
this 6 ft., 200-pound Methodist street preacher from Virginia
could be seen—and heard—expounding the Gospel to huge
crowds outside the saloons at Portsmouth Square, or on the
wharves as each shipload of new gold seekers arrived. This is an
excerpt from his *California Life Illustrated* (New York, 1859).

Life and death at City Hospital

AFTER GOING THROUGH THE pay rooms, I was next con-
ducted across a yard to a separate one-story building, about thirty by
forty feet in size, divided into two wards, each containing from forty
to fifty sick men. Here the city patients, proper, were confined together
as closely as possible, and allow room between their cots for one
person to pass. I thought the up-stairs rooms were filthy enough to
kill any well man, who would there confine himself for a short period;
but I now saw that, in comparison with the others, they were entitled
to be called *choice* rooms, for the privilege of dying in which a man
who had money might well afford to pay high rates. But these "lower
wards" were so offensive to the eye, and especially to the olfactories,
that it was with great difficulty I could remain long enough to do the
singing, praying, and talking I deemed my duty.

The ordinary comforts, and even the necessaries of life in California, in those days, were very rare and costly; and to the patients were
things to be remembered in the experience of the past, only to add, by
contrast, a keener edge to their present sorrows.

The nurses were generally men, devoid of sympathy, careless,
rude in their care of the sick, and exceedingly vulgar and profane. One
hundred dollars per month was about as low as anything in the shape
of a man could be hired, and hence hospital nurses were not only the
most worthless of men, but insufficient in number to attend ade-
quately to their duties.

I remember a poor fellow, by the name of Switzer, died in one of
these wards, who told me that he lay whole nights suffering, in

addition to the pains of mortal disease, the ragings of thirst, without a drop of water to wet his lips. A cup of tea was set in the evening upon a shelf over his head, but his strength was gone, and he had no more power to reach it than a man on a gibbet. He was a Christian, too, a member of the Congregational Church, and I have no doubt went from there to heaven. When he got to that country in which "there is no more death, neither sorrow nor crying," and looked back to the place where he left his corruptible body, the contrast must have filled him with unutterable surprise.

The most prevalent and fatal disease in California at that time was chronic diarrhea and dysentery, a consumption of the bowels, very similar, in its debilitating mortal effect upon the constitution, to consumption of the lungs. Men afflicted with this disease have been seen moping about the streets, looking like the personification of death and despair, for weeks, till strength, and money, and friends were gone, and then, as a last resort, they were carried to the hospital, to pass a few miserable weeks more in one of those filthy wards, where they often died, I was told by the patients, in the night, without any one knowing the time of their departure. In the morning, when the nurses passed round, they found and reported the dead. A plain coffin was immediately brought, for a supply was kept on hand, and laid beside the cot of the deceased, and he was lifted from the cot just as he died, laid in the coffin, and carried out to the dead cart, the driver of which was seen daily plodding through the mud to the graveyard, near North Beach, with from one to three corpses at a load.

While many lingered on the confines of death for weeks, I have often seen men enter those horrible wards with apparently very slight indisposition, and within a few days wilt down and die. I wondered that *any* could survive in such a place for a longer period. The city was then paying for the care of those patients five dollars per day, an amount, one would think, sufficient to furnish a motive, if not to cure and discharge the patients, at least to prolong their lives as long as possible; but I suppose they made as profitable a speculation out of the multiplication of new cases as they could do by protracting the lives of the old ones; and hence, no matter how fast they died, others took their places, who for a time, perhaps, required less attention.

It turned out that the old man who piloted me through the hospital on my first visit was an old ship master, Captain A. Welch. He introduced me that day to his friend Captain Lock, who died soon after, having after my visit professed to find peace through Jesus, and a preparation for heaven. Captain Welch told me that seeing his friend neglected, he said to the doctor: "Captain Lock has had no attention for forty-eight hours, and is dying from sheer neglect."

"Well," replied the doctor, "let him die, the sooner the better. The world can well spare him, and the community will be relieved when he is gone." He died that night. Before his death he gave his clothing to his friend Captain Welch, but the captain told him he would not touch a thing he had while he was alive, but as soon as he was gone the nurse relieved the captain of any trouble with the effects of the deceased man.

The doctor fell out with Captain Welch, because he spoke his mind so freely, and threatened to turn him out of the hospital.

"Yes," said Captain Welch, in reply, "I saw Captain—— pay you for the ten days he had been in here eighty-six dollars, and after his death you collected the same bill from his friends. Now, sir, if you want me to show you up, just turn me out."

The doctor then took his cot from him, and the captain said: "Doctor, where shall I sleep, sir?"

"Sleep there on the floor," replied the doctor, pointing to a corner where they laid out the dead, when it was too late in the evening, or the weather too bad, to remove them directly from their cot of death to the dead cart.

The captain said he lay there one night with four corpses around him, and could hardly get his breath. I have heard patients complain of very foul play towards those who had money, but sick men are apt to be sensitive and suspicious, especially in such a place as that, and I always hoped those things were not so bad as represented; but from what I saw I had my fears for the safety of any man's life who had money, in the hospital at the time of which I speak.

The hospital changed hands several times, however, within a few months, and one or two good physicians, and I believe honest and kind-hearted men, had for a short time the care of the sick, and were really working a reform in the old hospital, before the whole care of the city patients was, in 1850, transfered to Doctor Peter Smith, in a new hospital, near the corner of Clay and Powell streets, where the sick had better accommodations, and more attention shown them.

Old Captain Welch was in the old hospital over a year, and would doubtless have died if he had been confined to his room, but he was out where he could get pure air most of his time. He had a very sore leg, and the doctor told him that it was mortifying and would have to be amputated. Finally several doctors came into his room with a table, and a lot of surgical instruments, and said to him, "Come, captain, we want to lash you to this table, and take off that bad leg of yours."

"I won't have my leg taken off," replied the captain.

"If you don't," said the doctor, "you are a dead man, or as good as dead, for that leg is mortified now."

"Well," said the captain, "if I die I'll die with both legs on me."

The doctor became enraged, and said to him: "If you don't obey orders immediately, and submit to the rules of this house, you shall leave it this day."

"Very well," rejoined the captain. "And that very day," said the captain to me since, "I took up my sore leg and walked off with it, and have not been back since." He is the same Captain Welch who since received a medal from some New-York citizens for his success in rescuing a number of the poor survivors of the wrecked "steamer San Francisco," and is now employed as a colporteur and Bible distributor in the city of New-York.

.   .   .

In the winter of 1849-50, we had a great many scurvy patients in the hospital; many of whom had been on long voyages, living for months on what the sailors call "old junk" and ship-bread; all the fresh meat they got was found in a live state in their bread. Poor fellows! they had come to a bad market, where potatoes were fifty cents per pound, and scarcely any other vegetables to be had at any price. There they were, confined in the bad atmosphere of the hospital, swallowing drugs and dry provisions, sinking down and dying daily.

One day, as I entered a large ward filled with such patients, I looked at them and thought a minute on their wretched condition, and then I said, "My friends, what are you doing here? You are cooped up in this miserable place, without fresh air, without sunshine, without exercise, and without vegetable diet. You will die, the last man of you, if you don't get out of this place. You had better be turned out in San José Valley to graze, like old Nebuchadnezar, than pine away and die in such a place as this. Now," said I, "I'll tell you what will cure you. On those sand-hills back of the city there grows a kind of wild lettuce," which I described to them. "If you will go out and gather that lettuce and use it, with a little vinegar, it will cure you." I knew the open air, and sunshine, and exercise would help them, and believed the prescribed salad the best thing for them within their reach.

It was an interesting sight to see those poor fellows under the inspiration of a new hope, crawling out and scrambling up the hills in search of my prescribed cure. The next week, when I called again to see them, I was really surprised to see how much their condition had improved. When I entered, some of the poor fellows wept, and others laughed, and after a grateful greeting they said: "You've saved our lives, sir; your prescription has done us more good than all the medicines and all the doctors in the city could do for us." The most of them soon afterward recovered and left the hospital.

Although he rarely solicited money for himself or for his ministry, Rev. Taylor would occasionally ask his congregation to contribute funds for people in distress, and it was not unusual in one evening to collect the boat fare for some destitute and disillusioned person who wanted to go home to his family and friends. After seven years in California, he continued his preaching in Europe, Egypt, Australasia, and South and Central America before being appointed missionary bishop of Africa. He retired in 1896 and returned to California, where he died in 1902.

A high point of life in San Francisco was the monthly arrival of a steamer bringing mail from the East Coast. In 1849, three months went by without one delivery of mail, until the *Panama* finally arrived with a cargo of 37 sacks containing 45,000 letters. Bayard Taylor, who had just returned from Monterey where he witnessed the drafting of California's first constitution, was staying with his friend the postmaster, Mr. Jacob B. Moore, when the steamer arrived, and he offered to help sort and distribute the mail. This is from his *Eldorado*.

Most letters sent to California from eastern states were mailed COD, presumably because there was a fair chance they might not reach the people they were intended for. The recipient then paid 40 cents per half ounce for postage.

Mail call!

A DAY OR TWO AFTER MY ARRIVAL, the Steamer Unicorn came into the harbor, being the third which had arrived without bringing a mail. These repeated failures were too much for even a patient people to bear; an indignation meeting in Portsmouth Square was called, but a shower, heralding the rainy season, came on in time to prevent it. Finally, on the last day of October, on the eve of the departure of another steamer down the coast, the Panama came in, bringing the mails for July, August and September all at once! Thirty-seven mail-bags were hauled up to the little Post-Office that night, and the eight clerks were astounded by the receipt of forty-five thousand letters, besides uncounted bushels of newspapers. I was at the time domiciled in Mr. Moore's garret and enjoying the hospitalities of his plank-table; I therefore offered my services as clerk-extraordinary, and was at once vested with full powers and initiated into all the mysteries of counting, classifying and distributing letters.

The Post Office was a small frame building, of one story, and not more than forty feet in length. The entire front, which was graced with a narrow portico, was appropriated to the windows for delivery, while the rear was divided into three small compartments—a newspaper room, a private office, and kitchen. There were two windows for the general delivery, one for French and Spanish letters, and a narrow entry at one end of the building, on which faced the private boxes, to the number of five hundred, leased to merchants and others at the rate of $1,50 per month. In this small space all the operations of the Office were carried on. The rent of the building was $7,000 a year, and the salaries of the clerks from $100 to $300 monthly, which, as no special provision had been made by Government to meet the expense, effectually confined Mr. Moore to these narrow limits. For his strict and conscientious adherence to the law, he received the violent censure of a party of the San Franciscans, who would have had him make free use of the Government funds.

The Panama's mail-bags reached the Office about nine o'clock. The doors were instantly closed, the windows darkened, and every preparation made for a long siege. The attack from without commenced about the same time. There were knocks on the doors, taps on the windows, and beseeching calls at all corners of the house. The interior was well lighted; the bags were emptied on the floor, and ten pairs of hands engaged in the assortment and distribution of their contents. The work went on rapidly and noiselessly as the night passed away, but with the first streak of daylight the attack commenced again. Every avenue of entrance was barricaded; the crowd was told through the keyhole that the Office would be opened that day to no one: but it all availed nothing. Mr. Moore's Irish servant could not go for a bucket of water without being surrounded and in danger of being held captive. Men dogged his heels in the hope of being able to slip in behind him before he could lock the door.

We labored steadily all day, and had the satisfaction of seeing the huge pile of letters considerably diminished. Towards evening the impatience of the crowd increased to a most annoying pitch. They knocked; they tried shouts and then whispers and then shouts again; they implored and threatened by turns; and not seldom offered large bribes for the delivery of their letters. "Curse such a Post-Office and such a Post-Master!" said one; "I'll write to the Department by the next steamer. *We'll* see whether things go on in this way much longer." Then comes a messenger slyly to the back door: "Mr.— sends his compliments, and says you would oblige him very much by letting me have his letters; he won't say anything about it to anybody." A clergyman, or perhaps a naval officer, follows, relying on a white cravat or gilt buttons for the favor which no one else can obtain. Mr. Moore politely but firmly refuses; and so we work on, unmoved by the noises of the besiegers.

The excitement and anxiety of the public can scarcely be told in words. Where the source that governs business, satisfies affection and supplies intelligence, had been shut off from a whole community for three months, the rush from all sides to supply the void, was irresistible.

In the afternoon, a partial delivery was made to the owners of private boxes. It was effected in a skillful way, though with some danger to the clerk who undertook the opening of the door. On account of the crush and destruction of windows on former occasions, he ordered them to form into line and enter in regular order. They at first refused, but on his counter-refusal to unlock the door, complied with some difficulty. The moment the key was turned, the rush into the little entry was terrific; the glass faces of the boxes were stove in, and the wooden partition seemed about to give way. In the space of an hour the clerk took in postage to the amount of $600; the principal firms frequently paid from $50 to $100 for their correspondence.

A familiar sight at the post office when mail arrived once a month.

We toiled on till after midnight of the second night, when the work was so far advanced that we could spare an hour or two for rest, and still complete distribution in time for the opening of the windows, at noon the next day. So we crept up to our blankets in the garret, worn out by forty-four hours of steady labor. We had scarcely begun to taste the needful rest, when our sleep, deep as it was, was broken by a new sound.

Some of the besiegers, learning that the windows were to be opened at noon, came on the ground in the middle of the night in order to have the first chance for letters. As the nights were fresh and cool, they soon felt chilly, and began a stamping march along the portico, which jarred the whole building and kept us all painfully awake. This game was practised for a week after the distribution commenced, and was a greater hardship to those employed in the Office than their daily labors. One morning, about a week after this, a single individual came about midnight, bringing a chair with him, and some refreshments. He planted himself directly opposite the door, and sat there quietly all night. It was the day for dispatching the Monterey mail, and one of the clerks got up about four o'clock to have it in readiness for the carrier. On opening the door in the darkness, he was confronted by this man, who, seated solemnly in his chair, immediately gave his name in a loud voice: "John Jenkins!"

When, finally, the windows were opened, the scenes around the office were still more remarkable. In order to prevent a general riot among the applicants, they were recommended to form in ranks. This plan once established, those inside could work with more speed and safety. The lines extended in front all the way down the hill into Portsmouth Square, and on the south side across Sacramento street to the tents among the chapparal; while that from the newspaper window in the rear stretched for some distance up the hill. The man at the tail of the longest line might count on spending six hours in it before he reached the window. Those who were near the goal frequently sold out their places to impatient candidates, for ten, and even twenty-five dollars; indeed, several persons, in want of money, practised this game daily, as a means of living! Venders of pies, cakes and newspapers established themselves in front of the office to supply the crowd, while others did a profitable business by carrying cans of coffee up and down the lines.

The labors of the Post Office were greatly increased by the necessity of forwarding thousands of letters to the branch offices or to agents among the mountains, according to the orders of the miners. This part of the business, which was entirely without remuneration, furnished constant employment for three or four clerks. Several persons made large sums by acting as agents, supplying the miners with their letters, at $1 each, which included the postage from the Atlantic side. The arrangements for the transportation of the inland mail were very imperfect, and these private establishments were generally preferred.

The necessity of an immediate provision for the support of all branches of Government service, was, (and still remains, at the time I write,) most imminent. Unless something be speedily done, the administration of many offices in California must become impossible. The plan of relief is simple and can readily be accomplished—in the Civil Department, by a direct increase of emolument, in the Military and Naval, by an advance in the price of rations, during service on the Pacific Coast. Our legislators appear hardly to understand the enormous standard of prices, and the fact that many years must elapse before it can be materially lessened. Men in these days will not labor for pure patriotism, when the country is so well able to pay them.

Mary Jane Megquier was one of the earliest women to establish a boarding house in San Francisco. She arrived in June
1849, to assist her husband, Thomas Lewis Megquier, in his
practice as physician, leaving their children with relatives and
friends in Winthrop, Maine. A selection of her letters was
published in 1949 by The Huntington Library Press under the
title *Apron Full of Gold*. A second edition, with new material,
is being published in 1994 by the University of New Mexico
Press.

The following letters to her daughter (Angeline Louise
Megquier), and to her friend Milton (J. M. Benjamin) are
reprinted here from the earlier edition, with the permission of
the Henry E. Huntington Library.

This picture was taken about 1853.

MARY JANE MEGQUIER (1813-1899)

"This land of
gold and wonders"

San Francisco, Nov. 11 [1849]

VERY DEAR FRIEND, MILTON,

Your kind letter was received last week, there can be no estimate made of the pleasure it gave us to hear from you and others of our kind friends in W. it being the first since we left the states. I suppose you have heard one thousand and one stories of this land of gold and wonders, they may differ widely but still all be true. Every one writes in some degree as he feels, some will get into business the moment they put foot on land, in three months will find themselves worth fifty thousand, while others whose prospects are much brighter, will in the same short space of time be breathing their last in some miserable tent without one friend, or a single dime to pay their funeral charges, they are tumbled into a rough box with their clothes on, in which they died, this has been the fate of thousands since I have been here, yet there never was a place where money is spent so lavishly as here, it is said that one million changes hands, every day at the gambling tables.

When we arrived the first of June there was but very few storehouses, all kinds of provisions were lying in every direction in the streets, carts running over bags of flour, and rice, and hard bread, pork selling at six dollars per barrel, now flour is selling at forty dollars per barrel, pork at sixty five. sugar we paid three cents a pound, when we came, is now fifty, and other things at the same rates, a pair of thick boots sold on Saturday for ninety six dollars. gold is so very plenty it makes but very little difference what they have to pay, There are but few arrivals now, some days in September, and October, there were twenty vessels arrived a day every one with more or less passengers.

The mines are yielding about the same as when first discovered but it is mighty hard work to get it, but they are bound to get it if they work, many, very many go there who never done a days work in their life, dig for a day or two without much success, get discouraged and return in disgust, say it is all a humbug, many are sick, and die there but it is not considered very unhealthy, This town is so situated when the thermometer is one hundred and fifteen in the mines there is a tremendous cold wind blowing here, I have had a fire every day for comfort, since I have been here, excepting a few days in the month of Sept. Oct which were delightful, now it is beginning to rain which makes the street nearly impassable, the mud is about a foot deep, the draymen have four dollars for a load of one hundred if they do not take it ten rods.

We have a fine store which is now nearly completed, the upper part will rent for one thousand a month a pretty little fortune of itself if rents continue as they now are, but it is doubtful, Our motto is to make hay while the sun shines, we intend to sell the first good offer and return forthwith, although there are many things here that are better than in the states yet I cannot think of staying from my chickens a long time, and it is not just the place for them at present, no schools, churches in abundance but you can do as you please about attending, it is all the same whether you go to church or play monte, that is why I like, you very well know that I am a worshipper at the shrine of liberty.

The land is very rich would yield an abundance if it was cultivated, but no one can wait for vegetables to grow to realize a fortune, potatoes are twenty cents a pound, beets one dollar and seventy five cents a piece, tomatoes, dollar a pound but we have them for dinner notwithstanding, we have made more money since we have been here than we should make in Winthrop in twenty years, the Dr often makes his fifty dollars, a day in his practice then we have boarders to pay our house rent, they make great profits on their drugs, to show you some of the profits on retail, the Dr bought a half barrel of pickle in salt, after soaking them, I put up fourteen quart bottles, sold them for six dollars more than we gave for the whole, which still left me the same bulk I had at first.

They are getting quite interested in politics, the locos* take the lead, they pretend they are no party men, but you will find they are very sure not to have a whig nominated to fill any office. The seat of government is established at San Hosea [San Jose], about 60. miles from this, in a most delightful spot where they have plenty of fruit and vegetables, articles which cannot be found here. ...

Jennie

San Francisco, April 19/50

DEAREST DAUGHTER

As we received no line from you by the last steamer I have not half the courage to write that I should if I could have a long letter from you every time the mail arrives, it gives me new courage to hear from you. We have now twenty in a family. I have an Irish woman to help me, she has a very pretty little boy which makes me think of you and the boys, it hurts my feeling to hear any one speak cross to him for I think some one may do the same by mine in my absence, I hope you are enjoying yourself as well as possible without your parents, I am living on the hope of seeing you all before another winter.

We are having our building raised, when it was built, it was up to the skies but filling up the street has made it quite under ground, but it gives us a fine view of the bay (over all the other buildings) which is filled with shipping from all parts of the world, and makes the cook room delightful as you have a fine view. I can stand by the stove and watch the porridge and take a look at the big ships, as they are rolling lazily on the water.

We had a nice little dance the other [night] at the store of one of our boarders. I was engaged four dances ahead, isnt that smart? I suppose you will have a good laugh to see your Mother tripping the light fantastic toe. I think you must be quite lonely in the states, it seems that they will soon be depopulated there is so many coming here. ...

I look anxiously at the arrivals every morning for the brig *Margaret*, almost every week brings some of our old friends from the states. We are getting ahead of any thing on the other side in the way of improvements. We have soft water carried through the streets every

---

* Democrats. (See Glossary.)

day, for which you only have to pay dollar and a half, a barrel, We have three daily papers put into our door handle every morning but they are all democratic, which is quite a trouble to your Father. We have concerts from Henri Herz, the pianist which are well attended at six dollars single ticket ...

San Francisco June 16. [1850]

DEAR DAUGHTER

... I am now without help again which makes me quite homesick, the husband of the woman I have had, came back from the mines and I was obliged to give her up, We have again been obliged to pack up our duds, expecting every moment to be burnt out, but as good luck would have it the fire was subdued before it reached us, but I am heartily sick of picking up and getting ready to move, I hope my next packing will be for the states although I shall be very lonely to sit down quietly for a half day, a thing I have not done in Cal, not even an hour, you will see a better account of the fire in the paper than I can have time to give you, We were out to a party the night before the fire at the St Francis Hotel, it was quite a splendid afair. ...

The fire has burnt the house we had our parties at, of course we shall have to dispense with them for the present, the people are getting discouraged some of them, others are all ready to try it again, they make their money so easy that they do not feel their losses as they do in the states. ...

I see by the paper that Bobby is burnt out but I have not seen him Dr Robinson was going to open a theatre the next night but was burnt out, he thinks fate is against him he was going to send for his wife by this steamer but I do not know what he will do now. ...

We were out in the harbor last week to a dance, had a tall time of course, ... you cannot imagine the tax it is to write in such a hub-bub as we are in all the time. ...

San Francisco June 30 [1850]

DEAR DAUGHTER

... I am most desperately vexed that I dont hear from you, ...

We are not burned up yet, but are expecting it every day, but we are in hopes to have enough left to take us home in the fall.

We are improving our streets the one we live on has become one of the busiest in the city, one morning while I was sweeping, for my own amusement I counted the persons that passed while I brushed down the stairs, they numbered two hundred and ten, the walk is crowded in the first part of the day, in the afternoon no one goes unless he is obliged too, the city is enveloped in a cloud of dust ... We have lots of fun of late, one of our boarders was very much offended at another, and there was what some would call a challenge passed between them but it finally ended in pulling hair and scratching a little but it afforded us any quantity of timber for small talk. ...

I am now sitting on my feet, writing on your Fathers trunk as my room is not large enough for a table if it was I have none for it. I want to buy only what I cannot possibly do without, it takes all the loose change to buy white kids, ribbons, shoes, ...

I should like to give you an account of my work if I could do it justice. We have a store the size of the one we had in Winthrop, in the morning the boy gets up and makes a fire by seven o'clock when I get up and make the coffee, then I make the biscuit, then I fry the potatoes then broil three pounds of steak, and as much liver, while the woman is sweeping, and setting the table, at eight the bell rings and they are eating until nine. I do not sit until they are nearly all done. I try to keep the food warm and in shape as we put it on in small quantities after breakfast I bake six loaves of bread (not very big) then four pies, or a pudding then we have lamb, for which we have paid nine dollars a quarter, beef, and pork, baked, turnips, beets, potatoes, radishes, sallad, and that everlasting soup, every day, dine at two, for tea we have hash, cold meat bread and butter sauce and some kind of cake and I have cooked every mouthful that has been eaten excepting one day and a half that we were on a steamboat excursion. I make six beds every day and do the washing and ironing you must think that I am very busy and when I dance all night I am obliged to trot all day and if I had not the constitution of six horses I should [have] been dead long ago but I am going to give up in the fall whether or no, as I am sick and tired of work, The woman washes the dishes and carpets which have to be washed every day and then the house looks like a pig pen it is so dusty, ... *Write. Write. Write.*

As the pioneer days of San Francisco began to recede into memory, disagreements occasionally arose over matters such as where this or that building used to stand, or what so-and-so used to wear. Then—as still happens today—people turned to their bartenders for answers. In the 1860s and 1870s they would most likely consult Theodore Barry (left) or Benjamin Patten (right), keepers of The Bank Exchange—a highly respected saloon for businessmen, on Montgomery Street. These two Puritan gentlemen from Boston established a new standard for saloons in the city, one that eschewed gambling and licentious paintings while serving only the finest wines and meals. After much urging from grateful customers, the two wrote a book, *Men and Memories of San Francisco in the Spring of '50*, which A. L. Bancroft and Company published in 1873. Here is the first of three excerpts from the book.

The candy man

A REAL "LONDON-CRY" CANDY MAN held forth in the early days on the west side of Montgomery, near Clay street. His little shop-on-wheels displayed its store of sweets, over which he waxed eloquent. His sonorous voice rang out, with a distinct and banging emphasis, that would not be ignored. He was something of a humorist, and made good local hits, going on with the most serious voice and grave face; his head lifted, but with downcast eyes, like one exhorting against time, for a good salary. His tall, black, narrow-rimmed hat could never have been built off English territory; his precise cravat and unrelenting shirt-collar were cockney; his telling tone and clear pronunciation, vaunting his goods, betrayed a long experience: "Hore-hound—Pep-per-mint—and—Win-ter-green! Large lumps! and strong-ly fla-vored!" A short, dead pause, and "'Ere they go!" This was three times given in a tone to excite the envy of a drill-sergeant or a stump-speaker; occasionally diversified with the assertion that Judge—— bought them; that Col.—— bought them; always naming some prominent individual.

One evening he amused the public by exclaiming, in a voice of unusual power: "Buy 'em up! Every body buys 'em! Tom B—tt—e's sweetheart buys 'em! 'Ere they go!" Busy-bodies lost no time in in-forming Tom of the distinction forced upon him. He strolled along, listening. Out it rang upon the air. Watching an opportunity to speak, unheard by others, he walked up quickly, saying, "Look here! you quit that, or I'll horsewhip you!" "All right!" said the itinerant in a soft voice—so unlike those vociferous lungs, bowing low and courteously; then, straightening up, he roared out in the well-known voice, "Tom B—tt—e's sweetheart does not buy 'em!!"

This moving excerpt from Barry and Patten's *Men and Memories* has all the melodrama of a story by Charles Dickens—an author widely read in 19th century California.

The little girl across the road

IN THE SUMMER OF 1850 we lived in a little cottage on Montgomery street, somewhere between Broadway and Vallejo; the precise spot we cannot tell, as there were no land-marks to designate street lines, the whole neighborhood being precipitous, rough and uneven, save where some little space had been leveled for a house or tent. There were very few habitations of any kind, after passing the line of Broadway.

Nearly opposite our domicile was a little tent, its only occupants, a woman and child. The mother was seldom seen; the daughter, a delicate, interesting child of eight or nine years, was often at the opening of the tent, shyly observing us, with childlike curiosity, as we went down to the city in the morning and returned at evening. The mother and child were dressed in poor, soiled, mourning garments, but their attire could not make them seem coarse or unrefined. In the occasional glimpse of the mother, we could discern the unmistakable lady—that something which all can see and none describe.

We never spoke with her, knew nothing of her, not even her name; but knew she was a well-bred, accomplished lady. She had a poor, jingley, old piano in the wretched, little canvas apology for a shelter; but she never indulged in any trashy music. Early in the morning and late in the evening we heard her practising, with the facility and grace of a musician—a style which even the muffling canvas could not hide. Sometimes, though seldom, she gave a little scrap of a sonata, a fragment of Mozart, Beethoven or Sebastian Bach, with exquisite effect, but never any trash.

In our daily and constant going and coming, we made friends with the little, lonesome-looking girl, so pale and quiet; and she was always watching for us, morning and night—a pure pleasure for us, so far from home and children. We often brought her some trifle— a toy, a little paper of confectionery, a cake or picture-book, which she received at first shyly, but with much pleasure; and after our better acquaintance, with an unconcealed delight, that made the moment as much to us as to her poor little fragile self—worth all the day beside.

One evening at our return we missed her, and lingered awhile to meet her, but she did not come. We went in to our dinner, but the little omission had made us less hungry than usual, and we dwelt upon our little friend's absence long into the evening. When morning came she was not there to welcome us, and we waited vainly, almost determined to step to the tent and satisfy our curiosity; but did not— turning down the hill, with reluctant steps, to our daily labor. We thought, all through the long September day, about our little friend, sure of meeting her when we went home; but again we were disappointed, and resolved to know in the morning all about our missing one. We questioned our host and his wife, but they had not noticed— believed they had seen neither mother nor child that day.

At midnight we were awakened by a woman's voice in agony of weeping, and supplicating prayer. Starting from our bed, we hastened to the window. All was still; not a sound came to our listening ears. The moon was wonderfully bright, revealing every object in the still, cool night, with great distinctness.

Thinking we had been awakened by a dream, we were turning back to bed, when a loud cry rang out upon the silent night—a wail so utterly despairing, that our heart stood still. It came from the little tent; there was a dull, reddish light through the canvas, unnoticeable before in the all-powerfull moonlight. Agonizing sobs followed the long, thrilling cry; the mother's voice calling her darling's name; the sound of oft-repeated kisses; then low moans and silence. The child was dead!

We hastily dressed and hurried to the spot. There were other voices in the tent; soft, soothing words from women's lips and from their hearts—kind, sympathizing neighbors, we knew, by the lighted, open doors near by. Knowing the poor, motherless woman was in gentle hands, we turned sadly away to wait for daylight. We longed to offer some sympathy or assistance; but it never would have helped the wretched mother, who was almost paralyzed with grief.

As we went down our daily path, our heart heavy with its first sorrow in this earthly paradise, we met a man carrying a little coffin on his shoulder. Stopping in the path, we stood uncovered, repeating in our heart, "The Lord giveth and the Lord taketh away: blessed be the name of the Lord!" and went on to the battle of life, with no courage in our heart.

When we came home at night, the place seemed strangely altered. A little, level place on the hillside, was all that remained to mark the spot where had been the tent, our innocent little friend, the mother's long days of anxious poverty, and her last night of hopeless agony. They were gone from our sight and knowledge, from everything but memory, forever.

Just three months after arriving in California following a grueling trek across the continent in a covered wagon, Sarah Royce, her husband, and their small daughter had to flee from Sacramento because of the flood of January 1850. They came down river by steamer to San Francisco, where they endured further hardships finding a place to live. The town was already full of refugees from Sacramento and of miners waiting out the winter.

Sometime in the 1880s, her son, Josiah, asked her to expand on the notes she had kept of her experiences in those pioneering days because he was writing a history of the state. His book, *California: A Study of American Character,* was published to great acclaim in 1886, and today it is still considered a classic account of California's emergence as a state. Sarah Royce's manuscript was published in 1932 by Yale University Press as *A Frontier Lady: Recollections of the Gold Rush and Early California.* Here is the first of two excerpts from that book.

This portrait was made several years after she arrived in California.

A lady at the Montgomery House

THE MORNING OF JANUARY 16TH, 1850, we anchored in the Bay of San Francisco, at some distance from the shore. Directly in front of us was Telegraph Hill, and very cheery did it look to me, after all the dreary scenes of the past few days; with its sides, not then torn and disfigured as they are now, but clothed with bright verdure, and bathed in warm sunlight. The old, red building on its summit looked quaint and interesting with a bright-colored flag floating above it. It became an object of still greater interest, when I was told it stood there as a signal-bearer, keeping up communication between vessels outside the Golden Gate, and men in the heart of San Francisco.

It seemed that our steamer could not safely approach any nearer the shore; so the unloading of freight and passengers was effected by means of lighters. It was nearly noon when we landed on one of the wharves. I had to sit for awhile in a warehouse office, while my husband went to inquire for rooms, where we might put up. After some time he returned looking rather puzzled. He said he had not been able to hear of a place where rooms, or even one room, could be got; but there was a public house not far off, where we could get dinner; and probably Mary and I could sit there for an hour or two, while he and Mr. A—— looked farther for rooms, or a house. Accordingly we walked, with not very elastic footsteps, to The Montgomery House, which Mr. A—— said they had been informed, was the best, if not the only hotel to be found within easy distance. It fronted on Montgomery Street not very far from Commercial. The building was long in proportion to its width, its frame work was frail, and was covered on the outside partly with boards, and partly with canvas, diversified, if I recollect rightly with sheets of zinc, in places that particularly needed staying, or had proved extra leaky. The inside was partly lined with cloth. The front door was in the middle of the gable end, and was reached by two or three rough board steps, from the decidedly muddy footpath which, then and there, was the sidewalk of Montgomery Street.

As we entered we were motioned to the right, where was a small room wholly without carpet, containing one table, and a very few chairs, and lighted by one window. This was the sitting room. The partition which separated it from the dining room behind it was of cloth. Across the little hall-way into which the front door opened, and directly opposite the sitting room door, was the bar room, a much larger apartment than the sitting room, and furnished with a box-stove, the only place for a fire in the whole house, excepting the cook stove in the kitchen; which latter apartment was behind the bar-room.

From the little hall-way, and facing the front door ascended a flight of stairs. At the top of these you found yourself in a hall extending the whole length of the building, and of just sufficient width to allow a passage by the side of the stairway to the front end. The partitions on each side were wholly cloth, and, at distances of about four feet apart along the whole length of the hall, on both sides, were narrow doorways. Looking into one of these doorways, you saw before you a space about two and a half feet wide and six foot long, at the farther end of which was a shelf or stand, on which you could place a candlestick, while you had just room to stand and dress or undress. At the side of this space were two berths, one above the other; and these berths, so situated, were the only sleeping accommodations afforded by this hotel.

Of course when I entered the house I had not the least idea of ever knowing anything about its sleeping accommodations. I supposed that in two or three hours, I should be in a private room, resting, preparatory to arranging a home nest. But when, after spending the afternoon searching, both the seekers returned and said nothing of the kind we wanted could be found; there was no alternative but to remain where we were.

The landlord thoughtfully proposed to the two lodgers who occupied the berths at the farther end of the hall, against the wall of the house, to give them up to us; thus placing us in the most private spot to be obtained; for which I certainly felt grateful. The next morning efforts to obtain a place to live were renewed, with similar results. An opportunity was offered of renting a whole house, which would be vacated in a few days, by a family going to the mines; but it was three times as large as we needed; besides being too lonely a place for me to be left alone in, while business was attended to.

Meantime, with all the discomforts of these surroundings, health was returning to me, and I was able to walk out a little with Mary. However, by turning to the right from the door, and going up a street which was then very steep, one soon got away from the water, and up to where there was a fine view of the Bay and the shores beyond. Up this hill I managed slowly to walk, and lead Mary, and very greatly did we both enjoy the warm sunshine, soft breeze and sparkling scene.

Chinese costumes of the mid-19th century.

Turning in a fresh direction, we came to where there were a number of odd looking shanties, several of them displaying in doors and windows strangely-shaped packages, many-colored boxes and, in some places, queer toys. It took me but a minute or two to see, that the people who stood in these doors, or walked busily about, were Chinese. I had seen but one or two since coming into San Francisco, and, before that, the only Chinese I had ever seen, was one who in my youth was brought by missionaries to America, and visited an Eastern city where I lived.

This little nucleus of the since celebrated China-Town of San Francisco was to me, that January morning in 1850, an unexpected sight; and I was for a few minutes as much amused as Mary; but the out-landish look of every thing, soon made me feel out of place; and I was hastening to find a street I could turn down, when an elderly Chinaman with a long queue and blue cloth sack came from a store door, with smiling face, addressed to me a word or two in broken English, then stooped down, shook hands with Mary and placed in her hand a curious Chinese toy.

Now came a rainy day or two, greatly magnifying all the disagreeable features of our surroundings. Everybody boarding at "our Hotel" was now obliged to keep within doors; and those not engaged in regular business had to spend the whole day, crowded into the little comfortless sitting room or huddled, as they could get chances, around the bar-room stove. There was necessarily much confusion; there were of course many there who were far from refined in manners; yet, I must say in all candor, that during those three very unpleasant days, I received no rough or discourteous word from anybody; I witnessed no offensive behavior; and, whatever there was of drinking at the bar, I saw no drunkards, either at the bar-room stove or in the sitting room. I was, repeatedly, very kindly invited to a warm seat at the stove with Mary; and never went there without finding room, cheerfully made.

But we could not live in this way long. Efforts were being made; but no place for us had yet been found. At last, on Saturday morning of this tedious week a new face appeared on the scene, introduced by Mr. A———. It was the Rev. Mr. W——— Pastor of a Protestant Church, organized in San Francisco but a few months before. He had heard that a family were staying at the Montgomery House who wished to get rooms for housekeeping; and he came to give information and make a suggestion which he thought would be a relief. He said a friend of his had just built a house on purpose to rent in tenements.* Only one tenement was yet finished and that one Mr. W——— was

* Apartments.

[236]

occupying with his small family; but another would soon be finished, which he thought we might get. Meantime, there was one room, besides his own apartments, which was habitable. We could no doubt secure that immediately, and we could board in his family until a place was ready for us to keep house. We were not long in availing ourselves of this hospitable offer, and before night we were safely sheltered, and our little comforts piled about us, in a room which, though unfinished, was more comfortable than any place we had occupied for many months.

The conveniences of civilized life, the comforts of home, can not be keenly appreciated, or even fully seen, by those who have never been, for a time, shut out from them. Repeatedly in the days that now followed, did I find myself feeling that I had never before known the brightness of the evening lamp-light, nor the cheeriness of the morning breakfast room, with all their orderly accompaniments; that I had never before realized the worth of quiet domestic life, unworried by ever-threatening dangers.

President Millard Fillmore signed the California Bill on September 9, 1850, admitting California into the Union, but the news did not reach San Francisco until October 18. The Washington debates had dragged on throughout the summer, with the outcome far from certain. At issue was California's stand against slavery at a time when the other 30 states were divided evenly on the issue. When news of acceptance finally reached San Francisco it was greeted with a sudden outpouring of jubilation, as Sarah Royce recalled in *A Frontier Lady*.

"Home again!"

In the fall of 1850 we were all excitement to hear the result of California's knock at the door of the Union; and as the day approached when the steamer would bring the decision, many eyes were strained toward Telegraph Hill. At length the signal went up—the *Oregon* was outside the heads and would soon be in the harbor. As she neared, another signal indicated that she carried flying colors, implying good news, and presently she appeared in sight to those, who like ourselves overlooked North Beach, gay with streamers and flags of all nations,—the Stars and Stripes most prominent, and, above them, straightened out by the generous wind which seemed to blow a long breath on purpose, floated the longest streamer of all, displaying the words "California Admitted"!

The roar of cannon rolled over the waters, and met answering roars from fort and ships. Everybody was laughing. "Now we were at home again!" cried one. "Yes," was the answer, "and remember, all, we must no more talk of going to 'The States' nor hearing from 'The States.' We are *in* 'The States'!"

Well do I remember the brisk tap at my door that morning, and the friendly voice that invited me up to a high veranda to take a look, through a large field glass, at the welcome steam-ship. For some minutes we stood there looking in silence—the sight brought thoughts too many and too absorbing for words. Then, with brief expressions of thanksgiving and mutal congratulations, we descended, meeting and answering, as we passed through the halls and porches, the laughing congratulations of our fellow-inmates.* This was in October of 1850.

---

* Other tenants in the apartment building.

A view of the city from Clay Street in 1850, painted by George H. Burgess for James Clair Flood in 1878.

A city transformed
1850-1851

It sometimes takes a visitor to notice the changes in a place. In several instances, people who left San Francisco and then returned after a brief absence have given us the most dramatic accounts of the town's rapid growth. One such person was Frank Marryat, an Englishman who arrived in June 1850 and spent two years in California, hunting game at the Russian River and quartz-mining at Tuttletown. Periodically he would visit San Francisco, and on each occasion he would marvel at the changes he saw. In this account, which is taken from his book *Mountains and Molehills*, he describes one such visit. The time is June 1851 and he has just sailed down river to San Francisco Bay from Sonoma after being away nine months.

A changed town

On landing at san francisco, I found so many changes on every side, that my knowledge of locality was at fault; wharves extended on all sides into the sea, and the spot where I last had landed was scarcely recognizable, it was now so far inland; the steam-paddy* had worked incessantly, and the front of the town still advanced into the bay.

The winter had been (compared with that of 1849) a dry one, and some of the streets having been graded and planked, the town was, under the worst circumstances, navigable for jack-boots.

What first struck me, among the many changes of a few months, was that the inhabitants generally were less eccentric in dress. When first I arrived, the people were most capricious in this respect; they wore, in fact, whatever pleased them, long hair and beards included; sobered down by circumstances, however, they had now quietly relapsed into the habits of ordinary mortals.

Places of rational amusement had sprung up, and replaced in a great measure the gambling-saloons, whose fortunes were rather on the wane from over-competition. There were clubs, reading-rooms, and a small theatre, called the Dramatic Museum. This last was sadly in want of actors, and as my time hung very heavily on my hands (I was awaiting the arrival of a vessel from England) I gave way to a vicious propensity that had long been my bane, and joined the

---

* A steam engine used to level the city's sand hills.

company as a volunteer. For about a month, under an assumed name, I nightly "Used Up" and "Jeremy Diddlered"* my Californian audiences, who never having fortunately seen Charles Matthews, did not, therefore, stone me to death for my presumptuous attempts to personate that unrivaled actor's characters.

I became, at last, so used to seeing my "last appearance but one" displayed on the advertising posters, that I began to associate myself with the profession altogether, and to believe my name was Warren; and what with the excitement of acting in leading parts, and the pleasant parties, and picnics, with our troupe, I forgot all about Russian River Farm, and became a very slave to the buskin.**

The dreadful experience of the place had made people so nervous respecting fire, that the sound of the fire-bell would cause every man to rush to his house, and get ready for the defense of his property; and as small fires on the outskirts of the town were of continual occurrence, there was scarcely a night but the deep-toned bell would keep the citizens on the alert. On these occasions the theatre would be deserted rapidly, while every other man would vociferate fire, but almost immediately the leading columns would return, with cries of "all over!" and "all out!" and the theatre would refill, and the performance proceed, until the "fire-bell" took them off again, which occasionally it would in ten minutes.

The market at this time was so overstocked with merchandise, that goods sold at auction at less than cost-price. Ready-made clothing, in particular, was cheaper in San Francisco than it was in New York or London. So that the storehouses being every where crammed with goods, great depression in trade existed. The city of San Francisco at this time was in debt about a million of dollars, and the Treasury being empty, scrip was issued bearing the ruinous interest of thirty-six per cent. per annum. But this state of affairs was remedied by funding the debt, and issuing bonds payable in twenty years, bearing interest at ten per cent. The citizens co-operated in this movement, and submitted to a heavy tax, and thus, in spite of repeated conflagrations following on a state of apparently hopeless bankruptcy, the energy of San Franciscans not only enabled the municipality to redeem

* Thoroughly exhausted, and swindled. (See Glossary.)
** An expression implying a deep involvement with acting. (See Glossary.)

annually a portion of their bonds, but placed the credit of the city on a firm and secure basis.

There were seven or eight churches already in San Francisco, all of different denominations—these were well attended on Sundays, but the price of pews was very exorbitant, reaching as high sometimes as ten pounds a month. Some of these churches were built entirely in a spirit of speculation; and on asking an acquaintance once what security he had for some money he had lent, he told me, so many shares in — Church; and the same building was afterward sold, I think, by auction, to satisfy its creditors. Now that ladies begin to flock into California so rapidly, the churches are crammed to overflowing on a Sunday. The Americans are rather strict observers of congregational worship, which has this drawback, however, that it here imposes the necessity of so many becoming hypocrites on the Sabbath; for as regards the amount of religious feeling that exists at this time, one can neither judge of it by the attendance or the absence of the people from public worship.

But I will say this for them, that as a nation they are most charitable, and that they are true friends to one another in adversity; *once* your friend, the American will share all he has with you, and risk his life in defense of your honor and name—more, he will not even permit merited censure to be passed upon you in his presence; and however suspicious of others worldly contact may have made him, he will repose his confidence in you like a child. And so common are these friendships, that the true generosity which cements them forms a prominent feature of the American character; but whether it springs from deep religious feeling or not is a question I do not care to argue.

A great proportion of the working-classes of America are Methodists, or of somewhat similar persuasions; they have their camp-meetings, read their Bible very generally, are given to psalm-singing, and have the appearance of being a religious people. I attended one of these camp-meetings. My old friend of the English barque, who wished to "rip up the cook," was officiating with "tears in his eyes." There was a great deal of excited praying; but the greater proportion of the people seemed to have come out for any purpose but that of worship; in fact, the scene was very lively, and if it had not been for the weeping priest, it would have been a merry picnic.

In the 1920s, a notebook containing 211 yellowing pages of tiny handwriting was discovered in Paris. It was the journal of Albert Benard de Russailh, and it described in detail his attempts to strike it rich in California in 1851-1852. In 1931, the Grabhorn Press printed Clarkson Crane's translation of the last 50 pages as a book for The Westgate Press under the title *The Last Adventure*. The excerpt that follows is the first of three from the book.

According to another journal (Ernest de Massey's *A Frenchman in the Gold Rush*), Benard "came out to make a fortune for a charming but penniless English girl whom he wished to marry. But since coming to California he has completely forgotten her."

Toothpicks and broken watches

T HERE IS NOTHING SO TEDIOUS and insipid as talking about oneself: it embarrasses the writer and bores the reader. But despite the drawbacks of the first person singular I shall have to use it, for I intend to tell everything that happened to me in this horrible California. If only for myself, all my impressions are of importance, and I shall not omit my least thought or action.

I have unpleasant memories of my first days in San Francisco. The customs inspection promised to be endless, and more than two weeks after my arrival I was still without my baggage and the small quantity of merchandise I had brought with me. We waited patiently in complete inactivity, passing the time as best we could. When the passengers of the *Joseph* were finally notified that the custom's officers had finished their work, I hurried down to the Long Wharf, determined to be the first on board and to get my belongings ashore as quickly as possible. My friend, Louis, was not with me: he had fallen into such apathy and discouragement that he was incapable of effort, and begged me to look out for his things.

I had a man row me out to the *Joseph* and began to lower our trunks and packing-cases into the small boat. But my troubles were not yet over. Among my baggage the customs officers had found some stationery goods and several cases of champagne, for which they wanted to collect as duty more money than I had. We stood arguing on the deck, while my half-loaded boat thudded against the ship's side; and I was giving up all hope, when a sudden idea struck me. Breaking open one of the cases of champagne, I pulled out a few bottles, and gave one to the chief inspector, a burly man with a red beard. Without a word, he smashed the neck on the bulwark, gulped down the wine, tossed the empty bottle overboard, and wiped his red beard with the back of his hand. The other officers crowded around me, and in a moment half a dozen corks popped and champagne splashed onto the deck. While they were drinking, I lowered the unopened cases over the side, dropped the stationery after them, and then lifted the case from which the bottles had been taken. The wine had done its work, and by this time the inspectors were too befuddled to notice what I was doing; and in a moment I was safely away from the *Joseph*. For a few bottles of champagne, I had saved $30 or $40 in duty.

The following day I spent unpacking my cases in preparation for my new career as shopkeeper. Early next morning, I conquered my vanity, put on a red flannel shirt, and went down to the Long Wharf, where I chose a good place, and with a few old boards rigged up my open-air shop. My goods were soon spread out to attract customers. I had many things of no particular value: brushes, gloves, perfumes, cutlery, colored shirts, and other articles; but it was enough to begin with; and my little stock transformed me into an important San Francisco merchant. After all, my shop was not much smaller than the best in town, and my different lines were fairly complete.

My business began superbly; my sales were steady, and I made good profits. I sold a pair of suspenders for more than six times what I had paid for them, and a toothbrush for ten times its cost. Jars of cold cream, bottles of *eau de Cologne* and perfume went for high prices, $1 or $1.50 apiece. It seemed quite magnificent. A hundred old magazine illustrations, which I had by chance stowed away in the bottom of my trunk, paid my hotel expenses for more than a week. Among them some caricatures by Gavarni, clipped five or six years before from *Charivari*,[*] brought me $2 each. But I made my biggest profit from a wholly worthless article. In Paris no restaurant charges for these articles, they are carelessly thrown away and trodden under foot, and a man will break twenty-five a day at lunch or dinner. I am speaking of toothpicks. I had brought with me two packages of them (about 248 small packs) for my own use, or to give away to my friends

---

[*] A French satirical magazine.

and acquaintances. One day I decided to lay several packs on my counter. They had scarcely left the box when a grave gentleman paused before my shop and began to examine my merchandise. He picked up the illustrations and a few other things, but laid them down again, and he seemed about to walk away, when his eye happened to light on the toothpicks. He reached for a pack, held it up, and said:

"How much?"

I was quite taken aback, for I had no idea what to charge. It had never occurred to me that anyone would buy them, and I had rather planned to give them away. But I remembered suddenly that in California nothing is given away; everything is sold. With as serious an expression as I could command, I replied:

"Half a dollar, sir."

He gave me a long look.

"It is not possible," he said finally. "That is very little."

At first, I thought he was joking. Then I feared that he would fly into a rage. I smiled and was about to say politely: "That is nothing for you, sir." But he quietly gathered up four packs, handed me $2, nodded pleasantly, and moved away.

My happiness was even greater than my amazement, and I congratulated myself on being such a good business man. Next day I laid out twice as many toothpicks for sale, and in a few minutes they were all snapped up at the same price. "If this is a country where toothpicks are valuable," I said to myself, "and if I have the only supply on the market, I must certainly take advantage of the situation and do something on a grand scale."

Elated by my success, I hurried home and sat up far into the night splitting the packs of toothpicks in two. After this process of division, packs originally containing twenty-four toothpicks had only twelve. The plan was excellent and I was not disappointed: in less than a week they had all gone for 50c a pack. I could hardly restrain my laughter whenever a man paid me half a dollar for only twelve. If I had a 1500-ton ship loaded to the gunwale with toothpicks, my fortune would have been made, and I could have gone home to France in a steamer. But, unluckily, I had only 496 packs.

For a while my shop was well patronized and my business flourished, for I was beginning to learn the tricks of the trade. I discovered the value of a friendly word here and there, a smile for a woman, a jest or a timely remark for a man, all of which helped to attract customers. Destiny seemed propitious. But my goods were nearly exhausted, and I knew that I should have to lay in a fresh supply, if I wished to continue operations.

An opportunity to replenish my stock soon presented itself. A passenger on the *Joseph* had brought with him a quantity of silver watches, some with open crystals, others of the hunting-case type. He had been able to get rid of some, but about three dozen remained, and he offered to sell me the lot. After a long discussion we came to terms: I bought the whole collection of large and small watches with their chains and keys for 100 francs a dozen, which made roughly nine francs and a few centimes apiece. Now I must confess that these watches were of unequal value: some ran for ten minutes, some for a quarter of an hour, others for half a day, and a few for even a whole day; but to make up for this it cannot be denied that many would not run at all. By chance, five or six turned out to be excellent (buyers later complimented me on my wares), and I still carry one of them myself, a large silver affair with a double case, which I pull out on occasion and proudly exhibit. Of course, it is rather capricious, like a flighty woman, and has many whims and impulses. But if it happens to stop for a while, the hands next day will travel twice around the dial to catch up, which persuades me that it is a watch with the best intentions.

When my purchase was made, I spread out my new merchandise, and before long a crowd gathered. Standing behind my counter, I shouted at the top of my voice that they all had come from the Royal Watch Company, and that they had been carefully tested; and I went so far as to guarantee them for five years. That is more than the houses of Brèguet or Lepine will do for their famous watches. All around me I heard men asking: "How much? How much?" As an abundance of watches had recently been shipped into California, they did not bring high prices; but I sold nearly the whole stock at from $3 to $6 apiece, depending on the sizes; and was satisfied with making more than a hundred per cent profit.

I then bought up a few odds and ends in auction sales, but had some difficulty in disposing of them. Realizing that my business was about to decline, I immediately cast about for some other way of earning a living. My little shop had brought me some of the money I so badly needed. On disembarking, I had only 3 francs 50 in my pocket. It is true that a friend offered to help me, but none the less the 3 francs 50 were all I actually possessed. When my hotel expenses were paid, about $100 remained from my business profits; and I knew that I should have to make money as quickly as possible, for the sum of $100 does not go far in San Francisco.

About this time a city ordinance was passed, forbidding sales in the streets and on the Wharf, and aimed directly at small open-air shopkeepers like myself. I wrote an article, discussing the ordinance from every point of view, and sent it to Monsieur Anselin, who was editing the French section of the *Daily True Standard*. The law was particularly unfair to newcomers, I stated, because it prevented them from quickly selling off whatever they had brought, and thus made it impossible for them to meet the expenses that would inevitably overwhelm them on their arrival. What would keep them from utter poverty, when their only means of living was taken away? No one could claim, I added, that these petty merchants, the value of whose stock was often little more than $10, could injure the well-established storekeepers. I recommended an immediate repeal of the ordinance.

My article appeared in next day's paper, and I went into the Café des Artistes on Commercial Street to read it over. I experienced a curious sensation at seeing my full name at the bottom of the page. When I heard someone near me ask a friend if he knew who this Monsieur Albert Benard was, my heart nearly stopped beating, and I sat there in fear, expecting them to laugh at my article. But I felt a thrill of pleasure, for another man remarked: "Surely this isn't by Monsieur Anselin. The style is quite different. This is very well written." Then, noticing my name, he added: "Ah, no wonder! It's by Monsieur Albert." All that day my excitement rose and fell: the first emotions of a future journalist, if only in California.

Of all the nationalities that flooded into San Francisco in those Gold Rush years, the French were the most influential in raising the town's standard of living. Rather than adapt to the crude existence that they found, they recreated the sophisticated ambience of Paris in their restaurants, stores, theaters, and gambling saloons. Their manners and the way they dressed were in contrast to everyone else's. Many Americans were alienated by this refusal to meld—they considered it an insult—but in time, these embellishments were assimilated into a lifestyle that ultimately defined San Francisco. In this excerpt from *Last Adventure*, Benard voices his opinions about—and occasional disdain for—various aspects of life in California, while at the same time he offers advice to anyone thinking of moving there.

A Frenchman's views

LIFE IN SAN FRANCISCO is not unusually difficult: men do not die of hunger if they are willing to work, and yet many of our compatriots here are far from being well-off. Before a man embarks on an adventure like this, he should think carefully of all the suffering and privations that may await him; he should crush out every bit of vanity and sensitivity, and get rid of prejudices that may be well enough in his own country but certainly are out of place here; he must be prepared for the petty mishaps that will befall him, and hard enough to overcome every possible obstacle. In short, he must have courage, energy, and a firm character. Don't think that everyone can blithely come here and adjust himself to this completely new existence. I've seen men go mad, and many others lose hope and drink themselves to death, finding no better end for their troubles. I've known some who were reduced by discouragement and boredom to such a condition of bestial torpor that they were utterly incapable of the slightest effort.

At the time of my arrival in San Francisco the cost of ordinary living was very high, but it is only fair to add that one could earn enough to pay one's expenses. In March, 1851, a fairly good dinner without wine cost $2.00, a bottle of wine, $1.50, which brought the price of an ordinary meal to $3.50 a person. For this amount, at Vefond's or at the Trois Frères Provençaux, I could have had an excellent dinner and the best wines. At the same period one could rent a corner of a bedroom for $1.50. You were given a blanket and had the right to wrap up in it and stretch your weary bones on the floor. Daily expenses ran up to $5.00. Everything else was in proportion: laundries charged $9.00 a dozen to do up shirts, although a new shirt cost only $2.00. The bootblacks working in front of the El Dorado, the Parker House, and the Union Hotel earned from $10.00 to $15.00 a day each. The negroes and other workmen who were always hanging around the Wharf charged $3, $4, or $5 to carry a trunk or two. A musician could earn two ounces ($32) by scraping on a squeaky fiddle for two hours every evening, or by puffing into an asthmatic flute.

You had to give one of the girls in a bar about as much to come and sit with you an hour or two, and if you wanted anything more from these nymphs, you had to pay 15 to 20 ounces ($240 or $320). But to make up for this, every kind of work was extremely well-paid. Almost any small business deal would eventually bring in very handsome profits. You earned money in proportion to what you spent, and you quickly got used to paying $3 or $4 for your dinner and no longer hesitated to spend five times as much as in France for a drink in the middle of the day.

There is a great bustle all day long. Men hurry about doing their business; deals are put through easily and quickly, even when they amount to $100,000 or $150,000, and they are helped along by drinks of brandy in any one of the numerous bars of the city. Practically all transactions are discussed and closed with a few drinks, which is the recognized method of coming to an agreement. When buyer and seller have once drunk together, the bargain is definitely concluded. Wagons and carriages crowd along through the ruts of the street, and the docks are packed with all kinds of goods, brought by ships from the ends of the earth, to be traded for gold dust. By evening everything changes and the night-life begins. Business-men and merchants, who work so hard during the day, can think of nothing better to do right after dinner than to push into the innumerable stuffy gambling-houses where in a flash they lose everything they have earned. A few of them, but not very many, go to the theatre to enjoy subtler emotions.

.   .   .

Theatres

The theatres and gambling-houses are the only places where one can spend the evening. On clear nights when the moon lights the dark city, one can stroll along the shore of the bay and on the wharves, and breathe a little fresh air; but I must add that such weather is rare, for

Miss Albertine, the pretty dancer; and Mr. Booth who is an extraordinary tragedian. One of Booth's great successes is Pizarro, or An Episode during the Conquest of Peru. French plays and light comedies, some of which I saw in Paris, are frequently translated and put on here, for example, Don César de Bazan, Le Joueur, and several amusing things from the Théâtre des Variétés: Le Chevalier du Guet, and Bruno le Fileur, among others.

I must mention here the Americans' strange manner of applauding a favorite actor or a good scene. In France, and everywhere else in Europe that I know anything about, we clap and sometimes shout bravo, and whistle only when we are disgusted. Actors at home are terrified and paralyzed if an audience whistles; Nourrit, once so well-known in Paris, is even supposed to have died from it. But with Americans, whistling is an expression of enthusiasm: the more they like a play, the louder they whistle, and when a San Francisco audience bursts into shrill whistles and savage yells, you may be sure they are in raptures of joy.

The circus is not so firmly established. It remains here a month, then tours the valley towns for a few weeks, and finally reappears in San Francisco. Circus people are all nomads, and need a change of air every day. This is particularly true of the bare-back riders. It is as if they had got so used to riding around on horse-back to amuse the public that they can't bear to stay long in the same place. Today they put up their tent in San Francisco, tomorrow evening they will be performing in Sacramento, a few days later in Marysville, and before a week has gone by they will have crossed the high mountains to pitch their camp and put on the show in Downieville.

The bare-back riders I've seen out here are no better than the wandering performers who drift through our provinces every summer and astonish the peasants at country fairs. As a matter of fact, Americans demand very little in the way of bare-back stunts. What they want is a good clown. When they see him kicked in the behind, they scream with laughter, and they love a fellow with plenty of jokes, who can roll around in the sawdust and make funny faces while his partner belabors him. An American clown always smears his face with paint, especially red and black, and wears the traditional costume: a tight shirt, yellow-spotted pantaloons, and a pointed hat. We all know how serious clowns are. Perhaps they think their great race would be dishonored if they made a laughing-stock of themselves without wearing a disguise and making their faces unrecognizable. The rest of the evening performance consists of a few acrobatic stunts, some songs, a display of fire-works, and a little bare-back riding.

I come now to the Adelphi Theatre, where every Sunday the French Troupe tries hard to put on something worth while. I confess that they do not always succeed, because they have very little to work with. The company is directed by three women, Mesdames Eléonore, Adalbert, and Racine. The other members of the troupe are Mademoiselle Alexina Courtois, Mademoiselle Bréa, Messieurs Richer, Paul Saspor- tas, Léon Prat, Yomini, Nitzel.

Naturally, we are not severe critics; it would be foolish to expect much art six thousand leagues from France; and we go to the Adelphi every Sunday evening eager to find everything wonderful. I should certainly be the last one to abuse these good ladies, as some of them treated me with great kindness, and, I might say, generosity. Need I add that it was not because of my personal charm? To them I was only a dramatic critic who had to be won over and muzzled, and I suppose they succeeded well enough. I can't help smiling when I think of the glowing write-ups I used to give them in Monday's paper, far better ones than Parisian stars usually receive.

The hypocrisy of the press? Oh well, perhaps. But they are nice people. I often pitied readers of my column in the *Daily True Stand- ard*, who hopefully took boxes for the next performance at the Adel- phi on the strength of my notice. Even though they know little about good acting, they must have cursed me and said I was a fool to praise a show that might deserve to be hissed. But, all things considered, this little theatre is not so bad, and is well patronized.

Before the May fire the Adelphi was on Commercial Street, in the heart of town, with a rear exit onto Clay Street. It boasted a parterre, orchestra seats, a balcony and gallery, and was fairly attractive, al- though simply decorated. The May fire quickly reduced the whole place to ashes, by chance sparing the house next door where I was living. Since then the theatre has been rebuilt on Dupont Street, be- hind Portsmouth Square and across from the Post Office. It is practi- cally the same, a little larger, with the whole balcony divided into boxes.

Only three members of the company really have talent, Madem- oiselle Racine, Monsieur Paul and Monsieur Richer. Mademoiselle

Racine is amazingly versatile, always ready for anything, soubrette, character part, duena, whatever is needed; and I've often hated to see her pretty face hidden under some ugly make-up. She has been trained in the best tradition, and acts naturally and with good taste. She is graceful, speaks her lines well, has vivacity and wit, and come pretty close to being a finished actress. The public all like her and I am enthusiastic myself. Her best plays are Mademoiselle de Liron and L'Image.

Monsieur Paul, who was once a director of the Théâtre Lyrique, Rue de la Tour d'Auvergne, is a first-rate comedian with lots of verve and intelligence. He is splendid in Le Comédien des Etampes and Les Vieux Péchés. Young Monsieur Richer has a pleasant voice. He is well fitted for the juvenile roles, and plays them conscientiously. As he takes part in nearly every performance, he has become a favorite with the audience, and contributes not a little to the theatre's success.

What can I say of Madame Eléonore and Madame Adalbert? Just what must be said of two women who have been on the stage for a long time (I was about to write too long a time), and who have never definitely arrived. Madame Eléonore is still able to use her old eyes to good effect, which gets over with the public, and Madame Adalbert dresses well enough to make up for the rest.

As for the other men, Yomini, Nitzel, and Léon Prat, the less said the better. They are useful in the cast, but the audience would willingly dispense with their usefulness, as we have often gathered from what may be politely called expressions of disapproval. Unfortunately, no one has been found to take their place.

On the whole, the French Troupe is about as good as one could expect in California; the ensemble is as satisfactory as possible, and the shows are fairly varied, made up usually of light skits or comedies, farces, short plays of a more serious nature, or musical interludes. The women directing the company will soon have been two years in California, and have not done badly from a financial point of view, as they now own the building, the lot, and the scenery. Perhaps they have not earned all their money in the theatre. People say that there are certain wealthy patrons of the arts in the background, worthy men who have endangered their own fortunes to make Mademoiselle Racine and her partners richer. But I shall say no more, lest I be accused of gossiping: I am only telling what everyone in town knows.

Women in San Francisco

When I first arrived here, there were only ten or twelve French women in San Francisco, but quite a number of American women had been here for some time, and were living in attractive houses with a certain amount of comfort and even luxury. They all had come from New York, New Orleans, Washington, or Philadelphia and had the stiff carriage typical of women in those cities. Men would look hopefully at them in the streets, at least men who had just come to California, but they much preferred the French women, who had the charm of novelty. Americans were irresistibly attracted by their graceful walk, their supple and easy bearing, and charming freedom of manner, qualities, after all, only to be found in France; and they trooped after a French woman whenever she put her nose out of doors, as if they could never see enough of her.

If the poor fellows had known what these women had been in Paris, how one could pick them up on the boulevards and have them for almost nothing, they might not have been so free with their offers of $500 or $600 a night. A little knowledge might have cooled them down a bit. But I'm sure the women were flattered by so much attention. Some of the first in the field made enough in a month to go home to France and live on their incomes; but many were not so lucky, and one still meets a few who have had a bad time and who are no better off financially than the day they stepped ashore. No doubt, they were blind to their own wrinkles and faded skins, and were too confident in their ability to deceive Americans regarding the dates on their birth-certificates.

Many ships have reached San Francisco during the past three or four months, and the number of women in town has greatly increased, but a woman is still sought after and earns a lot of money. Nearly all the saloons and gambling-houses employ French women. They lean on the bars, talking and laughing with the men, or sit at the card tables and attract players. Some of them walk about with trays of cigars hanging in front of them; others caterwaul for hours beside pianos, imagining they are singing like Madame Stoltz. Occasionally, you find one who hides her real business and pretends to be a dress-maker or a milliner; but most of them are quite shameless, often scrawling their names and reception-hours in big letters on their doors.

There is a certain Madame Cassini who runs a collar shop and claims to be able to predict the past, present, and future and anything else you like.

All in all, the women of easy virtue here earn a tremendous amount of money. This is approximately the tariff. To sit with you near the bar or at a card table, a girl charges one ounce ($16) an evening. She has to do nothing save honor the table with her presence. This holds true for the girls selling cigars, when they sit with you. Remember they only work in the gambling-halls in the evening. They have their days to themselves and can then receive all the clients who had no chance during the night. Of course, they often must buy new dresses, and dresses are very expensive out here.

For anything more you have to pay a fabulous amount. Nearly all these women at home were street-walkers of the cheapest sort. But out here, for only a few minutes, they ask a hundred times as much as they were used to getting in Paris. A whole night costs from $200 to $400.

You may find this incredible. Yet some women are quoted at even higher prices. I may add that the saloons and gambling-houses that keep women are always crowded and are sure to succeed.

The famous beauties of San Francisco today are Marguet, Helene, Marie, Arthemise, Lucy, Emilie, Madame Mauger, Lucienne, Madame Weston, Eleonore, Madame St. Amand, Madame Meyer, Maria, Angèle, and others whose names I have forgotten.

There are also some honest women in San Francisco, but not very many.

.   .   .

Public dances

It is easy for pleasure-loving people to find amusement in San Francisco. There are the French and American theatres and the circus; women and good restaurants abound; and the streets swarm with horses and carriages. For a time there were no public dances. Shortly before my arrival [1851] this defect was remedied by the proprietors of the California Exchange, who had the happy idea of giving dances in this large hall where much business is transacted by day and which is used as a stock-exchange. Now absolutely nothing is lacking, and a perpetual carnival reigns.

These entertainments are usually fancy-dress balls, and take place twice a week, on Wednesdays and Saturdays. They are very popular. Although Americans are generally awkward and unbending, they enjoy dancing, and above all they love to watch other people dance. All the women in town appear, French, American, and Mexican; the men gather in crowds; and one often sees beautiful costumes richly adorned with lace, which the women make themselves or order from dress-makers for each occasion. A masked ball naturally permits a certain freedom, but here the feverish atmosphere of the city produces an abandon I have never seen elsewhere. Three distinct quadrilles are always in progress simultaneously, French, American, and Mexican, and the races mingle only in waltzes, polkas, and gallops. The American quadrille is danced with Anglo-Saxon stiffness and impassivity; the Mexican with a southern languor and indolent grace; but the French quadrille is a centre of genuine gaiety and animation.

I often notice how American men steal away from their own group and enviously watch the vivacious French women, who do not hesitate to let themselves go, when they see they are being admired. I am occasionally reminded of our balls at the Salle Valentine on the Rue St. Honoré. There is one important difference: Parisian rowdies often come to blows; but in San Francisco hardly an evening passes without drunken brawls during which shots are fired.

The music is fairly good and is certainly noisy. Eight or ten pass-able musicians play all the popular dance tunes for quadrilles, waltzes, and polkas. The price of admission is $3.00, and, as I have said, the hall is always crowded.

The "Mr. Booth" referred to was Junius Brutus Booth, Sr.—at that time America's greatest tragedian—who performed to great acclaim in San Francisco in 1852. His son Edwin Booth began a spectacular career as a tragedian in San Francisco, and another son, Junius Brutus Booth, Jr., managed local theaters. Their brother, the infamous John Wilkes Booth, who assassinated President Lincoln in 1865, did not perform in San Francisco.

The caption to this 19th century French cartoon read, "Monsieur Williaume exports to California an article that is in great demand." The sign in the background advertises a matrimonial service offering "an assortment of widows."

Very little is known about Dolly Bradford Bates, other than that she was from Kingston, Massachussetts, that she sailed from Baltimore with her husband on July 27, 1850, and that she survived three fires at sea before finally arriving in San Francisco at the end of April 1851—just a few days before the town was almost entirely gutted by fire. All of this she chronicles in her book, *Incidents on Land and Water, or Four Years on the Pacific Coast* (Boston, 1857), which was published under the name "Mrs. D. B. Bates." This excerpt describes her arrival in town. Her description of the May 3-4 fire closes the volume.

"Why don't you kiss me, Bessy?"

SUCH A HURRY, SUCH A BUSTLE, so much excitement! We are nearing the wharf at San Francisco. What crowds of men assembled upon the pier, ready to rush on board as soon as the steamer is made fast! I almost envied those who were going to meet loved friends. We knew none, to give us a cheerful greeting, in that city of strangers.

Mrs. B——, a lady who was accompanied by her husband, and myself seated ourselves upon deck, to witness the meetings. So many joyful tears were shed, such heartful embraces! Fathers caressing little ones they had never seen; they in turn frightened half out of their wits at finding themselves in the arms of such frightful objects. Sometimes we could scarcely repress the tears at witnessing some affecting scene; at others, constrained to laugh outright at some really ludicrous sight. One delighted husband said, "Why don't you kiss me, Bessy?" She stood gazing at this hirsute representation of her better half in utter astonishment; then timidly ejaculated, "I can't find any place."

"Oh!" said Mrs. B——, sportively, "they will all get a kiss but you and me." Almost instantly a gentleman sprang to her side, cordially greeting her, and even bestowing a kiss. I was almost stupefied at such audacity, for at first she seemed not to recognize him. Soon the air of astonishment, and even of alarm, resigned its place upon her countenance to the glad smile of recognition. He was an old friend, whom she had not seen for years. He thought he recollected her countenance; then the sound of her voice confirmed his preconceptions. I felt greatly relieved when I found it was not the custom in California for the gentlemen to kiss all the ladies they fancied, whether acquainted or not.

Happy Valley, in 1849.

My husband and myself, by invitation of the captain, concluded to remain on board that night. He insisted upon our occupying his room in his absence, as business called him ashore. "Everything," said he, "is at your disposal, except my tooth-brush."

Next morning, upon going ashore, my husband met a cousin of ours, who was residing in Happy Valley. He came immediately on board, and insisted upon our going at once to his house. This cordial invitation we at once accepted. Mr. B—— had emigrated to California in 1849, and there married.

How unique to me seemed everything in San Francisco, when first I paced its sandy streets leading to Happy Valley! They were building up the water-lots rapidly. The old ship Niantic, of Boston, seemed quite up town. Upon the deck of this condemned ship was reared quite an imposing edifice, bearing the signature of the Niantic Hotel. Streets were extended far beyond it, bayward. The interstices between some of these streets were not yet filled. I grow dizzy even now, thinking about it. In our haste to reach Happy Valley, and avoid, as far as lay in our power, those interminable sand-hills, it was proposed to cross one of those interstices on a hewn timber, which, at least, must have been nearly one hundred feet, and at a height of twelve feet, I should think, from the green slimy mud of the dock. I succeeded pretty well, until about half-way over, when, finding myself suddenly becoming very dizzy, I was obliged to stop, get down on my knees, and hold on to the timber. I was afraid to proceed, lest I should fall into the mud and water below, and, for the same reason, unable to retrace my steps. After much crying on my part, and coaxing and scolding on the part of the gentleman, I succeeded in reaching the terminus of the timber. That was my introduction into the town of San Francisco in 1851.

Upon leaving, three years afterwards, I traversed that same locality. It had become the richest business part of the city. There were nicely paved walks, bounded on either side by massive granite and brick structures, an ornament to the city—the pride and the glory of the energetic pioneers, representatives from every state in the Union.

Dolly Bates and her husband spent much of their time in California operating a hotel at Marysville, in the heart of the gold country. Her book, which appeared in 11 editions between 1857 and 1861, offers a rare insightful account of the Gold Rush from a woman's perspective.

The area between Mission and Market streets, and First and Second streets, was known in those days as Happy Valley. The sand dunes that used to provide shelter from the winds have since been leveled.

The first of the major fires to devastate San Francisco began at Dennison's Exchange, seen here nestled to the right of the larger Parker House.

Fire!
1849-1851

Théophile de Rutté was one of the last people to write of the "old" San Francisco before a large portion of it was destroyed in the first of six major fires that devastated the city between December 1849 and June 1851. He arrived on the *Resolutie* on October 27, 1849, and in December he climbed Telegraph Hill to take a closer look at the town. What he saw that night and the day after is described in his journal, which remained virtually unknown until it was published in France in 1979.

In 1992, the Sacramento Book Collectors Club published an English translation by Mary Grace Paquette, entitled *The Adventures of a Young Swiss in California*. This excerpt is reprinted with permission of the Sacramento Book Collectors Club.

De Rutté came to California as a businessman, not as a gold prospector. He later became the first Swiss consul to California and Oregon. His memory of the date was at fault: this fire began early on the morning of December 24, 1849.

Christmas inferno

ALL WAS CALM AROUND ME, calm because it was a sacred day of rest, calm also because the sun was setting and dusk was casting its spell on nature. Through the pureness of the air, the pale lights and dark shadows made the details of this grandiose scene stand out like the fine brushwork of a painting by Greuze. On the eastern side of the bay, behind Yerba Buena Island, extended the fertile hills of Contra Costa dotted with dwellings partially hidden in thickets of live oaks, and farther on the horizon appeared the outlines of tree-covered mountains. The ferryboat which connected San Francisco and Contra Costa had just left the Oakland wharf and was moving silently across the bay in a billowing cloud of smoke.

At my feet stretched out this mushrooming city, grown out of the Mexican pueblo like a mighty oak out of an acorn, as if to demonstrate not so much the wondrous power of gold, but rather the unstoppable and prolific expansion of a free people. The original crescent of Yerba Buena had disappeared and the sand of the surrounding hillsides had already filled it in to facilitate the growth of the city. The North Beach end now met Rincon Point with a line of giant wharves stretching out into the bay on pilings, each crisscrossed with a series of transversal docks. A fleet of ships, the finest and sleekest in the world, lay at anchor in a long line.

Toward the south, it was an entirely different picture. In the foreground swamps and green meadows rose to meet the gentle slopes of the San Bruno Mountains. In the middle of the plain stood the little village of the Mission, with its massive old bell tower, a reminder of a different age and civilization. Mission Dolores, founded in 1776, at one time formed, with the pueblo of Saint Francis of Assisi and the presidio, the obligatory triad of all Spanish settlements—a unique symbol of a social order in which the representatives of the divine and royal orders worked hand in hand to watch over the walled-in world of an unarmed people.

In the middle of the bay, amid sluggish waves, were anchored several store ships, floating warehouses whose dark hulls dominated a flotilla of smaller boats and barges. To the left and right, to the north and south, my gaze took in the immensity of the gulf and disappeared in the countless inlets on the distant horizon. It was all marvelous and I would have gladly repeated the words of Faust: "Linger a while, so beautiful art thou!" Night was falling and soon the city seemed to be draped in that luminous mist which envelops all modern cities, forming a vague and mysterious backdrop pierced by the black masts of a thousand different ships. The breeze which passed over this human beehive brought back the drone of movement and life. In the distance it frothed the sea with phosphorous ripples, until finally the sound of the Angelus from the Catholic church reminded me that it was time to rejoin the faithful.

I went home scarcely suspecting that in a few hours half of this city I had been admiring would be nothing more than a pile of ashes. At one in the morning between Christmas and the 26th of December the cry of "Fire!" so terrifying for the city of San Francisco built of wood and canvas, echoed in the air and spread rapidly from person to person and street to street. More than once I had heard the clamorous and insistent call of the fire bell because conflagrations were common in San Francisco. But the one I was about to witness was monstrous, a huge inferno that would consume 300 buildings. It began between Clay and Sacramento streets. This was the district of wine and vegetable stalls and also of lumber merchants. Alcohol and wood! The most voracious fire could not have sought a more potent combination! Fed by a strong north wind, the flames took giant strides. We had been living in our house on Spring Street for a week, and perched on the rooftop, I watched the fire drawing near. It was a horrible and yet spectacular sight. With each new rum, brandy or grog shop it devoured, the fire doubled in intensity and at the same time changed color. It resembled a superb display of Bengal lights* with reds, yellows and

---

* A brand of fireworks.

blues, or else a giant punchbowl ignited by Satan and continuously stirred by the demons of hell. Add to that a habit the Americans have when an entire neighborhood is on fire: they throw kegs of powder into the middle of the conflagration to raze the houses and isolate the fire. Indeed, the buildings collapse, but all too frequently fiery debris tumbles to the other side of the street and sets on fire the houses opposite, which, built of wood and superheated from their proximity to the blaze, catch on fire like matchsticks.

Moreover, when the inferno is as large as it was on December 25, there is no stopping it. The city was lacking in cisterns, and with remarkable perspicacity, when a fire wants to erupt, it chooses the time of low tides. But, even without water, there exists to bring comfort to those afflicted, a company of firemen exceedingly well organized, made up of volunteers from all social classes, from bankers to porters, who devote themselves selflessly and with great courage to the saving of their city. As soon as the alarm is sounded, they race to the scene of the fire with their magnificent engines, and when water is lacking, they battle the enemy with powder, axe and hook.

The wind led the fire from north to south. By three in the morning it was separated from us only by the width of a single street, but this was California Street, the widest in San Francisco, and the fire, in spite of repeated attempts, could not cross it. From the roof of the house, I watched a building made of iron located nearly opposite ours. It was brought at great expense from England where it had been constructed and was reputed to be fireproof. Consequently, people carried, rolled, shoved and stockpiled in it anything of value. The capitalists brought their gold, the jewelers their gems, and cloth merchants their velvets and silks.

Unfortunately, the iron building stood in the middle of a block of wooden houses which caught fire. Soon the flames enveloped the iron building, licking it with their fiery tongues, and then the metal began to turn bright red, to twist and groan, just like the wooden houses, and of this giant strongbox and the riches it held, all that remained was a kind of misshapen cage, so shrunken and shriveled that it would have been impossible to determine its former purpose.

Finally, about six in the morning, the fire was controlled. It had lasted five hours, detroyed 290 buildings, numerous tents and stalls, and caused incalculable losses.

Bayard Taylor witnessed the Christmas Eve fire from the deck and rigging of a Peruvian brigantine as he sailed through the Golden Gate on his way back east. Here is how he described the blaze and its aftermath in *Eldorado*.

A spark in the fog

I WENT ON DECK, in the misty daybreak, to take a parting look at the town and its amphitheatric hills. As I turned my face shoreward, a little spark appeared through the fog. Suddenly it shot up into a spiry flame, and at the same instant I heard the sound of gongs, bells, and trumpets and the shouting of human voices. The calamity, predicted and dreaded so long in advance, that men ceased to think of it, had come at last—San Francisco was on fire! The blaze increased with fearful rapidity. In fifteen minutes, it had risen into a broad, flickering column, making all the shore, the misty air and the water ruddy as with another sunrise. The sides of new frame houses, scattered through the town, tents high up on the hills, and the hulls and listless sails of vessels in the bay, gleamed and sparkled in the thick atmosphere.

Meanwhile the roar and tumult swelled, and above the clang of gongs and cries of the populace, I could hear the crackling of blazing timbers, and the smothered sound of falling roofs. I climbed into the rigging and watched the progress of the conflagration. As the flames leaped upon a new dwelling, there was a sudden whirl of their waving volumes—an embracing of the frail walls in their relentless clasp— and, a second afterwards, from roof and rafter and foundation-beam shot upward a jet of fire, steady and intense at first, but surging off into spiral folds and streamers, as the timbers parted and fell.

For more than an hour, while we were tacking in the channel between Yerba Buena Island and the anchorage, there was no apparent check to the flames. Before passing Fort Montgomery [at Battery and Green streets], however, we heard several explosions in quick succession, and conjectured that vigorous measures had been taken to

[275]

prevent further destruction. When at last, with a fair breeze and bright sky, we were dashing past the rock of Alcatraz, the red column had sunk away to a smouldering blaze, and nothing but a heavy canopy of smoke remained to tell the extent of the conflagration. The Golden Gate was again before us, and I looked through its mountain walls on the rolling Pacific, with full as pleasant an excitement as I had looked inwards, four months before, eager to catch the first glimpse of the new Eldorado.

[Three days after it had left, the ship drifted back into the bay with a broken rudder and a small leak in the hold. The fire had destroyed the wharves, so the ship had to anchor off the beach, forcing its passengers to wade ashore.]

A light southern breeze springing up, enabled us to reach the anchorage west of Clark's Point in the night; so that next morning, after landing on the beach and walking through a mile of deep mud, I was once more in San Francisco.

I hastened immediately to Portsmouth Square, the scene of the conflagration. All its eastern front, with the exception of the Delmonico Restaurant at the corner of Clay-st. was gone, together with the entire side of the block on Washington-st. The Eldorado, Parker House, Denison's Exchange and the United States Coffee House— forming, collectively, the great rendezvous of the city, where everybody could be found at some time of the day—were among the things that had been. The fronts of the Verandah, Aguila de Oro, and other hells on Washington-st. were blackened and charred from the intense heat to which they were subjected, and from many of the buildings still hung the blankets by means of which they were saved.

Three days only had elapsed since the fire, yet in that time all the rubbish had been cleared away, and the frames of several houses were half raised. All over the burnt space sounded one incessant tumult of hammers, axes and saws. In one week after the fire, the Eldorado and Denison's Exchange stood completely roofed and weatherboarded, and would soon be ready for occupation. The Parker House was to be rebuilt of brick, and the timbers of the basement floor were already laid. The Exchange had been contracted for at $15,000, to be finished in two weeks, under penalty of forfeiting $150 for every additional day. In three weeks from the date of the fire, it was calculated that all the buildings destroyed would be replaced by new ones, of better construction. The loss by the conflagration was estimated at $1,500,000—an immense sum, when the number and character of the buildings destroyed, is considered. This did not include the loss in a business way, which was probably $500,000 more. The general business of the place, however, had not been injured. The smaller gambling hells around and near Portsmouth Square were doing a good business, now that the head-quarters of the profession were destroyed.

Notwithstanding there was no air stirring at the time, the progress of the fire, as described by those who were on the spot, had something terrific in its character. The canvas partitions of rooms shrivelled away like paper in the breath of the flames, and the dry, resinous wood of the outer walls radiated a heat so intense that houses at some distance were obliged to be kept wet to prevent their ignition. Nothing but the prompt measures of the city authorities and a plentiful supply of blankets in the adjacent stores, saved all the lower part of the city from being swept away. The houses in the path of the flames were either blown up or felled like trees, by cutting off the ground timbers with axes, and pulling over the structure with ropes fastened to the roof. The Spanish merchants on Washington street, and others living in adobe houses in the rear, were completely stupefied by the danger, and refused to have their buildings blown up. No one listened to them, and five minutes afterwards, adobes, timbers and merchandize went into the air together.

A very few persons, out of the thousands present, did the work of arresting the flames. At the time of the most extreme danger, hundreds of idle spectators refused to lend a hand, unless they were paid enormous wages. One of the principal merchants, I was told, offered a dollar a bucket for water, and made use of several thousand buckets in saving his property. All the owners of property worked incessantly, and were aided by their friends, but at least five thousand spectators stood idle in the plaza. I hope their selfish indifference is not a necessary offshoot of society here. It is not to be disputed, however, that constant familiarity with the shifting of Fortune between her farthest extremes, blunts very much the sympathies of the popular heart.

A fifth fire struck late at night on May 3, 1851, this time level-ing almost the entire town. According to Bancroft's *History of California*, the number of premises destroyed ranged from "over 1,000 to nearly 2,000, involving a loss of nearly twelve million dollars, a sum larger than that for all the preceding great fires combined." The following cameo is an excerpt from Barry and Patten's *Men and Memories.*

He who hesitates. . .

W E REMEMBER, AS WELL AS if it were but yesterday, being in front of Jo. Bidleman's fine, three-story brick, fire-proof store, on the east side of Montgomery street, between Washington and Jackson, when the fire of May 4th, 1851, reached it. Every one said, "Oh, the fire will stop there! It can't get through those walls and shutters!" But when the dreadful heat had turned its all-devouring breath upon the firm, thick walls, and bolted, massive shutters, the moments of suspense for the spectator were but few. He saw, along the iron window-shutter's edge, a line of thin, smoky fringe, like an angora edging for a lady's robe. For a moment it slowly curled about the window-casing; then, with a sudden puff, the delicately waving border quickly changed to a thick frame of wool-like smoke. The doubled sheets of bolted iron trembled and filled out like window-curtains shaking in a breeze, then burst their fastenings, belching long-tongued flames, that soon consumed the costly structure.

We ran away from the fearful heat to the corner of Jackson street, and stopped to look upon the walls, melting like snow drifts, piled upon the edge of a long sleeping crater, suddenly aroused to angry violence. Our faith in "fire-proof" was shaken. Turning away, we saw the deep hollow on the northwest corner of Jackson and Montgomery— a weedy basin in dry weather, a murky pool in winter—filled with goods of all descriptions, rescued from the flames. We looked around, thinking how strange that all those goods should have been hurried there to save them from fire, and left wholly unprotected, no one watching them; the owners returned for more; gone for some refreshment, wearied to sleep, or what not? No one was there; all seemed deserted; and yet, half a block away, the shouts of frenzied men and bellowing roar of flames were unabated. Lying upon some boxes in the promiscuous pile, we saw the silver-plated frame and plate-glass of a jeweler's show case, with its velvet lining, and diamonds in their various styles of setting,—rings, brooches, pins, ear drops and bracelets, displayed in their caskets, as when spread for sale.

We thought the people mad—leaving those jewels there—and proposed taking them from their caskets, wrapping them in our handkerchiefs, and advertising them, after the fire. One thought we'd better leave them alone; another said: "Don't open the case! some one might be concealed among these piles of goods, watching them; and, taking us for thieves, shoot us!" We fell back at this, arguing the question. One said that he was sure he knew the goods; they were Hayes & Lyndall's, in Clay street; and, knowing them to be good fellows, it was wrong in us to leave their goods to be stolen; to which another answered: "It isn't reasonable to suppose they are left unguarded."

While thus conversing, we had slowly moved from the immediate neighborhood of the treasure, half-turned towards, and looking at it, when a gang of drunken, shouting vagabonds—just such as hung about the dens on the hillside at the heads of Montgomery and Kearny streets—came along Montgomery, from the burning buildings, and, sauntering into the hollow, saw the show-case and sprang upon it, tearing it open, snatching the contents, pushing and fighting for their booty, and yelling in drunken, thieving triumph.

A frantic rush to save personal belongings as the May 3-4, 1851 fire moves toward the wharves.

As we discerned in earlier excerpts from his *Last Adventure*, the Frenchman Albert Benard de Russailh was not enamored of San Francisco. In retrospect, one can hardly blame him. He arrived in March 1851, and within the first few months he was burned out of two homes and a job as newspaper reporter on the *Daily True Standard*. His version of the May and June 1851 fires—the first of which almost killed him—is one of the most dramatic eyewitness accounts we have of those tragic events.

A city in ruins

NOTHING IS MORE TERRIBLE than the raging of elemental forces. Human strength is impotent against their brute power; and there always comes a moment when men must surrender and sadly watch destruction overwhelming position, wealth, and future hopes. Only yesterday the city was crowded with laughing and nearly happy people. Business was flourishing; pleasant houses lined the streets, gay with flags of every nation; bankers were heaping up profits from bold speculation; workmen were laboring honestly to support their families; the arts were springing into life, as well as the lowest vices. Now there are only ruins, desolation, and poverty, and death with its ugly train. Vanitas vanitatum.* All the hard-earned wealth has vanished; the great stocks of merchandise brought at such expense from the ends of the earth are piles of ashes. Everything is gone. In a few hours the fire has razed the city, and now one can see only charred, tottering walls that will crumble into dust at the first breath of wind.

Between ten and eleven o'clock on the evening of May 3, the ominous shout of warning was heard in Portsmouth Square, and was immediately repeated all over town. Fire! Fire! Everybody rushed out of doors and ran toward the danger point. The fire had begun in a paint-shop on Clay Street opposite the plaza. The flames spread rapidly through the oil and other inflammable material, gained the upper floor, and caught the adjoining houses. The engines arrived as quickly as possible, and the firemen did their best, but their helplessness was

---

* Vanity of vanities; everything man does is in vain. (Latin)

soon apparent. A strong wind was blowing; the fire was out of control; the painter's house collapsed almost immediately; and with terrific velocity the flames jumped across the street onto Kearny, and began to burn there as well as on Clay. A sudden change of wind made us hope that the business section could be saved and that the fire could be confined to the hill toward the north. But we were disappointed: the wind had only momentarily slackened, and soon it began to blow more violently than ever, driving the flames simultaneously into Commercial and Sacramento Streets. In an instant the houses along these streets were destroyed, and Montgomery Street and the Long Wharf were the next to go.

Before long the city was surrounded by a huge network of flame from which it seemed impossible to escape. It was a terrible and magnificent spectacle: Washington, Sansome, and Bush Streets were roaring furnaces; the larger buildings crumbled like card-houses. The Parker House, the Union Hotel, the Empire, the Adelphi Theatre, the Customs House, the American Theatre were soon heaps of smoking ashes. Everybody was terror-stricken. Frantic people ran to and fro, trying to save what they considered their most valuable possessions. They snatched from the flames documents, ledgers, chairs and tables, pieces of jewelery. Carriages and wagons interlocked in hopeless confusion, and many horses, terrified by explosions of powder, broke from the vehicles and galloped madly away, dragging bits of harness.

Frequently, a man would run back into a half-burned house and would be overcome by smoke or caught by the flames. We shall never know how many people were killed while trying to save their belongings. And the discouragement caused by the fire was more terrible than the property losses, reducing many individuals to utter despair. Certain ghastly memories will never fade from my mind. On Washington Street a man went mad and blew his brains out: the loss of his house and possessions, and the destruction of his business had been too much for him.

In the same neighborhood another man, who had been completely ruined, and who was without a roof, loaded his revolver and, in a moment of insanity, shot his wife and child, and then killed himself above their bodies. I remember seeing a man with his clothes aflame rolling about in a muddy gutter and dying in agony. For more than two weeks San Francisco was a pile of smoking ruins.

I must not forget to tell of an incident that nearly cost me my life. About half way down Commercial Street I had a bedroom which I also used for an office during the day and where I did most of my journalistic work. Some time before, I had furnished the place simply, so that I might receive business callers; and now it contained a bed, a writing-table, some chairs, and a rather shabby sofa. When I realized that the fire was heading straight for Commercial Street, I hurried home and carried a bundle of my lighter things to a safe spot far from the flames, and then returned to save what remained: the bed and bedding, a few chairs, and a trunk containing part of my linen and clothes.

By this time the back of the house was on fire; the roof was blazing, and the whole structure seemed about to collapse, but I foolishly decided to dash in and save what I could. Just as I stepped into my room, the ceiling crashed down onto my head; I staggered around half-stunned and bleeding from cuts on my forehead and nose; then fell to the floor and lay in a daze with flames and smoke all around me. Luckily, I came to myself after a few seconds and managed to get away.

On the street again, I roamed about for a while in exhaustion, covered with sweat and badly bruised. Among the panic-stricken crowds I thought of my mother and gave thanks to God for having saved me from death. My problem now was to find a temporary shelter, for I had stowed away my few rescued belongings in a brick house and could only abandon them to fate. Remembering the Hotel de l'Alliance, where I had spent my first night in San Francisco, I made my way there, threw a mattress on the floor, and stretched out on it, determined that nothing could make me get up. I was so weary I could not have stirred even if the fire had reached the hotel. I slept like a log until evening, nearly twelve hours at a stretch. For more than three weeks I bore the marks of the blows I had received.

The day after the fire, and through all the following week, you could see people returning to the blackened sites of their houses and digging around in the hot ashes for the remains of gold or silver articles that had been melted by the great heat of the flames. The city presented a most miserable appearance: there were innumerable funerals of those who had died from injuries; men wandered like lost souls among the ruins, hunting for traces of familiar streets. The Americans,

[285]

especially, suffered from the forced inactivity, and began to think of rebuilding their houses as soon as the fire should be completely extinguished.

Seven or eight days later, more fortunate than Sodom or Nineveh, which had been destroyed by the fires of heaven, the city of San Francisco began to rise again. One may say of San Francisco, as of the Phoenix, *e cinere suo rediviva.** Surprisingly enough, before a week had passed, the streets were once more marked out; houses were going up everywhere on still smoking ruins; and, although the inhabitants had learned from sad experience that wooden structures were excellent food for the flames, they were rebuilding in wood. Before long the chief buildings of San Francisco were up again: the Parker House, the Union Hotel, Delmonico's, the Empire soon rose more splendid than ever to the astonishment of the public. It was as if one had gone to bed among the ruins and awakened next morning to find a new city. Such is American activity. Even while his house is burning, an American will think only of how to rebuild it. He lets his friends save the furniture, jumps on his horse, and gallops like mad to the next town, so that he can arrive before the news of the fire and buy building material before the prices have gone up.

As I have said, there was nothing for anybody to do after the disaster. We had to give the last flames time to go out, and wait for the builders to put up the houses or for the merchants to start their business again. The day after the fire, unwilling to remain idle, another young man and myself set up a tent in Portsmouth Square, at the corner of Kearny and Washington Streets, and made a table out of two empty barrels and four planks. I then laid in a supply of glasses, bottles of wine, cognac, whiskey, gin, and rum, added a box of cigars, some crackers and cookies, and soon had a first-rate shop. What I really needed, of course, was plenty of toothpicks, but I had no more. When everything was ready, I opened up and waited for patrons, and I did not have to wait long, for the bars had all been burned and the drunkards could find nothing to drink. (I may add that they abound in San Francisco. Americans drink tremendously, and love strong liquor.) They all gathered around my shop to quench their thirst, and tried to find relief from their troubles in a bottle of whiskey. Although

* Risen from its own ashes. (Latin) (See Glossary.)

tending bar was a new experience for me, I did very well for a few days. I sold everything for five times its cost, and for a while cleared $5 or $6 a day. But soon I had a number of competitors; the profits began to fall; and one night I shut up shop for good, went home, and began to think of something else I could do.

.   .   .

The May fire had pretty well shattered my hopes of success as a newspaper man; I had lost most of my belongings; and I had narrowly escaped being roasted alive like good Saint Laurent, whom Matthieu Loensberg quaintly placed in his calendar on the day of my birth, the tenth of August. The catastrophe had revealed the danger of living in the center of town, and I had determined to find a house that would be farther from danger in case another fire should break out. After much searching, I had discovered a little cottage half-way up the hill on the northern end of the city. It was clean, pleasant, and comfortable; the air was good; and I liked it so much that I had rented it and moved in with a bed, a table, and three or four chairs. For a while I had been living agreeably in my new quarters.

Although the cottage had certain good features that San Francisco houses rarely possess, it also had a number of serious faults. For example, it was situated part way up the hill, in a nearly isolated district, and I had as neighbors some of the most dangerous men in the city, who rented the tumble-down shacks for almost nothing. Practically every night I was awakened by pistol shots. As I always went well-armed, and tried never to come home late, these bandits did not trouble me; and after a month I felt quite at ease, and hoped that I was safe from fire. Another drawback was the number of rats that infested my cottage. But they are everywhere in San Francisco as in all wooden cities, and there was nothing to be done. Whenever they let me alone, I slept peacefully.

On Sunday, June 22, at eight o'clock in the morning, I was suddenly awakened by shouts of "Fire! Fire!" When this cry is heard in San Francisco, there is no time to lose: in a moment one may be caught. At the first warning I sprang out of bed, dressed quickly, and went out onto the street to see where the fire was burning. Thick clouds of smoke drifted by and the flames were only a few yards away. I had just time to run back to my room, bundle together a few clothes that were hanging on the wall, pile them into my valise, and escape through the back door. Once more, I had to leave my furniture behind.

My cottage was on the corner of Virginia Alley and Broadway, and the fire had broken out across the street in a lumber-yard. I am sure an incendiary was responsible, for that is usually the case here. My little house was soon ablaze, and before long the whole quarter was burning, from Stockton Street onto Jackson, and then along Dupont Street. La Polka, Barroilhet's gambling-house on Dupont and Pacific, was immediately destroyed; the flames raged among the wooden buildings, swept down Pacific Street, and simultaneously turned in another direction and burned upper Washington Street, and all the houses around Portsmouth Square that remained after the May fire. A good part of Kearny and Sansome Streets was laid waste and the whole district between Pacific Street and Cunningham Wharf. At first we thought the whole city would go, but luckily the wind drove the flames toward the north. Several warehouses were soon in ashes, and some outlying shacks; then the fire burnt itself out against the bare hillside.

Once again San Francisco was in ruins. The fire destroyed four or five American churches and the French church. The French consul's house on Jackson Street was threatened, and only saved by a miracle. The business losses were tremendous: many warehouses, and a large number of ships used for storage purposes, went up in smoke. The damage done by these two conflagrations was estimated as high as $40,000,000. It was a hard blow for commerce and industry. The city now seemed dead, and there appeared to be no hope that its former prosperity would return. Everyone without established business fled from San Francisco, as if it were a doomed city, and went to try their luck in the neighboring towns or in the mines. What else was there to do? How I yearned to be able "to take the coach and go back to Flanders," as Voltaire advised the Flemish actor to do. During a performance of one of Voltaire's tragedies, the actor forgot his lines and kept repeating the first half of the speech: "What shall I do? What course remains?" "Take the mailcoach and go back to Flanders!" cried Voltaire in anger. I could not solve my difficulties so easily. As much as I hated the idea, I had to stay among the ruins of this terrible city.

> Disillusioned with his lack of success, Benard sailed from San Francisco a year later. He died of cholera before reaching France.

A sixth major fire raged across the town on June 22, 1851.

In this excerpt from her book, *Incidents on Land and Water,* Mrs. Bates tells of one family's terror in the May 1851 fire— and of the steadfast resolve that followed. Throughout San Francisco, pluck and perseverance were the watchwords as people struggled to rebuild their lives and their town.

Life after the big fire

THE SCENES I WITNESSED THAT DAY might wring tears from a heart of stone. Men who, a few short hours before, were worth thousands and hundreds of thousands, now sat weeping over the ashes of their once splendid fortunes. Some who were not possessed of sufficient self-command and fortitude to meet and brave life's severest trials, had sought consolation for every woe in the intoxicating cup; others sat, the images of mute despair, their grief too profound to permit a tear or sigh to escape as a mitigation of their deep-seated sorrow; some had already commenced fencing in their lots, although the smouldering ashes emitted an almost suffocating heat. These hasty proceedings were at that time expedient, to prevent their lots from being jumped; for these were the days of squatter memory, when possession was nine-tenths of the law.

We were in pursuit of Mr. and Mrs. B——. With her I had formed a close intimacy on board the steamer. Her husband, previous to the fire, was established in a lucrative business, but who had now shared the fate of all. Where was Mrs. B—— and her little daughter Nelly? They were obliged to run in their nightclothes. Mr. B—— deposited two or three trunks of their most valuable clothing in one of those fireproof buildings, and, of course, they were burnt, leaving them nothing which they could call their own out of their once abundant supply. Mrs. B—— that night sought and found protection at an hospital kept by a friend of hers, a doctor from New York. The building was situated upon the summit of one of the many hills which surround the city, and about a mile from where she had lived. This distance she ran, without even shoes or stockings, almost dragging her little girl along, who was so terrified as to be almost incapable of supporting herself.

After learning her whereabouts, I hastened to see her, and found her, where she was obliged to remain for the time being, in bed. I supplied her with a few articles of clothing from my limited wardrobe; but she being a much taller person than myself, we were really at a loss how to make her appear respectable, unless she would consent to make her debut in Bloomer costume. "Necessity is indeed the mother of invention;" and, after some crying, and a good deal more laughing, we had her equipped for a promenade. Then Nelly was released from "durance vile;" but it would have puzzled wiser heads than ours to have designated her costume. Poor child! how she lamented the fate of all the nice things which she had brought from home! This was her first grief. The proposition was made to us from Mr. and Mrs. B——, to go to housekeeping in company with them, and take boarders. No time was to be lost: after a fire in California was the time for immediate action. That day we found an unoccupied house, a little over the ridge of the hills.

The owner of this domicile had gone to the States; the agent for which was also absent in the mines. Therefore, our husbands had the audacity to take quiet possession; and, before night, we were duly installed in our new house. Perhaps some of my readers may have the curiosity to know how we so readily furnished our intended boarding-house, while nearly the entire city was in ruins. Well, in the house we found two bedsteads, with a miserable straw bed upon each; quite a good cooking-stove, with a few appurtenances attached; a pine table, constructed of unplaned boards; and old boxes, in lieu of chairs. Dishes, knives and forks, and spoons, we had picked up from the heterogeneous mass of half-consumed rubbish upon the former site of Mr. B——'s store. But, at such a time as that, if one could get anything to eat, he never stopped to see if his fork was blessed with one prong or three; and, if the knife was minus a handle, it was just as well, provided the blade was good. And then, too, a person was not particular about enjoying the luxury of both cup and saucer, if at any time there were more people than dishes. The next day, our husbands secured us as many boarders as we could accommodate with meals: a lodging they sought elsewhere.

We were to receive twelve dollars per week for board. Don't laugh: that was cheap board, when you take into consideration the exorbitant price of provisions. For butter we paid one dollar and a half per pound; beef steak, twenty-five cents per pound; and all else in proportion. Vegetables were sold by the pound, and dearly sold, too. I never prepared a meal, but what I thought of the old woman who had but one kettle in which to cook everything. We made coffee in the tea-kettle mornings; and, at night, made tea in the same.

There was a well of water at some distance from the house, near the foot of the hill; and, oh, what a deep one it was! The bucket, which would contain two pailfuls, had to be drawn to the top by a windlass. The united exertions of Mrs. B—— and myself were scarcely sufficient to bring it to the top. Oh, how we have laughed, and tugged, and laughed, until we could tug no longer, over that old well! Our husbands were busily engaged at the store-lot clearing and fencing it, and erecting a temporary building, to be in readiness to receive a fresh supply of goods which was daily expected to arrive, and which, fortunately for Mr. B——, had had a longer passage than usual.

Our boarding-house in San Francisco will never be forgotten; and, when reverted to, will invariably call up a smile, even if we are entertaining those provoking imps, the blues. Many times since, I have met some of those boarders at the tables of fashionable hotels; in which case, I was sure to receive some compliment in reference to the good dinners they had eaten from the old pine table, minus the table-cloth.

Glossary

Many of the words used by 19th century writers either have fallen from general use or have changed their meaning. The following definitions are offered as a guide for today's readers.

* These words are explained elsewhere in the glossary.

alcalde. The highest officer of local government during the Spanish and Mexican periods. The duties covered those of mayor, justice of the peace, and police officer. Elected each year by the people of the area, the alcalde was subordinate only to the governor's military representative. For a brief period after they occupied California, the Americans continued this system of government, electing their own alcaldes and councils, or *ayuntamientos*.*

Alta California. Under Spanish rule, California was divided in two: Baja (Lower) and Alta (Upper) California. The upper portion was ceded to the United States after the U.S.-Mexico war, and the lower portion—a peninsula separating the Gulf of California from the Pacific Ocean—remained part of Mexico.

Alta California, The. San Francisco's most influential newspaper from 1849 through 1891.

ap. (Thomas ap Catesby Jones) The Welsh equivalent of the Scottish and Irish *Mac*—i.e., son of.

argonauts. The early non-Spanish pioneers of California—the term implying an association with the mythological Jason and his argonauts who sought the Golden Fleece.

ayuntamiento. A council established by the Spaniards, and later by the Mexicans, to rule the *pueblos**, or towns. At the time of the American occupation, an ayuntamiento consisted of 12 elected officials, including the *alcalde**. The Americans continued this form of government until the adoption of California's constitution.

buskin. In early Athenian plays, actors portraying tragic characters often wore high, thick-soled boots called *buskins*. In contrast, comic actors wore low shoes, called *socks*. Hence the phrase "to put on the buskins," meaning "to assume a tragic role." When Frank Marryat wrote that he had become "a very slave to the buskin," he implied that he was deeply immersed in his acting.

Californio. Students of California history do not agree on the definition of this word. For some, it applies exclusively to the Spanish and Mexican people who lived in California before U.S. occupation in 1846. For others, it applies also to Americans and Europeans who were resident during that period. In an early attempt at colonization, Mexico emptied its jails of criminals and political agitators and sent them north, creating a sharp contrast with the wealthy Mexican families that had emigrated there. In time, the children of these early settlers—including sons and daughters of the ex-convicts—developed their own sense of identity with the new land. In their struggle for autonomy they became ambivalent toward Mexico, to the extent that they preferred to call themselves *Californios* rather than *Españoles* or *Mexicanos*. The term was in widespread use in the 1830s-1880s, according to Leonard Pitt's *The Decline of the Californios: A Social History of the Spanish-Speaking Californians, 1846-1890.* (University of California Press, 1966.)

cap-à-pie. From head to foot. (French)

Celestials. A popular term in the mid-19th century for the people of China, based on the old name for that country, *Celestial Empire*.

e cinere suo rediviva. "Having revived from its own ashes," loosely translated as "risen from its own ashes." (Latin)

embonpoint. In pre-weight-conscious days, this was a complimentary term for plumpness, or a well-nourished appearance. French, for "in good condition."

faro. A game of chance in which players bet on the order in which certain cards will appear when taken from the top of the deck.

fore cabin. A cabin in the forward end of a ship.

forepeak. The forward end of a ship.

forecastle. The forward end of a merchant ship where the crew lives.

frocks. Woolen sweaters worn by sailors.

hell. An archaic word for a gambling house.

hors de combat. Disabled; out of the fight. (French)

in durance vile. Forced confinement; imprisonment; constraint.

instanter. At once; immediately; forthwith.

jacks. A nickname for sailors.

Jeremy Diddlered. Swindled (colloq.). After a fictional character who appeared in an 1803 play (*Raising the Wind* by James Kenney) and an 1850 novel (*The Kickleburys on the Rhine* by W. M. Thackery). Today we would say *diddled.*

jollies. A nickname for marines.

Kanaka. A native of the South Sea Islands, although in the context of this volume, the term refers specifically to a person from Hawaii.

kids. Wooden tubs used for serving food to sailors.

lansquenet. A card game that originated in Germany.

locos. In 1835 members of the Democratic party were nicknamed *locos-focos*—the brand name of a match that a faction of Democrats used to light candles when the gas lights at New York's Tammany Hall were extinguished during a particularly boisterous debate.

monte. A game of chance in which the players bet on matching cards that are turned up one at a time by the dealer.

Mormon. A member of the Church of Jesus Christ of Latter-day Saints.

nil hi nil hi. A variation of *willy-nilly*, which the *Oxford English Dictionary* defines as "whether it be with or against the will of the person or persons involved; whether one likes it or not; willingly or unwillingly." Willy-nilly is believed to have originated in one or all three of the Old English expressions *will he nill he*; *will ye nill ye*; *will I nill I*. In that sense, *nill* meant the opposite of *will.*

nonce. "For the nonce" was an affected way of saying "for the occasion," or "for the time being."

pea-jacket. A short coat made of coarse wool, usually worn by sailors.

plastic display. In the sense used by Vicente Pérez Rosales, this term refers to a tableau, or a display of women posing like statues.

poncho. A cloak resembling a blanket with a slit in it for the wearer's head.

pulpería. A store selling food and liquor. (Spanish)

presidio. A military encampment established by Spain to protect a neighboring mission from attack.

pueblos. Towns established by the Spanish to attract settlers to their overseas territories. They were administered by a civil form of government, with officials being elected annually by the people. The earliest California pueblos were San Jose and Los Angeles. In contrast, San Francisco began as a military region governed from the *presidio.**

quartz mining. When the initial pick-and-pan search for gold along the river beds reached saturation point, miners had to bring in expensive and elaborate machinery to delve deeper into quartz veins to reach the precious metal.

quilgee handle. See *squilgee.*

quill-driver. Pen-pusher. See also *square the yards.*

ranchos. Tracts of land granted to settlers, first by the Spanish and then by the Mexican governments. Under Spanish rule titles to the land remained with the crown, but the Mexicans granted full rights to the individuals. In many cases wealthy Mexican families combined their holdings to create ranchos extending over several thousand acres, creating California's first aristocracy.

rancheros. The people who lived on, and ran, the *ranchos.**

roulette. A game of chance involving a spinning wheel. Players bet on which slot a ball will rest in when the wheel stopped spinning.

scurvy. A disease caused by a lack of ascorbic acid, manifested in spongy gums, loosened teeth, and pain in the limbs. It was common among the crews and passengers of ships not carrying sufficient supplies of fresh fruits and vegetables.

sinnet. Nautical term for a kind of flat, braided cordage, or rope, formed by pleating together several strands of rope-yarn, coarse hemp, grass, etc. This is then used in the rigging of a ship. *Lay* is a variation of *lathe* and is an obscure way of saying "to weave." When Richard Henry Dana wrote "the boys ... laid up grass into sinnet" he meant that they made rope for the ship's rigging.

slug. During the Gold Rush days this word was used variously for a nugget of gold and a large gold coin minted privately in California.

snake. A hollow belt worn by miners to carry their gold, sometimes worn in addition to the conventional belt.

square the yards. In nautical terms, a yard is a long spar that supports and extends a square sail. Usually when a square-rigged ship is in harbor, its yards are set *square*—that is, at right angles to the fore-and-aft lines of the ship. Richard Henry Dana's expression "square the yards with the bloody quill-driver" could translate into today's "getting even with the (bleep) pen-pusher."

squilgee. Nautical term for a mop. *Squeegee* is a variation. The "quilgee handle" intended for use as a weapon in "The night they cried 'To arms!'" is probably a mop handle.

steam paddy. A steam-driven engine used to scoop sand from the hills of San Francisco and dump it into the bay, thus accomplishing two ojectives—leveling the hills and filling in the bay. Apparently called *paddies* because they did the work of several Irishmen.

supercargo. A ship's officer in charge of the cargo and responsible for commercial transactions during the voyage.

tapis. "On the tapis" is from the French *sur le tapis*—on the tablecloth (or carpet)—meaning "under discusssion," or "being considered."

tenement. An early term for an apartment building.

traps. Personal belongings; portable furniture; baggage.

used up. Thoroughly exhausted; tired out; worn out. (Colloq.)

vara. A unit of measure in Spain, Portugal, and Spanish America, varying in length according to locality, but usually about 33 inches.

viand. An item of food.

waistcoat. A close-fitting, sleeveless garment worn by men under their coats. Although it is still called a waistcoat in England, in the United States it is now called a *vest*.

warp. As a noun, this refers to the rope or hawser which, when attached at one end to a fixed object, moves or hauls a ship from one place to another. As a verb, it refers to the action of moving or hauling the ship in this manner, usually when the ship is in a harbor.

Whitewashed Yankee. In his book *Mountains and Molehills* (1855), Englishman Frank Marryat defines a Whitewashed Yankee as an educated person who could do well in his own country but who could do better by immigrating to the United States and becoming an American citizen. The term was a compliment, though it didn't sound like one, wrote Marryat. He added, "It is from this educated class of naturalized subjects that the aspirants for office step forward, and under all the circumstances, I am not surprised that a large sect of Americans now oppose them."

yclept. A Middle English word for named, or known as. Elizabethan writers used it as a literary archaism; later it was used as an affectation.

Yerba Buena. A sweet-smelling herb that grew wild over the shores of early San Francisco. The name was applied to a cove and briefly superceded the original name of the town. (See "What's in a name?") The name was also applied to an island in the bay.

Resource notes

Finding the individual pieces for this volume was one thing. Researching the background and verifying many of the statements made by the writers was another. Fortunately for scholars of California history there are several reliable sources to turn to, including the works of Hubert Howe Bancroft, Charles E. Chapman, John W. Dwinelle, Zoeth S. Eldredge, Theodore H. Hittell, Francisco Palóu, Josiah Royce, and Franklin Tuthill. Then of course there is *Annals of San Francisco* by Frank Soulé, John H. Gihon, and James Nisbet. I delved into all of these at some point, although I did most of my research in Bancroft's 7-volume *History of California*, and in the *Annals*.

I chose not to use superscript numbers in my text. Instead, I tried to anticipate the instances where readers might want to check my sources, and I have listed them here according to the page numbers on which they appeared.

For the sake of brevity, book titles are abbreviated, as with "Bancroft 5:194-196" (H. H. Bancroft's *History of California* volume 5, pages 194-196). Complete titles and dates of publication are listed in the Bibliography.

CHSQ = California Historical Society Quarterly.   n = footnote.

Page:

20 Population growth—Bancroft 5:646n and 6:168n
23 "the Spanish town and settlement of St. Francisco"—Vancouver 3:14
23 U.S. communiques urge capture—Bancroft 3:399-400; 5:194-199
23 Cermeño names *La Bahía de San Francisco*—CHSQ 20:316-317
25 Portolá's sighting of Drake's Bay—Costansó 115-117
25 Confusion about two San Francisco bays—Bancroft 1:157-159
25 Ayala's instruction to seek strait linking the bays—Bancroft 1:245-247
26 Establishment of New San Francisco at Sonoma—Bancroft 2:496-505
26 Francisco Solano a missionary in Peru—*New Catholic Encyclopedia* 13:414-415
26 Naming missions "Dolores" and "Sonoma"—Bancroft 1:294-295n; 2:504-505
26 José Figueroa establishes civilian settlement at Yerba Buena—CHSQ 27:60

75 Hinkley and Ridley opposed the revolt—Bancroft 5:136
89 Quote from "Judges and Criminals"—*Golden Era*, November 13, 1853
105 *Portsmouth* returns to San Francisco in August—Rogers 101
115 The Skinners take on catering at City Hotel—Bancroft 5:680
246 Quote from de Massey's "A Frenchman in the Gold Rush"—CHSQ 6:46

Bibliography

The majority of these books have been out of print for many years, although original copies and reprints may be found in libraries, private collections, and antiquarian bookstores. I have attempted to indicate which books have been reprinted when and by whom, but the list is not complete. Your local librarian or bookstore (new, second-hand, or antiquarian) might be able to assist you with specific titles.

✓ indicates which books were either excerpted or cited in this volume.

Asbury, Herbert. *The Barbary Coast: An Informal History of the San Francisco Underworld.* New York. 1933.

✓ Ayers, James J. *Gold and Sunshine: Reminiscences of Early California.* Boston. 1922.

✓ Bancroft, Hubert Howe. *History of California.* 7 vols. San Francisco. 1884-1890.
Reprinted, in facsimile. Wallace Hebberd, Santa Barbara. 1963.

✓ Barry, T. A., and Patten, B. A. *Men and Memories of San Francisco in the "Spring of '50."* San Francisco. 1873.
Reprinted as *San Francisco, California, 1850.* Foreword by Joseph A. Sullivan. Biobooks, Oakland. 1947.

✓ Bates, Mrs. D.B. *Incidents on Land and Water, or Four Years on the Pacific Ocean.* Boston. 1858.

Beebe, Lucius, and Clegg, Charles. *San Francisco's Golden Era: A Picture Story of San Francisco Before the Fire.* Howell-North, Berkeley. 1960.

✓ Benard de Russailh, Albert. *Last Adventure: San Francisco in 1851.* Translated from original journal by Clarkson Crane. 475 copies printed for The Westgate Press by Grabhorn Press, San Francisco. 1931.

Brewer, William H. *Up and Down California in 1860-1864.* Edited by Francis P. Farquhar. Yale University Press. 1930.
Reprinted in 1949 and 1966 by University of California Press, each with slight changes to the notes.

✓ Brown, John Henry. *Reminiscences and Incidents of the Early Days of San Francisco (1845-1850).* San Francisco. 1886.
Reprinted by Grabhorn Press, with introduction and reader's guide by Douglas Sloane Watson. 1933.
Reprinted by Biobooks as *Early Days of San Francisco, California.* Index compiled by Alameda Public Library. Foreword by Joseph A. Sullivan. 1949.

Bryant, Edwin. *What I Saw in California: Being the Journal of a Tour ... in the years 1846, 1847.* New York. 1848.
Reprinted by Fine Arts Press, Santa Ana, with notes, index, and bibliography by Marguerite Eyer Wilbur. 1936.
Reprinted as a Bison Book by University of Nebraska Press. Introduction by Thomas D. Clark. 1985.

✓ Burnett, Peter H. *Recollections and Opinions of an Old Pioneer.* New York. 1880.
Reprinted as *An Old California Pioneer* by Biobooks. Foreword by Joseph A. Sullivan. 1946.

✓ Chapman, Charles E. *A History of California: The Spanish Period.* New York. 1921.

✓ Coburn, Jesse L. *Letters of Gold: California Postal History Through 1869.* The U.S. Philatelic Classics Society, Inc. Canton, Ohio. 1984.

✓ Costansó, Miguel. *The Discovery of San Francisco Bay: The Portolá Expedition of 1769-1770.* Edited by Peter Browning. Great West Books, Lafayette. 1992.
Originally published as *The Portolá Expedition of 1769-1770: Diary of Miguel Costansó,* edited by Frederick J. Teggart. University of California. 1911.

✓ Cross, Ralph Herbert. *The Early Inns of California, 1844-1869.* Cross & Brandt, San Francisco. 1954.

✓ Dana, Richard Henry, Jr. *Two Years Before the Mast: A Personal Narrative.* Harper & Brothers, New York. 1840.
Revised by the author and republished by University Press; Welch, Bigelow & Co., Cambridge, Massachusetts. 1869.
This title has been reprinted several times and may still be in print somewhere.

✓ De Rutté, Théophile. *The Adventures of a Young Swiss in California: The Gold Rush Account of Théophile de Rutté.* Translated and edited by Mary Grace Paquette. Sacramento Book Collectors Club. 1992.

Dillon, Richard H. *Embarcadero, 1849-1906; True Sea Adventures from the Port of San Francisco.* Ballantine Books, New York. 1959.

✓ Downey, Joseph T. *Reminiscences of San Francisco: Filings From an Old Saw.* by "Filings" [pseud.]. A series that appeared in the newspaper *Golden Era* between January 9 and July 3, 1853.
These pieces were reprinted in book form as *Filings From an Old Saw: Reminiscences of San Francisco and California's Conquest* by "Filings." Edited by Fred Blackburn Rogers. John Howell, San Francisco. 1956.

✓ ———. *Odds and Ends, or Incidents of a Cruise in the Pacific in the U.S. Ship Portsmouth from January 1845 to May 1848* by "Fore Peak" [pseud.]. This hand-written journal was published in book form as *The Cruise of the Portsmouth: A Sailor's View of the Naval Conquest of California.* Edited by Howard Lamar. Yale University Press. 1958.

Duvall, Marius. *A Naval Surgeon in California, 1846-1847: The Journal of Marius Duvall.* Edited by Fred Blackburn Rogers. John Howell, San Francisco. 1957.

✓ Dwinelle, John W. *The Colonial History of San Francisco.* San Francisco. 1867.
Reprinted in facsimile by Ross Valley Book Co., Albany, California. 1978.

✓ Farnham, Eliza W. *California In-doors and Out: or, How we Farm, Mine, and Live Generally in the Golden State.* New York. 1856.
Reprinted in facsimile with an introduction by Madeleine B. Stern. Women on the Move series. Nieuwkoop, De Graaf. 1972.

✓ Frémont, John C. *Geographical Memoir Upon Upper California, in Illustration of his Map of Oregon and California.* 1849.

Gentry, Curt. *The Madams of San Francisco: An Irreverent History of the City by the Golden Gate.* Doubleday, New York. 1964.

Grey, William. [pseud.] See White, William F.

Harlow, Neal. *California Conquered; the Annexation of an American Province, 1846-1850.* University of California Press. 1982.

✓ Heizer, Robert Fleming. "Archaeological Evidence of Sebastián Rodrigues Cermeño's California Visit in 1595." Article in California Historical Society's *Quarterly*, vol. 20, no. 4, pp. 316-317.

Hittell, Theodore H. *History of California.* 4 vols. 1885-1898.

Hunt, Rockwell D. *California's Stately Hall of Fame.* The College of the Pacific, Stockton. 1950.

Lewis, Oscar. Comp. & Ed. *This was San Francisco: Being First-hand Accounts of the Evolution of One of America's Favorite Cities.* David McKay Company, New York. 1962.

———. *San Francisco: Mission to Metropolis.* Howell-North, Berkeley. 1966.

Lotchin, Roger W. *San Francisco, 1847-1856: From Hamlet to City.* Oxford University Press, New York. 1974.

✓ Marryat, Frank. *Mountains and Molehills; or, Recollections of a Burnt Journal.* London and New York. 1855.
Reprinted in facsimile from first American 1855 edition, with introduction and notes by Marguerite Eyer Wilbur. Stanford University Press. 1952.

✓ Megquier, Mary Jane. *Apron Full of Gold: The Letters of Mary Jane Megquier from San Francisco, 1849-1856.* Edited by Robert Glass Cleland. The Huntington Library Press. 1949.
Reprinted with introduction by Polly Welts Kaufman, who supplies new insights into the life of Mary Jane Megquier. University of New Mexico Press. 1994.

Muscatine, Doris. *Old San Francisco: The Biography of a City from Early Days to the Earthquake.* G.P. Putnam's Sons, New York. 1975.

✓ Perkins, William. *Three Years in California: William Perkins' Journal of Life at Sonora, 1849-1852.* Introduction and annotations by Dale L. Morgan and James. R. Scobie. University of California Press. 1964.
Originally published in Spanish as *El campo de los Sonoraenses: Tres años de residencia en California, 1849-1851.* Buenos Aires. 1937.

✓ Phelps, William D. *Fore and Aft: or, Leaves From the Life of an Old Sailor.* by "Webfoot" [pseud.]. Boston. 1871.

✓ Pitt, Leonard. *The Decline of the Californios: A Social History of the Spanish-Speaking Californians, 1846-1890.* University of California Press. 1966.

Revere, Joseph Warren. *Naval Duty in California.* Biobooks, Oakland. 1947.

Richards, Rand. *Historic San Francisco: A Concise History and Guide.* Heritage Press, San Francisco. 1991.

✓ Richardson, Steve. "The Days of the Dons: Reminiscences of California's Oldest Native Son." Series of 42 installments in San Francisco *Bulletin* between April 22 and June 8, 1918. Edited by James H. Wilkins.

✓ Rogers, Fred Blackburn. *Montgomery and the Portsmouth.* John Howell, San Francisco. 1958.

✓ Rosales, Vicente Pérez. *We Were 49ers! Chilean Accounts of the California Gold Rush.* Contains excerpts of Perez's *Diario de un Viaje a California* which was originally published in 1878. Translated and edited by Edwin A. Beilharz and Carlos V. López. Ward Ritchie Press. 1976.

✓ Royce, Sarah. *A Frontier Lady: Recollections of the Gold Rush and Early California.* Yale University Press. 1932.
Reprinted as a Bison Book by University of Nebraska Press. 1977.

✓ Shaw, William. *Golden Dreams and Waking Realities: Being the Adventures of a Gold-seeker in California and the Pacific Islands.* London. 1851.
Reprinted in facsimile by Arnos Press, Inc., a New York Times Company, as one of The Far Western Frontier series. 1973.

✓ Skinner, James Horace. *Reminiscences of James Horace Skinner.* Photocopy of manuscript at Historical Department, The Church of Jesus Christ of Latter-day Saints, Salt Lake City, Utah.

✓ Soulé, Frank; Gihon, John H.; and Nisbet, James. *The Annals of San Francisco.* New York and San Francisco. 1854.
Reprinted in facsimile together with *Continuation of the Annals of San Francisco.* Introduction by Richard H. Dillon. Index. Lewis Osborne, Palo Alto. 1966.

Starr, Kevin. *Americans and the California Dream, 1850-1915.* Oxford University Press, 1973.

✓ Taylor, Bayard. *Eldorado: or, Adventures in the Path of Empire.* 2 vols. New York and London. 1850.
Reprinted with introduction by Robert Glass Cleland. Western Americana series. Alfred A. Knopf, New York. 1949.
Reprinted in facsimile with biographical introduction by Richard H. Dillon. Lewis Osborne, Palo Alto. 1968.

✓ Taylor, William. *California Life Illustrated.* New York. 1858.

✓ Vancouver, George. *A Voyage of Discovery to the North Pacific Ocean, and Round the World.* 6 vols. London. 1801.

Watkins, T.H., and Olmstead, R.R. *Mirror of the Dream: An Illustrated History of San Francisco.* Scrimshaw Press, San Francisco. 1976.

✓ White, William F. *A Picture of Pioneer Times in California, Illustrated with Anecdotes and Stories Taken from Real Life* by William Grey [psued.]. Privately printed. 1881.

Wilcox, Del. *Voyagers to California.* Seal Rock Press, Elk, California. 1991.

Index

Whereas the editorial style throughout this volume has been to retain the spelling of names and words as found in the original pieces, today's standard spelling is employed in this index. The preface, glossary, and resource notes are not included. Bold face figures indicate illustrations.

More San Francisco Memoirs
1852-1899: *The ripening years*

The story continues
as San Francisco rebuilds after the fires
and settles down to become "everybody's favorite city."
It is the time of the Vigilantes, and of Civil War.
A new social elite is developing,
with grand homes and elegant dances.
A popular Sunday attraction is an excursion
along the planked road to Mission Dolores,
or a carriage ride over the sand dunes to the Cliff House.
And, of course, there are earthquakes!
People who were there tell us what it was like.

LONDONBORN PUBLICATIONS
P.O. Box 77246, San Francisco, CA 94107-0246

About the author

Malcolm E. Barker first saw San Francisco as he sailed through the Golden Gate on board a British liner one February morning in 1960. At the time, he was working in the purser's office of P&O's *Iberia*, which was on a round-the-world cruise. The ship returned to San Francisco several times during the next 12 months, and on each occasion Barker fell more and more under the city's spell. In 1961, he signed off the ship and flew back to live there as an immigrant.

It is not surprising then that he should feel an affinity with the immigrants who had sailed through that same narrow strait more than a hundred years earlier.

His fascination with the minutiae of the city's past began almost immediately. When he was unable to find a publisher for a collection of 1860s newspaper stories about two stray dogs, he founded Londonborn Publications and produced the book himself. The success of that book—*Bummer & Lazarus: San Francisco's Famous Dogs*—led him to the idea of publishing a series of books about little-known aspects of San Francisco's history, beginning with the present volume.

He is also the author and publisher of *Book design & production for the small publisher*.

Cover design: David R. Johnson & Malcolm E. Barker
Text design: Malcolm E. Barker
Copy editor: Jackie Pels, Hardscratch Press
Typefaces: Adobe Minion and Minion Expert, set 11/13
Printed and bound by Thomson-Shore, Michigan,
on 60-lb. Joy White Offset acid-free paper.